STEVEN SPIELBERG
AND PHILOSOPHY

The Philosophy of Popular Culture

The books published in the Philosophy of Popular Culture series will illuminate and explore philosophical themes and ideas that occur in popular culture. The goal of this series is to demonstrate how philosophical inquiry has been reinvigorated by increased scholarly interest in the intersection of popular culture and philosophy, as well as to explore through philosophical analysis beloved modes of entertainment, such as movies, TV shows, and music. Philosophical concepts will be made accessible to the general reader through examples in popular culture. This series seeks to publish both established and emerging scholars who will engage a major area of popular culture for philosophical interpretation and examine the philosophical underpinnings of its themes. Eschewing ephemeral trends of philosophical and cultural theory, authors will establish and elaborate on connections between traditional philosophical ideas from important thinkers and the ever-expanding world of popular culture.

SERIES EDITOR

Mark T. Conard, Marymount Manhattan College, NY

BOOKS IN THE SERIES

The Philosophy of Stanley Kubrick, edited by Jerold J. Abrams
Football and Philosophy, edited by Michael W. Austin
The Philosophy of the Coen Brothers, edited by Mark T. Conard
The Philosophy of Film Noir (paperback edition), edited by Mark T. Conard
The Philosophy of Martin Scorsese, edited by Mark T. Conard
The Philosophy of Neo-Noir, edited by Mark T. Conard
The Philosophy of The X-Files, edited by Dean A. Kowalski
The Philosophy of Science Fiction Film, edited by Steven M. Sanders
The Philosophy of TV Noir, edited by Steven M. Sanders and Aeon J. Skoble
Basketball and Philosophy, edited by Jerry L. Walls and Gregory Bassham

STEVEN SPIELBERG AND PHILOSOPHY

WE'RE GONNA NEED A BIGGER BOOK

Edited by Dean A. Kowalski

THE UNIVERSITY PRESS OF KENTUCKY

Scholarly publisher for the Commonwealth,
serving Bellarmine University, Berea College, Centre
College of Kentucky, Eastern Kentucky University,
The Filson Historical Society, Georgetown College,
Kentucky Historical Society, Kentucky State University,
Morehead State University, Murray State University,
Northern Kentucky University, Transylvania University,
University of Kentucky, University of Louisville,
and Western Kentucky University.
All rights reserved.

Editorial and Sales Offices: The University Press of Kentucky
663 South Limestone Street, Lexington, Kentucky 40508-4008
www.kentuckypress.com

15 14 13 12 11   5 4 3 2 1

The Library of Congress has cataloged the hardcover edition as follows:

Steven Spielberg and philosophy : we're gonna need a bigger book /
edited by Dean A. Kowalski.
    p. cm. — (The philosophy of popular culture)
 Includes bibliographical references and index.
 ISBN 978-0-8131-2527-5 (hardcover : alk. paper)
 1. Spielberg, Steven, 1946—Criticism and interpretation. 2. Motion
pictures—Moral and ethical aspects. I. Kowalski, Dean A.
 PN1998.3.S65S84 2008
 791.4302'33092—dc22
                                    2008026318
 ISBN 978-0-8131-3389-8 (pbk. : alk. paper)

This book is printed on acid-free recycled paper meeting
the requirements of the American National Standard
for Permanence in Paper for Printed Library Materials.

Manufactured in the United States of America.

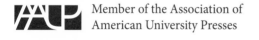   Member of the Association of
American University Presses

Contents

Part III: Realism, Mind, and Metaphysics

Acknowledgments

I remain indebted to Mark Conard, Steve Wrinn, and (especially) Anne Dean Watkins at the University Press of Kentucky. They, and all of their colleagues at UPK, remain unsurpassed in their dedication and loyalty to their authors. While I am grateful for the quality efforts of all the contributing authors, I owe a tremendous debt of thanks to Professor Joseph Foy. I have no finer colleague than he. My wife, Patricia, continues to be a constant source of strength and encouragement. My parents, Bruce and Susan, remain subtle stalwarts of support.

I have been incorporating film and television in my classroom for more than a decade. My students have always appreciated this; indeed, many subsequently inspired me to commit fully to this way of teaching philosophy. That inspiration now culminates in the fruition of this book. I thus dedicate this book to my students. I recall philosophy majors and minors from Dubuque and Indianapolis: C. Ashton, E. Bader, W. D. Bentley, E. Comstock, A. Fisher, S. Franks, K. Fry, A. Giese, V. Grider, J. Haire, E. Huff, W. E. Koron, S. Kutsch, T. Lazzaro, C. Neblett, K. Perhach, E. Phillips, K. Storey, S. Takacs, and K. Zeilenga. More recently, and at the risk of offending some, I note: J. Boeck, M. Carrillo, E. Colvin, K. Ellis, J. Gorman, L. Hlaban, M. Kleppe, D. Koller, D. Krause, S. Krause, C. Majdoch, L. Q. McDonald, B. Mikulice, E. Mosely, D. Myszewski, S. Pfenninger, B. Retzlaff, J. Schroeder, and C. Vouga. Space constraints do not allow me to continue. However, if you remember and appreciate the term "phledgling philosopher," then this book is dedicated to you.

"For 'Phledgling Philosophers' Everywhere"

Introduction

Dean A. Kowalski

No film director has had more impact on popular culture than Steven Spielberg. This volume acknowledges that fact. In its pages, you will find thirty years of Spielberg's directorial efforts explored and assessed through the lens of philosophy. What you will also find (surprisingly, perhaps) is that philosophy is not so much something that you "have" as something that you "do." Within each essay, the contributing authors discuss philosophical issues—"doing" philosophy—in metaphysics (the study of ultimate reality), epistemology (the study of knowledge), ethics (the study of right living), axiology (the study of value, of which ethics is one facet), aesthetics (the study of art and beauty), political philosophy, feminism, and mind, among other areas. Because we are teachers as well as scholars, each essay is written for those new to philosophy; thus, the discussions invariably presuppose very little philosophy background.

The first section, "Philosophy, the Filmmaker, and the Human Condition," contains five essays. Gary Arms and Thomas Riley provide a proper introduction to the book. Arms pens part I of the essay, providing an analysis of Spielberg's literary choices, and focusing particularly on *War of the Worlds* (2005) and *Minority Report* (2002). In the process, Arms provides us some insights into Spielberg's approach to filmmaking. Riley authors part II of the essay, signaling the turn to philosophical exploration of Spielberg. Riley focuses on ethical issues in Spielberg's films, especially *War of the Worlds* and *Empire of the Sun* (1987). He spells out how philosophical analysis is importantly distinct from other sorts of analysis: philosophers attempt to establish conclusions about nonempirical or conceptual matters via (objective) reasoning and logical argumentation. Michel Le Gall and Charles Taliaferro provide insights into the *Indiana Jones* movies (1981, 1984, 1989),

E.T. (1982), and *Hook* (1991) via the history of philosophy, and in particular Plato and Socrates. No other discipline relies so heavily on its history as does philosophy. In fact, studying the history of philosophy is another way of "doing" philosophy. By knowing what the greats of philosophy concluded about a topic we "stand on the shoulders of giants" so as to better see our own philosophical surroundings. Le Gall and Taliaferro therefore invite you to explore some of Plato's texts, including the *Republic, Euthyphro,* and *Crito.* There is no better start to learning the history of philosophy.

These two essays should prove to be excellent preparation for the remaining essays. The third and fourth essays of the section provide aesthetic assessments of Spielberg's films. They should be of particular interest to film scholars and philosophers of film. John Wright introduces us to Emmanuel Levinas's idea of the "other" and explains how Spielberg attempted to capture this idea in his films, especially *Close Encounters* (1977), *E.T.,* and *Schindler's List* (1993). Christopher Trogan and I revisit Spielberg's first "summer blockbuster," *Jaws* (1975). We draw out its vivid connections to the issue of whether our emotional responses to fiction are rationally defensible. Tim Dunn closes part I with an analysis of *A.I.* (2001) as a commentary on the meaning of life. He parts with many critics of the film, arguing that Spielberg's rendering of what was originally Kubrick's project is underappreciated. Dunn believes that *A.I.* offers powerful—and perhaps tragic—insights into the human condition.

The second section, "Values, Virtue, and Justice," explores some of the more significant ethical insights that can be gleaned from Spielberg's corpus. James Spence begins this section by exploring *Jurassic Park* (1993) for its connections to the idea of equating what is good with what is natural. He utilizes the thought of Scottish philosopher David Hume to argue that attempts to ground moral goodness in nature are difficult to maintain. In the next essay, Roger Ebertz assesses the moral character of Oskar Schindler in *Schindler's List* via Aristotle and Immanuel Kant. Ebertz argues that Schindler largely fails as a good person on Kant's ethics, but fares better on an Aristotelian account of moral goodness, even though some doubts about his moral character remain. In the subsequent essay, Robert Clewis offers a novel interpretation of Spielberg's *Saving Private Ryan* (1998) and *The Color Purple* (1985). Rather than interpret these films via utilitarianism or deontology (as is typically the case, especially with *Saving Private Ryan*), Clewis argues that an "ethics of the family" approach also proves to be insightful.

The last two essays of part II turn to the interconnected issues of rights and justice. David Baggett and Mark Foreman use *Amistad* (1997) as a springboard to discuss the philosophical foundation of basic human rights.

This allows them to explore the ideas of John Locke, an English philosopher whose ideas greatly influenced the framing of the Declaration of Independence. Joseph Foy's essay on *Munich* (2005) brings this section to a close. Foy carefully and skillfully analyzes Spielberg's controversial film about the 1972 Munich Olympics massacre and Israel's subsequent covert response. He argues that, despite Spielberg's assurances to the contrary, Spielberg implicitly provides us his own views on counterterrorism. In the process, Foy raises interesting issues about just war theory and other ethical implications of military engagement.

The third and final section, "Realism, Mind, and Metaphysics," turns to issues dealing with how things fundamentally *are* rather than what is right, good, or just. In the first essay of this section, Keith Dromm focuses on the realism that often marks Spielberg's films, with *Saving Private Ryan* being a prime example. Dromm begins with an analysis of what it means for a film to be realistic, and in this way offers us further glimpses into aesthetics. His piece finishes with an exploration of some of the more significant philosophical ramifications of "cinematic realism." Alan White deftly canvasses basic positions in the philosophy of mind regarding the nature of consciousness and the mind-body problem. He creatively but forcefully argues that Spielberg's plot device in *A.I.* of David's (Haley Joel Osment) imprinting on Monica (Frances O'Connor) is crucial to better appreciating the prospects for artificial intelligence. It also proves to be the key for a deeper appreciation of the film itself. This section concludes with an analysis of *Minority Report*. The essay begins with a rendition of the freedom and foreknowledge problem and argues that the problem may be more apparent than real. It is further argued that *Minority Report* conveys a distinctive sort of knowledge about our future choices; Agatha (Samantha Morton) and the other precogs seem to have what might be called knowledge of the "conditional future." The essay concludes with an exploration of Spielberg's textual choice to close down Precrime (breaking with Philip K. Dick's original story) and offers reasons in favor of and against his decision.

The book ends with an appendix that facilitates discussion about Spielberg's work and its connections to philosophy. Five Spielberg films are highlighted: *Schindler's List, Amistad, A.I., Minority Report,* and *Munich.* For each film there is a plot summary and subsequent discussion questions that are ideal for film clubs, book club discussion circles, and film or philosophy classroom use.

Finally, there is an emerging issue in the philosophy of film and the philosophy of popular culture about whether a film "does" philosophy in a way analogous to professionally trained philosophers. If "doing philosophy" necessarily requires constructing arguments and defending their premises via logical analysis, it seems unlikely that popular film accomplishes *that*. (Perhaps only the most intellectually challenging documentaries might reach this high standard.) But it cannot be denied that movies raise philosophical questions and sometimes offer suggestions about their answers; if they did not, books like this one would never see the light of day. The real question, then, is to what extent a popular film *begins* to do philosophy. Some of the contributing authors are skeptical of whether film even begins to do philosophy; others are more sympathetic to the idea that it achieves important strides in this direction. We leave it to you, as one of your philosophical achievements, to decide this issue for yourself. It is our hope that after studying the pages that follow, you will be in a better position to defend your answer.

Part I

Philosophy, the Filmmaker, and the Human Condition

The "Big-Little" Film and Philosophy

Two Takes on Spielbergian Innocence

Gary Arms and Thomas Riley

Film—at least good film—can be assessed in a myriad of ways. In this essay we attempt to help the reader better understand and appreciate Steven Spielberg's choices as a filmmaker. Part I conveys pertinent literary and psychological insights, and part II offers relevant philosophical assessments. Through this combination, we intend to offer the reader an enriched conception of what Spielberg's movies have in common and how one goes about mining their surprising philosophical depths.

Part I

Steven Spielberg's favorite kind of film (the modern world's favorite, too) is the melodrama, especially that variety of melodrama known as the "action film." Melodramas portray the struggle between good and evil; the two forces violently contend, and good always wins. Spielberg's fondness for this sort of material has often attracted criticism. As Mark Kermode remarks at the beginning of his TV documentary *An Interview with Steven Spielberg*, "there are those who find Spielberg showy, melodramatic and, worst of all, sentimental."[1] Lester Friedman in his book *Citizen Spielberg* notes that "even sympathetic commentators routinely liken the energetic director to Peter Pan or Huck Finn, lumping him with archetypal figures who refuse to grow up."[2] In the minds of some critics, the melodrama seems a low form of narrative, one designed to appeal to the childish. The melodrama seems juvenile and artificial when compared to realism or tragedy.

Spielberg is America's most commercially successful maker of cinematic melodramas. In his most famous films (*E.T.* [1982], *Jurassic Park* [1993], *Jaws* [1975]), virtuous protagonists flee from, and eventually triumph over, terrifying villains. In *E.T.*, an alien from outer space, assisted by a brave boy, escapes from a variety of faceless adult officials (most of the time we see only their legs and flashlights). In *Jaws*, three men fight an enormous shark. In *Jurassic Park*, two children successfully escape the jaws of a T-rex and a pair of velociraptors. Asked to describe his 2005 film *War of the Worlds*, Spielberg told an interviewer: "It's about a family trying to survive and stay together, and they're surrounded by the most epically horrendous events you could possibly imagine."[3]

The formula for many of Spielberg's most famous films is innocence in great jeopardy. Normally, innocence is represented by children and their families. The parents are often separated or divorced. Spielberg's fondness for broken families seems connected to the divorce of his own parents, which occurred when he was sixteen. In an interview with Stephen Schiff, Spielberg described his parents' marriage as never a very happy one: "My dad was of that World War II ethic. . . . He brought home the bacon, and my mom cooked it, and we ate it. I went to my dad with things, but he was always analytical. I was more passionate in my approach to any question, and so we always clashed."[4] Arnold Spielberg is often described as a preoccupied, hard-working, rather distant man who caused his son to feel neglected.

Spielberg's films are full of missing or neglectful fathers and lonely children; this sort of material often provides the emotional heart of his films. "There is nothing wrong with being sentimental," Spielberg told interviewer Kermode. Defending his use of children and broken families, he stated: "Without these more personal emotional subconscious themes, these films wouldn't be as successful with audiences."[5] For Spielberg, the intact, loving family is a primary value; the story that his films often tell is that of the endangered broken family, the family that must struggle to survive terrifying peril. The happy ending at the conclusion of many of his films occurs when the enemy of the family is destroyed and the family returns to health.

As Spielberg's comment implies, there is a sound commercial reason that so many of his films focus on broken families and children. Films are extremely expensive to make. A modern action film will cost anywhere between $100 million and $200 million. According to the Internet Movie Database (www.imdb.com), Spielberg's *War of the Worlds* cost $132 million. Peter Jackson's *King Kong* (2005) cost more than $200 million. Films this expensive are risky to finance and must be aimed at the widest possible audience. It helps if they focus on children. They should either have children in central roles, as with the *Harry Potter* films (2001, 2002, 2004, 2005, 2007), or tell melodramatic adventure stories designed to appeal to young people, like the

X-Men series (2000, 2003, 2006) or the Lord of the Rings trilogy (2001, 2002, 2003). This strategy makes commercial sense because spectacle-oriented melodramas that focus on young people can be appreciated by adults *and* children. Most modern adults proudly retain a remnant of their child self, their inner child. The reverse is not true of children. What child contains an inner adult? Most children, if forced to watch a film for "grown-ups" (e.g., *Munich* [2005], *Crash* [2004]) will soon grow bored. For this reason, an exciting film aimed at young people potentially will gain a much larger audience than a film with a complicated adult problem at its center. There is a way, however, to combine realistic family problems with sensational and fantastic material, to combine the emotional upheavals experienced by the members of a broken family with the thrills of melodrama. Spielberg is the master of this mixture.

Filmmakers often refer to films that focus only on realistic emotional and social problems as "little films." Such films (e.g., *Little Miss Sunshine* [2006]) feature the acting and writing and have few special effects; they are made with relatively low budgets. Action films with huge budgets, full of special effects, explosions, and monsters, are called "big films." Talking about Spielberg's *War of the Worlds*, its star, Tom Cruise, described the film as "the biggest, smallest movie that we've made."[6] Spielberg compared the film to David Lean's *Lawrence of Arabia* (1962) and added, "I thought that [*Lawrence*] was the biggest smallest movie I'd ever seen. It has the most intimate, sensitive, personal, up-close story, and yet it was told against some of the greatest [scenes] we'd ever beheld in 70 mm."[7] Spielberg has mastered this particular art, the art of making big-budget thrillers that also contain realistic family conflict, the art of "big-little" films.

In Spielberg's case, we may suspect that the commercially sensible focus on broken families caught up in exciting melodrama is supported by a psychological need to explore and revisit his personal trauma. At least, there seems little doubt that psychologically Spielberg remains intimately connected to the intense feelings he experienced in his adolescence, and that he has become adept at exploiting such feelings in order to make gripping films.

The topic of the broken family provides a filmmaker with enormously sympathetic material. In the United States, we often hear, something like one half of marriages end in divorce. Those of us who work with college students are highly aware that a great many of our students are the children of divorced couples. They are often affected emotionally by these divorces. Almost all of us are touched by divorce; we are divorced ourselves, or the children of divorce, or have somehow witnessed the effects of divorce at close hand. Spielberg's remembered trauma, the divorce of his parents, is very similar to the experience of huge numbers of modern filmgoers.

ADAPTING *MINORITY REPORT*

In the film *Minority Report* (2002), the source material, the original novella by sci-fi writer Philip K. Dick, is altered in significant ways. The screenplay was written by Scott Frank and Jon Cohen, but it had to meet with Spielberg's approval. Spielberg hesitated about making the film until he found the right script; not until then did he call his star, Tom Cruise, and tell him, "Yeah, I'll do *this* version of the script."[8] There are numerous differences between the Dick novella and the screenplay, but the most noticeable is the script's inclusion of a highly personal story about a broken family. It is this that transforms *Minority Report* from a typical "big" film to a trademark Spielbergian "big-little" film.

From the Dick version of the story comes the concept of Precrime (criminals are captured *before* they commit murder), as well as the idea of precogs (humans who are able to predict the future). Potential murderers are identified by the precogs; these "criminals" are arrested by the enforcers of Precrime and then imprisoned. In both versions of the story, the protagonist, Anderton, who works for the Precrime organization, discovers that he is suspected of a murder that has yet to happen; he must flee to save his life while struggling to learn why he is being set up. (As is typical of Hollywood adaptations, the middle-aged and out-of-shape protagonist of Dick's story is transformed by the film into a handsome and youthful movie star [Tom Cruise].) In the Dick version of the story, Anderton has a wife who he fears is cheating on him, but there is no mention of any children. His primary motivation is to save his own life, and to save his invention, Precrime. The screenplay contains several revealing alterations.

In the film, the protagonist's psychological profile is dominated by the fact that his beloved son Sean, a child who appears to have been no more than five years old, was kidnapped and then almost certainly abused and murdered by a human monster who was never captured. We learn that the loss of his son became Anderton's primary professional motivation. He joined the Precrime unit in order to prevent similar murders. Anderton has become a superb professional in his role as an investigator and enforcer of Precrime, but the loss of his son remains an open wound. In his spare time, he gets high on an illegal drug known as "Clarity" and watches holograms of his lost son. He so badly needs to reconnect with the missing child that he has become addicted not only to the drug but also to these holograms. Anderton's marriage dissolved after the kidnapping, and he seems to have nothing to live for except his job. The screenplay of *Minority Report* also provides the protagonist with a boss, the director of Precrime, Lamar Burgess (Max von Sydow), who ruthlessly exploits Anderton's emotional vulnerability in order to set him up for murder. Anderton is tricked into believing he has discovered the man who kidnapped his son and, upon finding the man, fills with murderous rage. This material about the missing son provides the film's story its emotional core. The protagonist of Spielberg's version seems vastly more sympathetic than the protagonist of the Dick story because we witness the suffering he must endure from the loss of his beloved child. Any parent can relate to this sort of subject matter; it is every parent's nightmare.[9]

While attempting to clear himself of his alleged future murder, Anderton kidnaps the precog Agatha (Samantha Morton). The film makes Agatha vastly more sympathetic than does Dick's novella. In Dick's story, the precogs are described as repulsive, "retarded" creatures able to do nothing but sit strapped to chairs and mumble their visions. In the film, they are described as "the innocents we now use to stop the guilty"; they float in a large, womblike pool and are cared for by an attentive babysitter who seems almost in love with Agatha. Once Anderton frees Agatha from the pool, she emerges as a genuine human being, a hypersensitive innocent afflicted with terrifying visions, exploited by the Precrime organization, and deprived of anything resembling an ordinary life. Constantly pursued by the Precrime officers (dressed very like storm troopers), the two of them flee from place to place. Although so weak she can barely stand upright, Agatha begins to talk and actually helps Anderton escape. Using her power of precognition, the fragile and innocent victim proves resourceful enough to save her rescuer.[10]

At the climax of the film, we learn that Agatha was taken from her mother by one of the founders of Precrime, the director Lamar Burgess. Since Agatha and the twins are the only functioning precogs in the country, Precrime could not exist without them. Although it is unclear whether or not Agatha is sister to the twins, several times we hear that Agatha is the best of the three precogs and are told the twins cannot function well in their role by themselves. Burgess, we learn, fearing he might lose control of the invaluable precogs, lured Agatha's mother, Ann Lively, to a lake by promising her he would return her child to her; in fact he lured her there only to murder her. The mystery of the set-up is finally solved when Anderton learns that Director Burgess, the founding father of Precrime, has ruthlessly destroyed a family, murdered an innocent mother, and kidnapped a helpless child in order to protect his organization. Adding these broken or endangered families to the Dick novella provides the film version of *Minority Report* its emotional power and allows it to be both a "big" and a "little" film.

At the conclusion of *Minority Report,* Spielberg shows us his two main families restored to health. The murderous Director Burgess is dead. Pre-crime is shut down forever. The three precogs live in an isolated cabin far from other human beings, where they read a great many books and seem happy and content. Although Anderton failed to save his lost son from the kidnapper, he has saved Ann Lively's innocent child, Agatha, from Director Burgess. Our last glimpse of Anderton reveals that he has reunited with his wife, and that she is eight months pregnant. We see the husband and wife in a tender embrace and feel confident that the happy family unit (father, mother, and child) will soon exist again.

ADAPTING WELLS'S *WAR OF THE WORLDS*

We find intriguingly similar characters in the film that Spielberg made three years after *Minority Report,* his adaptation of H. G. Wells's *War of the Worlds.* When asked to describe the film, Spielberg told an interviewer: "It's nothing you can really describe. The whole thing is very experiential. The point of view is very personal."[11] In an interview with Paul Fischer, Spielberg contrasts his early film *Close Encounters of the Third Kind* (1977) with the later *War of the Worlds.* He thinks of *Encounters* as a young man's film: "*Close Encounters* is about a man whose insatiable curiosity develops into an obsession that drew him away from his family and, only looking back once, made him walk into the mothership. Now I wrote that before I had any kids. So I wrote that blithely. Now I have seven kids. Today I would never have the guy leave his family and go onto the mothership. Today I would have the guy do every-thing he could to protect his children."[12] If *Close Encounters* is a film made by a childless young man about a father who abandons his family to go on a quest, *War of the Worlds* is a film made by a middle-aged man with seven children that describes a father who does everything he can to protect his children. One might even suspect that, at least in terms of its portrayal of fathers, *War of the Worlds* is a kind of apology for *Close Encounters.*

Spielberg's films solve the dilemma of how to make popular genre mov-ies (sci-fi thrill rides) and at the same time make "personal" films, movies that focus on the filmmaker's emotions and interests, by mixing personal material into adventure stories. When Spielberg decided to transform H. G. Wells's classic sci-fi adventure into a "personal" film, he transformed it into a story about a father desperately trying to protect his children. The Wells novel has become a personal story, a story about the two Spielbergs—the young one who could abandon his family for a dangerous adventure, and the middle-aged man who will do anything to save his kids.

Spielberg's intriguing image of two Spielbergs is worthy of further exploration. Spielberg was talking about two versions of himself, but we may wonder whether the two father-types that he contemplates are really based on himself and his own father, Arnold. His male characters who neglect or abandon their children seem based at least partly on the latter. In his book *Citizen Spielberg*, Friedman notes that Arnold "was a World War II veteran, electronics engineer, and early computer pioneer who paid little attention to his son. In numerous interviews, Spielberg reveals how emotionally distant his father was during adolescence: 'I always felt my father put his work before me. I always thought he loved me less than his work, and I suffered as a result.'"[13]

In an interview, Spielberg stated that he had wanted to turn *War of the Worlds* into a movie ever since he bought the only surviving script of the Orson Wells radio play. After reading the radio play he concluded it "would make an amazing movie." Unfortunately, a bunch of "scavenger films came out that sort of picked the bones of H. G. Wells over the years, and when *Independence Day* came out, I said, 'Well, maybe I won't make it.' Because they kind of picked the bones of that, you know. They didn't pick it clean, and they picked different bones than I would have chosen to pick from the original H. G. Wells book, but that kinda put me off for a while."[14] Spielberg's enthusiasm for the project was rekindled when he pitched three movie ideas to Tom Cruise and Cruise responded enthusiastically to that of *War of the Worlds*.

Spielberg does not so much find a few "unpicked bones" in the Wells novel as film a script that includes material entirely missing from the book, the kind of personal material that Spielberg always seems eager to explore. In the Wells novel, the protagonist is a single man, a "moral philosopher." In the Spielberg version, he becomes a divorced, blue-collar crane operator with two children. Spielberg's version shows the protagonist experiencing a significant character arc. He changes from an inattentive father who is estranged from his children to one who is passionately connected to them and will do anything to protect them. In other words, he seems to change from an "Arnold Spielberg" sort of father into the kind of child-centered and heroic father that Steven Spielberg much prefers.

Spielberg has described his film as a highly personal story that focuses on character. It may seem odd to describe a story about an invasion of monstrous aliens in this way, but for Spielberg "this one was 100 percent character." Whereas *Minority Report* was "fifty percent character and fifty percent very complicated storytelling with layers and layers of murder mystery and plot,"

War of the Worlds was "a character journey."[15] It is revealing that Spielberg thinks in these terms of this big-budget action spectacular with its explosions and giant tripods. He has made his "big" film into a "big-little" film, one that combines spectacular scenes full of violence and horror with a number of "small," intimate scenes that focus on realistic family drama. In their script for *War of the Worlds,* Josh Friedman and David Koepp departed from the source material by adding children and a divorced father; it is this inclusion of the broken family that gave Spielberg a way into the material.

Ray, the character played by Tom Cruise, has a young daughter Rachel, played by Dakota Fanning. Fanning was the hot child actor at the time *War of the Worlds* was being cast, and she is used in the film primarily to demonstrate fear and vulnerability. She is the child who loves her father, the daughter who desperately needs his help. The young actress has enormous eyes that seem easily to fill with glistening tears; she can scream so loudly and shrilly one might expect her voice to shatter windows. Fanning is an instinctive actress with a startling range of expression, but for the most part Spielberg uses her in this fairly simple way—to register extreme fear. This is similar to the manner in which he used another girl actress, Ariana Richards, in his super-hit *Jurassic Park.* In both of these films, the actresses give fathers or father-types an opportunity to save them from great danger.

It is Ray's son Robbie (Justin Chatwin) who seems to remain like the young version of Spielberg (or like Steven's preoccupied father). Like the protagonist of *Close Encounters,* after the invasion of space aliens the young man becomes obsessed. Robbie is appalled by the destructive deeds of the monsters and their tripods. The entire human species seems on the verge of being ruthlessly dominated and exploited, even exterminated. He has to help his fellow human beings even if it means leaving behind his family, his dad and little sister. When he encounters an army attempting to fight back against the aliens, he tries to join it by hitching a ride. Realizing her big brother is eager to abandon her, Rachel shoves him hard and cries, "Who is going to take care of me?!" Robbie stays with his father and sister for a while longer, but eventually the young man responds to a higher calling and has to leave them. He seems to love his little sister, but cannot resist the chance to fight the monsters. For Robbie, the twin calls of adventure and duty to his country are irresistible.

The two children are important in the film, but the central emotional journey portrayed in *War of the Worlds* is that taken by Ray. In some ways, Tom Cruise seems an odd choice for this character, since he hardly seems like a blue-collar worker. It is even harder to take the perpetually boyish Cruise seriously as a father, but that is the point. He seems immature and self-absorbed. We quickly assume his immaturity explains why he has lost his wife to a more mature and financially successful man. This new husband even seems to be a better father and provider than Ray; the children are obviously fond of the man and are not at all eager to spend a weekend with Ray.

It is easy to see why the children do not trust their father, because Ray seems barely prepared to care for them. He has almost no food in the house and seems unable to cook. The kitchen is occupied by a disassembled car engine. His only way to entertain his alienated son is to drag him into the tiny back yard and force him to play catch. There is so much rivalry and bad blood between the son and the father that the boy Robbie can barely manage to be polite to Ray. The antagonism between them is symbolized by the fact that Robbie wears a Red Sox cap in pointed contrast to his father's Yankees cap. Robbie challenges his father at every opportunity. The son is nearly grown, and yet Ray barely knows who he is. For a father, Ray is oddly unfamiliar with basic health questions involving his children. When Rachel rejects the sandwich he fixes her and explains she has an allergy to peanut butter, Ray responds, "Since when?" Rachel replies, "Since birth!" One could describe the rest of the film as a quest in which an incompetent father tries desperately to return his children to their mother, but by doing so finally becomes a "true father," one who will risk his own life to save his children from harm.

Once Ray transforms into a heroic and caring father, the role of the family-deserting "Arnold-type father" is taken up by his son, who is determined to fight the aliens even if it means abandoning his father and sister. When Ray realizes his son is bent on joining the resistance, he does all he can to keep Robbie part of their little family. In one of the film's more powerful scenes, we see Ray tackle Robbie and violently hold him on the ground. Ray is literally lying on top of the boy while the son is begging his father to please let him go. In this scene, Ray is terribly torn, faced with a "Sophie's Choice" decision. Another man and woman find Rachel all alone and try to take her away with them. Ray must give up one of his children or risk losing both of them. He chooses to protect Rachel, his most vulnerable child, and watches Robbie run away to join the military.

We see the extreme of Ray's devotion to Rachel in the scene in the basement, when they encounter the crazy, maniacal character Harlan Ogilvy (brilliantly played by Tim Robbins). This character seems a more extreme version of Robbie: he is obsessed with the desire to fight back against the alien invaders and is dangerously reckless. Ogilvy's hatred of the aliens is certainly understandable, but if he is to be a good father, Ray must focus entirely on keeping his daughter safe. When Ray concludes that Ogilvy is

War of the Worlds, Paramount Pictures, 2005. With the ensuing global threat of extra-terrestrial invasion, once-absent father Ray Ferrier (Tom Cruise, *center*) realizes the immediate threat to his daughter's (Dakota Fanning) life in the form of crazed Harlan Ogilvy (Tim Robbins). (MovieGoods, Inc.)

so insanely focused on revenge that he endangers their lives, Ray is forced to kill him to keep him quiet. Never before has he done anything so violent, but in these extreme circumstances, when the safety of his child is at risk, he can actually commit murder. This murder is accomplished off-screen. Before he attacks Ogilvy, Ray makes his daughter close her eyes and sing a song to herself. Rachel is so innocent and fragile that she must be protected from not only the sight of murder, but also the sound.[16]

Anyone who sees *War of the Worlds* is likely to remember the film's many scenes of spectacular and horrific violence: the lightning bolts striking the earth, the enormous tripods rising up from fissures in the ground, the death rays that transform human beings to dust in a moment, the sprays of blood, the thudding explosions, and the fleeing mobs of people. Yet, it is the "small" human drama of one man trying to prove he is indeed a father who will do anything to save his children that gives this film its emotional center.

The conclusion of *War of the Worlds* is similar to that of *Minority Report*. Once the monsters are gone (they die, as they do in the novel, because of microbes), Ray and Rachel find their way to the home of Rachel's grand-parents, where they discover Ray's ex-wife and her new husband. The little girl and her mother embrace. The mother silently mouths the words "thank you" to Ray. Robbie suddenly appears too. In one of the film's final shots, we see the father and son embracing. We receive the usual happy and sentimental ending of the melodrama. The broken family is healed. We gather that, although the wife will continue to be married to her second husband, Ray will now be a useful part of this extended family. He has proved himself worthy; he is a true father.

FATHER KNOWS BEST?

As Lester Friedman comments, "Spielberg's screen children usually discover that father never knows best. Their dads either remain forever distant, forsake the family, neglect their offspring, or run off to pursue goals and people beyond the family unit."[17] One may find these distant and neglectful fathers in *Minority Report* and *War of the Worlds,* but in these later Spielberg films the director tells a different story. One gathers he is now telling the story not merely of Arnold, his distant and preoccupied father, but of the ideal and courageous parent we all hope to be, the father who is committed to his children, the dad who refuses ever to abandon them, the parent who will do anything to protect them.

Spielberg's action melodramas mix the intimate and highly personal stories of broken families, of single parents and wounded children, with the big, violent sequences for which action films are famous. They are "big" films certainly, but they are also "small, personal" films. Comparing the source material to the final films allows us to see how this was accomplished. Philip K. Dick's *Minority Report* is transformed from a story about a childless man attempting to save himself and his Precrime organization into a story about a family traumatized by the tragic loss of a son.[18] H. G. Wells's novel *The War of the Worlds* features a single man, a moral philosopher who has no children; but Spielberg transforms the childless hero into a neglectful and self-absorbed father forced by circumstances to become a true father, one who will literally risk his life to save his children.

Spielberg's "big" movies are really "big-little" films. They are action melodramas full of thrilling chase scenes and state-of-the art special effects, but they are also personal films that allow Spielberg to explore his own feelings and experiences, particularly those having to do with broken families, with single parents and frightened, grieving children. Spielberg is America's master of the "big-little" film.

Part II

Considering the films of Steven Spielberg, we have before us a body of cinematic literature, any piece of which is between one hundred and two hundred minutes of layered sounds and images that have been assembled under the strictest possible control. Each scene is edited together from multiple "takes," each of these takes having been recorded with multiple cameras and from multiple angles; the duration of each shot is carefully regulated for maximum dramatic effect and so that both the scene and the film as a whole have a discernible "pace"; each bar of music is composed to match and enhance the mood of the scene; and in the technologically sophisticated setting of current filmmaking, every frame can be adjusted for everything from color to composition. For whatever else one might say about him, Steven Spielberg does not appear to take a casual approach to filmmaking: we should rest assured, I think, that nothing appears in a Spielberg film that Spielberg does not want to be there. For a filmmaker like Spielberg, each and every facet of the final product somehow "expresses the filmmaker's vision."

DESCRIPTIVE-INTERPRETIVE AND PHILOSOPHICAL ANALYSES

Expressing a vision obviously means more than seeing to it that the film has the look that the director intended. It means that the film gives voice and image to those ideas (big and small) that ring true to the filmmaker. Once a person begins to understand how much goes into making a film and how much control over the desired effect an accomplished filmmaker like Spielberg can have, it seems obvious that the better we "know" both the film and the filmmaker, the better we understand the film. I would call this kind of groundwork a "descriptive-interpretive" analysis.[19]

When done carefully and thoughtfully, analyses like these call our attention to the details of a film; they provide us with a great deal of insight into the person who is making all these choices, but they also get us a long way toward understanding what the film is saying. It changes the way I understand a Spielberg film to know that as a boy he thought of his father as a remote figure, for example; to recognize that this experience may have influenced the way he depicted Ray in *War of the Worlds* or John Graham (Rupert Frazier) in *Empire of the Sun* (1987); to understand what made Spielberg's films commercially successful; to notice that he is relatively consistent from one screenplay to the next in the way he deviates from original source material, and so on. I would argue that this knowledge contributes to a deeper understanding of what Spielberg's films are saying.

There are no guarantees, of course, since "what a film is saying," especially in the case of a densely layered, well-crafted film like *Empire of the Sun* or *A.I.* (2001), is often a complex matter not expressible in a relatively small number of declarative sentences. This much is certain: it is not easy to be "right" about what a complex film is saying; however, it is possible to get it right, and we ought to try to see to that as much as we can. Getting the descriptive stuff right is a way of minimizing the chances that we are making some fundamental mistake about what a film is saying. This is where a detailed and insightful descriptive account is of the greatest value: it allows us to make reasonable inferences about "what the film is saying," or "what Spielberg wants the film to say," or even "what audiences (including critics) seem to think the film is saying."

A philosophical account, on the other hand, will likely build on our best descriptive-interpretive account of "what the film is saying" to carefully consider, given a certain interpretation, "whether what the film is saying is, in fact, true." This will not be easy for a number of reasons—not the least of which is, once again, that what the film is saying is sometimes difficult to express in terms that lend themselves to analysis. But that is not really the point. What we should be clear about is that philosophical analysis is a different kind of undertaking than descriptive-interpretive work.[20]

To sum up: descriptive-interpretive analyses begin, as one might expect, with descriptions of the factual state of affairs. To a certain extent, the measure of this phase of the analysis is the accuracy with which it captures the way the facts really are. As I outlined above, in the case of a film this means a tremendous number of things: the technical aspects of the film itself, the plot details, allusions to other creative works or historical events, the screenplay's divergence from original source material, and the director's own reports of his or her intentions, among others. We do our best to get all that right. Most of those who study a film do not stop there, however. They proceed through the accumulation, selection, and organization of this evidence to draw (hopefully) reasonable "interpretive" inferences. Much like a practitioner of a social science, the one carrying out a descriptive-interpretive analysis of a film will, based on the potentially very large amount of descriptive data, reach certain conclusions about the thematic content of the film. There is, as we know, a good deal of room for interpretive disagreement; but there is also a principled way of telling which of the interpretations on offer is to be preferred. The interpretation that makes the best use of the available descriptive data is, by and large, the best interpretation. What else would a reasonable interpretation be, if not the one that accounts for as much of the available information as possible, that makes all the pieces fit while allowing the film to speak for itself, that offers no contradiction to what the director has said on the record about the film, and so on?

Then what kinds of questions fuel the philosophical analysis of a film? If a descriptive analysis is also interpretive, what is left for a philosophical analysis of a film to accomplish? Isn't spinning out theories concerning "what it is all about" exactly what philosophers are supposed to do? Contrary to popular misconception, no. In much the same way as the interpretive moment of an analysis relies on the descriptive moment as its jumping-off point, a philosophical analysis of a film's themes takes its cues from the best available interpretive conclusions. Only once our best interpretive conclusions have been reached (as the result of authoritative descriptive-interpretive analyses) do the philosophical analyses begin. Suppose, for example, that we interpret Spielberg in *A.I.* to be saying, "Our technological reach has exceeded the grasp of our moral concepts." We immediately recognize a substantial number of questions, all of which are a crucial part of a complete appreciation of the film's themes, and all of which go well beyond the scope of the descriptive-interpretive process. Is it possible for a being like the synthetic boy to be "conscious"? What duties do we have toward apparently sentient though nonliving beings? Should we be permitted to make everything we can make? At that point, descriptive-interpretive methods can take us no further. The myriad questions that force themselves on us when we take Spielberg's putative claim seriously require an entirely different kind of analysis. These are philosophical questions that can only be adequately addressed using the methods of philosophy.

Those methods are, unfortunately, not so straightforward to enumerate. A casual list to pique the reader's interest would include the following: conceptual and linguistic analysis, where the possible meanings of our most fundamental notions and ways of talking are unpacked as carefully as possible; logical analysis, where the structures of arguments are examined to see if our controversial views follow from the reasons we give in support of them; phenomenological analysis, where we take stock of the character of our conscious experiences, from which, if we are careful, we can draw certain conclusions about the nature of the objects of those experiences; and thought experiments, which are a great way to work out what is possible ("what-if's") and what is necessary ("must-be's") and what follows from these, and are an obvious fit when analyzing movies. Philosophical investigations have a different character than descriptive and even interpretive investigations, because the subject matter of philosophy lies beyond the scope of description and interpretation. Philosophy is less concerned with the way things are than with the way things ought to be, or could be, or must be.

One of the dividends of a careful reading of the essays in this volume would be to get a sense of how descriptive-interpretive and properly philosophical analyses of a film differ.

PARENTAL OBLIGATIONS IN *WAR OF THE WORLDS*

As Professor Arms points out in the first section of this essay, the crucial "little film" aspect of *War of the Worlds* is the father's moral journey. Ray passes from delinquent dad, who is neither prepared nor all that willing to take care of his children, to a person who is, as Arms puts it, "a useful part of this extended family," "a true father" who has proved himself worthy. The film is crafted in such a way that the central "redemptive" transition of the film—what Arms rightly calls the film's "emotional core"—is Ray's recognition and acceptance of the deep and potentially very dangerous obligations he has as a father.

From the outset we should notice one relatively obvious thing: Ray's transformation as a character does not come in his recognizing some kind of "universal and neutral" obligation or some larger brotherhood-of-man kind of obligation. On the contrary, we start to feel some sympathy for Ray—we begin to root for him and he really comes to life as a character—when he begins to recognize the "special" obligations he bears toward his children as their father.[21] As the film progresses and the disaster approaches, and as Ray starts to abandon the selfish and immature person of the opening scenes of the movie, we the audience see some promise. He starts to place the interests of his kids ahead of his own. Moreover, we want Ray to put his kids' interests not just ahead of his own interests, but (especially as the situation deteriorates) over the interests of virtually everyone else they encounter. We will not be satisfied with Ray—he will not be redeemed for us—until he has expressed his willingness to do whatever it takes to honor those special obligations that he ignored so blatantly as the delinquent dad in the movie's opening scenes. This transformation reaches a climax when Ray carries out the violent but calculated murder of Harlan Ogilvy in the cellar to prevent him from inadvertently disclosing their location. Paradoxically, Ray becomes "good" precisely in the horrific decision to take another person's life with his bare hands for the sake of his special obligation to his daughter.[22]

OBLIGATIONS TO ALL CHILDREN IN *A.I.* AND *EMPIRE OF THE SUN*

Spielberg also seems to want us to believe that grown-ups have special obligations to children even if those children are not our own. In *A.I.*, Spielberg self-consciously ratchets up both the sympathy we feel for the robot-child David (Haley Joel Osment) and the sense of "innocence in great jeopardy" we are familiar with in his films. He accomplishes this by placing the wrench-ing scene in which David's surrogate mother Monica (Frances O'Connor) abandons him in the woods right along side the postapocalyptic "Flesh Fair" scene, where "mecha" are wantonly and violently destroyed. There is a great deal of emotional and moral tension in David's abandonment by Monica (who should know her obligations better, Spielberg might say), which is only aggravated by the peril David immediately lands in.

Enter the film's most interesting character, the fugitive Gigolo Joe (Jude Law)—an otherwise perfectly amoral love-mecha who, by the time his part in the drama is ended, shows himself to be a "hooker with a heart of gold." Joe the mecha redeems himself for us by recognizing the moral imperative to protect David even when "Mommy" the human did not. The important thing to notice here is that, rather than having the kind of obligations on which Spielberg builds *War of the Worlds, Empire of the Sun,* and the rest of his "parent" movies, Joe and David have no familial relationship, no friend-ship, no special bond whatsoever at their first meeting beyond the fact that they are both mecha and both in a heap of trouble. Joe shows no evidence that he feels any obligation to all mecha the way he does toward David, and although we in the audience are repulsed by the humans' behavior at the Flesh Fair and wish that all the captured mecha would be released unharmed, we urgently want Joe (and the other mecha in the cage) to place David's interests first.[23] Joe's redemption as a character comes in his recognizing the moral potential in protecting David in his quest for the Blue Fairy. As Joe's time on the lam runs out and he is lifted off to his doom by the police aircraft, we recognize his moral goodness. It is not because he and David are family or friends, nor for any other apparent relation that they stand in, but because Joe recognized something about David and acted on it in spite of the grave risks to himself.[24]

The same themes of parental obligations and obligations to all children are developed through a very different set of characters in a very different Spielberg film: the feckless father, John Graham, and his accidental surro-gates in *Empire of the Sun.*[25] In addition to the story of the twelve-year-old protagonist Jim (Christian Bale), what captures our attention in *Empire of the Sun* is once again the opportunities for redemption encountered by the other characters (both parents and strangers) as they interact with this preco-cious boy. The film's opening scenes are set in the surreal British enclave of Shanghai—a throwback to the security and privilege of a nineteenth-century British colony—in the days immediately preceding the Japanese invasion of China in 1941.

At the outset of the film, Jim's parents are indulgent but remote and relatively inattentive, not unlike all the other adults in the Grahams' social circle. Jim's father is an inoffensive but unsympathetic character who, in spite of the signs of impending danger on every side, seems more concerned with keeping up appearances—and burning what looks like evidence of shady dealings—than with ensuring his family's safety. The storm clouds gather for John Graham as he takes no steps to remove his family from danger, even as the explicit warnings from friendly voices accumulate. The family faces real danger—not for the last time—when Jim accidentally stumbles across a hostile regiment of Japanese soldiers. Only the presence of mind of the Grahams' family friend prevents a disastrous turn of events for the boy. Added to Jim's father's failure to recognize his obligation to move his family away from danger, we witness his inability to cope with a flesh-and-blood threat. This father is both too clueless to remove his family from danger and too weak to protect them when the danger materializes.

When the clouds finally burst and the Japanese march into Shanghai, Jim gets separated from his parents as they are attempting, much too late, to escape. Jim's father has failed to meet his obligations to his family—not so much out of immorality (as with others of Spielberg's cinematic fathers) as from self-absorption, inattention, and weakness. John Graham's failure is amplified in the film's final scene, in which he first fails to recognize his own son, walking directly past him among the other refugee children looking to be reunited with their parents, and then remains at a distance as mother and child embrace. Remote as ever, unable to participate in the family's reunion, John Graham is an unredeemed character because of his failure to live up to his special obligations.[26]

Following his separation from his parents, Jim returns to his family's home in the British enclave to discover the evidence (in a beautifully cinematic piece of filmmaking) of his parents' capture. Alone and hungry, Jim ultimately has to leave the empty house to fend for himself on the streets of Shanghai. Enter Basie (John Malkovich), the street-smart opportunist, scavenger, and survivor who plays Fagin to Jim's Oliver. Basie's character arc is unlike others we have seen from Spielberg in its almost grim lack of sentimentality. He is the perfect stranger who clearly recognizes something in this boy that ought to be protected. However, much worse than merely failing to live up to his special obligations to Jim because of weakness or self-absorption, Basie actively manipulates Jim for his own purposes. At one point he sends Jim on a "mission" in the knowledge that Jim might accidentally trigger a landmine; and ultimately he uses the information collected

Empire of the Sun, Warner Bros. Pictures/Amblin Entertainment, 1987. Spielberg implicitly raises the question of obligations to the innocent by depicting the dysfunctional association between Basie (John Malkovich, *left*) and Jim (Christian Bale). (MovieGoods, Inc.)

on Jim's mission to escape from his own predicament, breaking his promise not to leave Jim behind. There is something of Gigolo Joe in Basie. However, unlike Joe, who not only *recognizes* the potential for redemption in meeting his special obligations to the innocent David but *acts* on that recognition as well, Basie is an almost entirely reprehensible character throughout the film. Basie is not just an unattractive character because he is unrepentantly self-serving; he is truly reprehensible because his self-service is at the expense of one who ought to be receiving his protection.[27]

One way to read Spielberg's overarching moral view in these films is this: Persons fail in character-defining ways when they do not take their special parent-child obligations (Ray in *War of the Worlds,* Anderton in *Minority Report,* John Graham in *Empire of the Sun*) or special adult-child obligations (Gigolo Joe in *A.I.,* Basie in *Empire of the Sun*) seriously enough. And redemption comes, at least in part, in recognizing and acting on these obligations, no matter how dangerous they are.[28] So Spielberg singles out at least two kinds of special obligations for consideration in his films: the indefeasible obligations that parents have toward their children and the obligations that all adults have toward children.

It is not hard to grasp Spielberg's reasons for placing child characters on the receiving end (as "patients") of these special obligations: The great majority of people in the audience will believe that obligations toward children are among the most pressing of all. Because of this, audiences will connect with characters that either recognize their special obligations to children from the outset or come to recognize them as the plot unfolds. But looking more closely at the breadth of Spielberg's work, I think there is a more interesting reason, too. Elements of his filmmaking and screenwriting indicate that he has an even stronger view of special obligations. We have already seen that Spielberg clearly does not believe that *only* parents are the relevant agents of special obligations. On closer examination, it is equally clear that children are not the only patients of special obligations for Spielberg. As we view Spielberg's films we recognize the merit of acting on all sorts of special obligations whose scope extends well beyond parent-child or adult-child relationships. I will return to the question of the scope of Spielberg's special obligations toward the end of this essay.

THE PROBLEM OF SPECIAL OBLIGATIONS

The special obligations that seem to have caught Spielberg's moral and artistic imagination have long garnered the attention of moral philosophers. As we have been discussing here, for Spielberg they are a compelling way to generate both the external conflicts (innocence in great jeopardy) and the internal conflicts (previous failures to live up to these special obligations) that can drive both the action and the main character arc in a film. For philosophers, on the other hand, these special obligations are noteworthy for the kind of havoc they can wreak on our attempts to generate a satisfactory general account of moral obligation.[29]

From the subjective point of view, it seems obvious that not all obligations are created equal. Some obligations are felt differently than others by the person making a moral decision, and up to this point we have been discussing the most deeply felt of these obligations as Spielberg makes use of them in his films. But what is it that causes us to feel these differences? What makes special obligations "special"? One way to pinpoint the particularity or context-relativity of special obligations is to contrast them with obligations that are general and not context specific. Are there any obligations we have that are perfectly general? Are there any obligations we have to everyone all the time? Moral philosophers have spilled a lot of ink on this question:

What do we owe each other, just in virtue of our shared humanity? It should come as no surprise, even without studying much moral philosophy, that there have been a number of different answers proposed to a question like this one, including the possibility that we do not owe each other anything at all. However, among those who hold that we do have at least some obligations to each other, one of the most persuasive answers goes like this: of the alternatives available to me, I ought to choose whatever tends to produce the best consequences for as many people as possible. This is the conceptual kernel of a view called "consequentialism."[30]

There are many different forms of consequentialism, but they all have one feature in common: they hold that the rightness of an action is a function of its tendency to produce consequences that are intrinsically valuable, where intrinsic value is value for its own sake and not as a mere means to some good other than itself. For example, if money is good because you can use it as a means to procure some other good thing, then money is extrinsically good and will not be a relevant moral good for the consequentialist. Money is good *for* something. It is not just plain good, so it is not intrinsically valuable. Acts that produce as much money as possible may very well be good, but they are not good in a morally relevant way, according to the consequentialist. Consider instead those acts that tend to produce happiness. If happiness is something that is sought not for "what you can get for it" but as something worth having "just because it is good," then happiness is intrinsically good. So, one way to cash out the general principle of consequentialism is this: I have an obligation to act on those alternatives available to me that tend to produce the greatest happiness for as many people as possible, because doing that will produce the greatest amount of (intrinsically good) happiness.[31]

We can see at first glance that consequentialism is a good fit for our common sense because it seems obvious to most that we ought to produce good with our actions. Likewise, consequentialism is in line with important moral principles like equality, because if consequentialism is true then no one person's interests are more important than any other's. If happiness is intrinsically good, I need to make as much of it as I can by my actions, no matter who gets the happiness that results. Consequentialism is radically egalitarian, in that once I take the intrinsic value of happiness (or wherever my analysis of intrinsic value takes me) seriously, I am obliged to do what tends to produce the most of it, even if I do not benefit at all. Philosophers call obligations like these "agent-neutral duties," since neither the agent's interests, nor her particular situation, nor (importantly) her relationships have any effect on these obligations. In this way, consequentialism is able to give a very general account of the obligations we all have to each other all the time, which is, as I mention above, just what the philosopher is after. Nothing that I carry around with me and nothing that anyone else carries around with them should interfere with my doing whatever, of the alternatives, produces the greatest net intrinsic value.

Having said all that, however, we should readily see that anything like a "special" obligation is going to be tough to reconcile with consequentialism because agent-neutral obligation is antithetical to the special obligations we find so compelling. To spell out consequentialism's radical egalitarianism with respect to special obligations goes like this: If consequentialism is true, then in a *War of the Worlds* scenario, for Ray, Rachel's well-being is no more intrinsically valuable than some other person's well-being (we will pick Mr. X for "extra"). This is true even if Mr. X is a perfect stranger to Ray. Because Rachel's well-being is no more intrinsically valuable than Mr. X's well-being, Rachel's well-being should be no greater motivation for Ray to act in a particular way than Mr. X's well-being. Since the only obligation Ray has is the agent-neutral obligation to act so as to produce the greatest net intrinsic good, and all other obligations are derived from this single general imperative, it is not difficult to imagine a situation where Ray may be obliged to act so as to benefit Mr. X instead of acting so as to benefit Rachel—as long as by acting in this way Ray is producing the greatest net intrinsic value. Ray's acting on Rachel's behalf under these circumstances would, in fact, be *morally wrong* on the consequentialist account, even though she is his daughter and Mr. X is a perfect stranger. All this is even easier to see when put in terms of numbers of patients: if Ray can benefit ten extras a little bit or Rachel a little bit then Ray is required to benefit the extras, since what we are talking about is *net* intrinsic value, and intrinsic value is treated as if it is additive on the consequentialist account.

The problem for consequentialism in all this, of course, is that most people think that if I am presented with the opportunity either to benefit someone with whom I have an important relationship or to provide an equal benefit to a perfect stranger, I really ought to act so as to benefit the person with whom I have an important relationship. We can put this difficulty for consequentialism in the form of a deductively valid argument.[32]

1. If consequentialism is the correct account of moral obligations then the only obligation I have is the agent-neutral obligation to act so as to produce the greatest net intrinsic good.
2. If the only obligation I have is the agent-neutral obligation to act so as to produce the greatest net intrinsic good then one *should never* act to benefit those persons with whom one stands in

important relationships when a greater net intrinsic good could be produced by acting otherwise (i.e., there are no special obligations).

3. One *should* sometimes act to benefit those persons with whom one stands in important relationships even when doing otherwise may produce a greater net intrinsic value (i.e., there are special obligations).

4. Therefore, consequentialism is not the correct account of moral obligations.

Consequentialism holds that all obligations are agent-neutral and none are what we might call "agent-relative"; that is, neither the existence nor the force of obligations varies as a function of the agent's interests, nor her particular situation, nor her relationships. This runs contrary to common sense, which seems to allow for the possibility that there really are agent-relative duties.

Consequentialists have made various attempts to reconcile their view with these commonsense special obligations, of course. They are philosophers, after all, so that is what we should expect! Perhaps the most obvious way to account for what appears from the subjective point of view to be a special, agent-relative obligation is to hold that either we are obliged to act for what are really agent-neutral reasons (the act that seems to be required for agent-*relative* reasons is, in fact, required for agent-*neutral* reasons), or it is not an obligation at all (our genuine agent-neutral obligation is obscured by our self-interest, for example) even though it seems like one.

Take the example of a parent's special obligations to her children. There will be times, according to the consequentialist, when a father like Ray ought to place the good of his child ahead of the good of any other person, but that will not be because of a special obligation he has relative to being a parent. It is because parents' attending in a focused way to their children's needs tends to produce the greatest good for the greatest number in the long run. It could be argued that a society in which parents routinely place the interests of their children on a par with the interests of other individuals in that society will be less likely overall to produce benefits for its individuals. Such a society will not flourish, and therefore its individuals will not flourish. Parents' inclination to take care of their children, when they have that inclination, serves to produce the greatest net intrinsic value in the long run. However, even though we may hope that we never find ourselves in such a situation, there will be times when parents may very well be required by consequentialist principles to place the good of others—even strangers—above the good of their own children. This may place Ray in a difficult situation emotionally or psychologically (and these factors are not irrelevant to the consequentialist), but these feelings will not overrule the more general obligation he has to produce what is intrinsically valuable for whomever may be affected. It may cause Ray—or any of us—a great deal of emotional or psychological distress to do the right (agent-neutral) thing, but nobody promised that doing what is right was going to be easy or that doing what is right would make us happy.

What this defense of consequentialism boils down to, then, is that what we believe to be special obligations are, in fact, "derivative obligations," or variants of our more general obligation to maximize intrinsic value. There is nothing special about special obligations at all—they are nothing more than our general obligations as applied to those people with whom we also happen to have certain kinds of relationships.[33]

SPIELBERG AND SPECIAL OBLIGATIONS TO THE INNOCENT

This consequentialist reply is a challenge: Are there genuine (nonderivative) special obligations, and if so, what makes them "special"? But there is at least one other question we must ask the defender of special obligations. If there are genuine special obligations, what is the *ground* of these obligations? The consequentialist has a ready answer to the question of the grounds of obligation: agent-neutral duties are grounded in the intrinsic nature of those to whom these duties are owed—the intrinsic nature of humans. What grounds the egalitarian principles instantiated in consequentialist duties, for example? The consequentialist's answer to this question will include something about the intrinsic equality of human persons, such that no person's interests are more important than any other person's. That is what all persons are like (they are equal), so that is the kind of obligation we have to them (to treat all persons' interests equally). So what is the ground of our claim that there are such things as agent-relative duties?

I think Spielberg provides something like an answer to the question of the ground of special obligations in some of his films, whether he has intended to or not. I think Spielberg believes that there is something special about people who are "innocent" and this specialness of the Innocent is what grounds the special obligations we have toward her. Although I am not sure how satisfactory this "answer" is, I would like to return to Spielberg's films again for a moment. Let us take stock of the special obligations represented there to see whether there are any additional insights to be had.

Professor Arms has convinced me that "innocence in great jeopardy" is among Spielberg's favorite devices for propelling his films toward their resolutions. We see it powerfully portrayed in the characters of Rachel in *War of the Worlds,* David in *A.I.,* and Jim in *Empire of the Sun,* as well as Carol Anne (Heather O'Rourke) in Spielberg's screenplay for *Poltergeist* (1982);[34] four children so very much in need of protection. As we indicate above, redemption for the adult or worldly characters comes through recognition and acceptance of their obligation to provide the protection these Innocents need. But Spielberg does not limit his representations of the Innocent to children. Consider Agatha in *Minority Report* and Viktor Navorski (Tom Hanks) in *The Terminal* (2004), for instance. Spielberg does not even limit his portrayals of innocence to humans—if E.T. is not the Innocent then no character in film ever has been! But what is it about all these very different characters that elicits this kind of response from an audience? What is it about them that grounds the special obligations their worldly counterparts seem to feel and hope they can live up to? The answer that Spielberg seems to put forward in some of his films is that there is something "special" about the Innocent—or perhaps even about innocence itself—that merits our special preferential attention.

To be innocent in a Spielberg film is, on a certain level, to be harmless, simple, and naive. Consider how you might describe the characters mentioned above as they are represented in their first ten minutes of screen time in any of these films. Spielberg establishes these characters as worthy of our preferential attention just by virtue of their being pure and without guile, incapable of dissembling or dishonesty, open and full of wonder. We are drawn in by these characterizations to believe that innocence is something to be preserved in itself. I am reminded in this context of perhaps the most compelling scene from *War of the Worlds,* mentioned in the first section of this essay. Once Ray has decided that Ogilvy is a danger to his own and Rachel's survival and that he must be killed, he blindfolds Rachel and tells her to cover her ears and sing her favorite song to herself. Ray seems to recognize the need to preserve Rachel's innocence. We admire Ray's bravery in doing something that he clearly did not want to do and was afraid to do, and at the same time we admire his attempt to preserve something worthy and important in his daughter. Spielbergian "redemption" seems to come in those moments when it finally becomes clear to the worldly or sophisticated character that there is something special about being innocent. More would need to be said to assess what looks like Spielberg's view here, but recognition that innocence in a person is, by itself, worth protecting and preserving may at least partially serve to ground the special obligations we have to those persons who have it.[35]

In a Spielberg movie, to be innocent is to be harmless, simple, naive, pure, open, and full of wonder; but it is also a good deal more. Innocence often comes with unique gifts of intuition and perception, often to a much greater degree than the sophisticated characters possess. Carol Anne in *Poltergeist* is the first to sense the presence of the spirits; Rachel from *War of the Worlds* is always already awake and aware when the alien danger is approaching even if everyone else is at ease or asleep; David in *A.I.* seems to have a great deal more insight about unconditional love than his surrogate family; and, in the most extreme case, Agatha in *Minority Report* is literally able to see into the future. At the risk of stretching the analysis beyond the reader's tolerance, I think Spielberg's Innocents see the world more clearly than the other characters. Their openness, wonder, intuitiveness, and perceptiveness place them in a unique relation to the truth. This insight into the truth is an important part of what inspires the more sophisticated characters to accept their obligations. The Innocent, being what she is, brings out what is best in these other characters; in the presence of the Innocent the redeemed character lives up to his "special obligations." Just as the consequentialist might want to say as a way to ground our agent-neutral obligations, "That is what *all* people are like, so those are the kinds of obligations we have to them," Spielberg might want to say as a way to ground our special obligations, "That is what *some* people are like, so those are the kinds of obligations we have to them." One way to "read" Spielberg's view in these films is that when we lose our innocence as adults we lose something else along with it, something that very much ought to have been preserved. In our finer moments we realize this, and, when given the chance, we act accordingly. We ought to act according to this realization even if doing so does not produce the greatest net amount of utility.

WHAT MAKES AN ACCOUNT "PHILOSOPHICAL"? (REPRISE)

As we have seen above, a philosopher might very well be open to the possibility that there are no special obligations. Spielberg's films, on the other hand, do not seem to allow for this possibility, although I would not argue that this is a weakness in his filmmaking. If my reading of Spielberg's films is correct, then he is not attempting to raise the question of whether or not special obligations hold. He is forcefully putting forward the possibility that human beings (and maybe even mecha!) are redeemed by recognizing and courageously embracing these special obligations, no matter how dangerous they may be. This is another way of saying that we *ought* to be moved by the special obligations that we feel toward the Innocent, and when we do not we have failed in an important way. This is one of the ways in which a philosophical look at these themes in the films differs from what I have called a descriptive-interpretive look (in which, for instance, we might talk about

Spielberg's early family life, the "origins" of his feelings in his early experiences). Where it is an integral part of our descriptive-interpretive analysis to account for the possible *origins* of Spielberg's interest in these themes, the question of origins does not come into a philosophical analysis. The philosopher wants an answer to a very different kind of question: Is Spielberg *right* when he presents his characters as having special obligations?

No one who is looking at Spielberg's films is likely to deny that audiences are attracted to and feel positively toward characters who live up to their obligations to the Innocent when they encounter her. But why does he choose to represent his characters in the ways he has? Why alter the original texts in the ways he has? Why juxtapose the images he chooses to cut in next to each other? And why do I tend to react to these features of Spielberg's movies the way I do? Without taking the questions of author motivation and audience reaction seriously it is hard to imagine that any relatively complete understanding of film as a popular medium is possible. A descriptive-psychological account of Spielberg's films must certainly take seriously what we know of Spielberg's history, of the ways he has described his own earlier experiences, and, inasmuch as it is possible to do so, of an audience's feelings about such things; in fact, the more accurately our view expresses what we know about such things as Spielberg's early life, his relationship to his parents, what he has said about his reasons for making the myriad writing and directing choices he has made, and so on, the better the account will be.

We need to be aware, however, that by their very nature descriptive-interpretive analyses can only go so far, and much of real interest and importance in Spielberg's films lie entirely beyond the scope of descriptive-interpretive analyses. Whether or not the claims about the agent-relative obligations implicit in Spielberg's plots and characterizations are true—that is, whether we actually *have* the special obligations that we seem to *feel*—is a very different kind of question that requires a very different kind of answer. This is exactly the kind of question that no litany of descriptive or psychological facts about Spielberg (or about Spielberg's many audiences) can answer. Questions of this kind call for the properly philosophical analyses that constitute the balance of this volume.

Notes

1. Mark Kermode, "An Interview with Steven Spielberg," *Best Online Documentaries,* http://best.online.docus.googlepages.com (accessed September 28, 2007).

2. Lester D. Friedman, *Citizen Spielberg* (Urbana: University of Illinois Press, 2006), 31.

3. Brad Miska, "On-Set Interview: Tom Cruise and Steven Spielberg for 'War of the Worlds,'" *Dark Horizons*, February 11, 2005, http://www.darkhorizons.com/news05/warworlds.php (accessed September 28, 2007).

4. Stephen Schiff, "Seriously Spielberg," in *Steven Spielberg Interviews*, ed. Lester D. Friedman and Brent Notbohm (Jackson: University Press of Mississippi, 2000), 186–87.

5. Kermode, "An Interview with Steven Spielberg."

6. Miska, "On-Set Interview."

7. Miska, "On-Set Interview."

8. *Minority Report*, DVD (Glendale, CA: DreamWorks, 2002).

9. The story of Chief Anderton and his missing son is not the only story about an endangered family in the film; it is augmented by several other stories of endangered or broken families, none of which exist in the Dick version of *Minority Report*. In the film, the first Precrime case we see involves a love triangle. An intact family of three (a father, mother, and son) are at breakfast, while outside in a nearby park lurks the family's menace—the wife's lover. This trio parallels the trio of Anderton's family, with the kidnapper replaced by the lover.

Another example involves Leo Crow, the man who Anderton thinks kidnapped and murdered his son. At the climax of the scene in which Anderton finally captures Crow, we learn that he did not commit the crime but is pretending to have done so to trick Anderton into murdering him. He has been told that his family will be highly rewarded if he participates in this charade. Crow forces Anderton to kill him, but only to save his family.

A third example involves the "family" of the precogs, Agatha, Dash, and Arthur (names borrowed from the mystery writers Agatha Christie, Dashiell Hammett, and Arthur Conan Doyle), which I discuss in the body of this essay. And as yet another example, the Precrime organization has a mother and father, its founders, whereas in Dick's novella, Anderton was the founder. Spielberg has commented that while making the film he thought of the von Sydow character, Burgess, as "almost a surrogate father of Tom's character" (see "The Players," Extra Features, *Minority Report*, DVD [2002]). Burgess is presented as a tragically flawed father who tries to frame his "son" for murder. The "mother" of Precrime, Dr. Iris Hineman, is encountered in a greenhouse and seems to be a botanist who specializes in the creation of predatory plants. These two "parents" appear divorced; the mother is no longer connected to the organization, and does not thoroughly approve of it. She is a paradoxical combination of a caring mother who provides Anderton with useful information, and an incestuous one who strangles her own plants and disturbingly kisses Anderton on the mouth.

10. There is a similar moment in Spielberg's *E.T.* In one of the film's most famous scenes, the apparently frail and helpless E.T. suddenly proves powerful enough to fly, and thus saves his savior.

11. Miska, "On-Set Interview."

12. Paul Fischer, "Interview: Tom Cruise and Steven Spielberg for 'War of the Worlds,'" *Dark Horizons*, June 23, 2005, http://www.darkhorizons.com/news05/war1.php (accessed September 28, 2007).

13. Friedman, *Citizen Spielberg,* 34.

14. Miska, "On-Set Interview."

15. Fischer, "Interview."

16. In a similar scene, when an alien inside a gargantuan tripod captures Rachel, Ray proves he is willing to give up his own life; he screams and makes noise until the alien captures him too. In the film's most unbelievable scene, Ray grabs hold of a convenient cluster of grenades and allows himself to be sucked up into the alien's maw. In a move that seems borrowed from a similar scene in *Men in Black* (1997), he blows up the alien and its tripod from the inside. Because of this heroic and self-sacrificing action, Ray and his daughter survive.

17. Friedman, *Citizen Spielberg,* 33.

18. Indeed, the movie, unlike the novella, plausibly portrays a series of broken families; see note 9.

19. It is not within the scope of this essay to address all the vexing difficulties of "intention" in a piece of film or literature. We are both very well aware of these difficulties, and that some will find our commitment to the value of what I am calling descriptive-interpretive analyses to be naive or quaint, but we are not convinced by any theoretical framework that would have us eliminate accounts of the artist's intentions from our analyses, for example. Contrary to some, we agree (with each other, at least) that interesting descriptive-interpretive analyses are not only possible but extremely valuable in coming to a more complete understanding of a work. It may be, for example, that we can never know what the director "really intended"; it may be that the director's intent may not really even be known by the director; and it may even be that there are no such things as "intentions" in the relevant sense—but these skeptical worries all seem highly exaggerated to us. Again, it is not easy to get it right, but it does not seem impossible, in principle, to get it right enough.

20. I will be talking about how these two kinds of analyses differ with respect to film, but by and large the same considerations would be true if I were talking about any other creative or practical endeavor. In my view it is dangerous to confuse philosophy and its methods with any of the social sciences (e.g., psychology, sociology, anthropology, history, economics) and their methods. It is, regrettably, a relatively common confusion, even in the work of some philosophers and social scientists. I believe that the very same goes for the natural sciences, but that will not detain us here.

21. We should also notice that Spielberg has made films where the central character ultimately feels this kind of universal obligation and acts accordingly. *Schindler's List* (2003) leaps to mind, for example, and the case can probably be made for *Munich* as well. Be that as it may, in my view Spielberg seems more comfortable with showing a character's development through acceptance of these especially forceful special obligations than through the acceptance of universal obligations.

22. *War of the Worlds* is obviously not the only film in which Spielberg makes use of the special obligations that parents feel toward their children as a means of propelling the central conflict forward. Once again, as Arms points out in his section, the kidnapping of Anderton's son while the child is in his care is the principal motivation for Tom Cruise's

character throughout *Minority Report*. We are led to think of Anderton's passion for justice, his obsessive work habits, the failure of his marriage, and his addiction to the illicit
drug "Clarity" as following, in a sense, from his failure to adequately protect his young
son those years ago. As an audience member, I am not fully resolved on Anderton—not
fully sold on him as "the good guy"—until he has come to grips with the reality that his
son is gone and until that realization becomes his resolve to protect those he is obliged
to protect in the present. He failed to protect his son in the past, he is consumed by the
mistaken belief that revenge in the present will somehow atone for this past failing, and
he is ultimately redeemed in accepting that his son is gone and in risking his own life
in the dangerous task of liberating and protecting the precog Agatha. Furthermore, our
satisfaction with him as a character is probably intended to be tied up with a bow in the
film's epilogue, where his family has been reconstituted as the focus of his most important
obligations, and his future as the redeemed "good father" looks bright.

23. The other mecha in the cage seem to feel the same, especially the "FemMecha
Nanny," who never leaves David's side.

24. The same kind of sentiment is represented in the otherwise violence-crazed
spectators at the Flesh Fair, who protest so vehemently when David is strapped to the
contraption that is intended to destroy him that the proceedings come to a halt. They
do not seem to care about the other mecha—far from it, in fact. Despite their strong
belief that he is a mecha (as are all "participants" in Flesh Fairs), the spectators do not
want David harmed because he seems too much like an orga child.

25. Thanks to Dean Kowalski for his careful reading of this essay and his numerous
suggestions, but especially for his recommendation that I take a look at *Empire of the
Sun*. Though neither a perfect film nor Spielberg's best, it is a beautiful and (I think)
vastly underappreciated gem.

26. Among Spielberg's recurring metaphors for this failed family is the precious
page from the *Saturday Evening Post* that Jim hangs over his bunk throughout his in-
ternment. In that famous illustration, entitled *Freedom from Fear*, Norman Rockwell
"depicts children safely sleeping, tucked warmly beneath their covers and protected from
harm by their parents. Although Jim literally carries a copy of this picture . . . wherever
he travels, his increasing difficulties make Rockwell's image function as more of an
ironic comment than a scrap of nostalgia. His parents utterly fail to protect him. . . . So
while the treasured Rockwell picture overtly sparks memories of the lavish world Jim
inhabited [before the invasion], it simultaneously reveals the growing distance between
the essential requirement of the father to be protector and [John] Graham's failure to
discharge his primary obligation." Friedman, *Citizen Spielberg*, 204.

27. Although Spielberg is known for his sentimentality, the ending of *Empire of the
Sun* is uncharacteristically dark. Jim is reunited with his parents, but there is no joy in
his eyes. After all that Jim has been through—not only the misery and deprivation but
also the manifold failures of those who ought to have been looking out for him—the
emptiness of his gaze in the closing scene is strikingly unsentimental. Jim is clearly
damaged goods, and I think Spielberg would have us lay that at the feet of those who
ought to have done better by him.

28. Although the discussion here and throughout this volume focuses primarily on films that Spielberg directed, one of the clearest examples of his use of this device is in his story and screenplay for the 1982 film *Poltergeist*. *Poltergeist* is a supernatural horror/thriller written by Spielberg but directed by Tobe Hooper (of the original 1974 *Texas Chainsaw Massacre* fame). It focuses on a poorly functioning (though not broken) family that takes up residence in a new house unfortunately built over a cemetery by an unscrupulous real estate developer. The unsettled spirits make contact, with their presence initially perceived ("They're here!") by five-year-old Carol Anne through the late-night static on the TV. The poltergeists' haunting begins innocuously and gradually, only to become progressively more destructive and violent. They ultimately go so far as to carry off Carol Anne bodily to the spirit world. The central arc of the story is then focused on the reconstitution of the family as they attempt to retrieve their youngest member from this "great danger."

When the film opens, the father (Craig T. Nelson) is very much the Spielbergian delinquent dad: remote, impatient with the simplest of his parental duties, irresponsible, and prone to drink too much. He is, in other words, that familiar Spielberg character whose defining flaw is a function of his failure to recognize his family obligations for what they are. Mom (JoBeth Williams) represents the more positive possibility: she is spontaneous and unswerving in her willingness to sacrifice whatever is necessary to rescue and protect her children, though she is certainly not without character flaws as well. Dad initially does not fare well by comparison in the eyes of the audience, but, as might be expected, we start to care about him as he begins to accept his parental responsibilities, even as the depth of those responsibilities begins to dawn on him. His character is redeemed by the end of the film in the acceptance of his special obligations to his daughter and his family and his acceptance of the risks he has to face to live up to those responsibilities.

29. Much more complete discussions of the problem of special obligations can be found in the philosophical literature. In the discussion that follows I rely in part on these works: Richard Fumerton and Diane Jeske, "Relatives and Relativism," *Philosophical Studies* 87 (1997): 143–57; Diane Jeske, "Families, Friends, and Special Obligations," *Canadian Journal of Philosophy* 28 (1998): 527–56; Thomas Nagel, *The View from Nowhere* (New York: Oxford University Press, 1986); and Samuel Scheffler, "Relationships and Responsibilities," *Philosophy and Public Affairs* 26 (1997): 189–209.

30. Spielberg has made films that seem to address the question of consequentialism directly. *Saving Private Ryan,* for example, is sometimes used as a vehicle for teaching the basic principles of consequentialism to beginning philosophy students. Is it reasonable for this whole platoon to entertain the risks it does in the course of the narrative in order to save one soldier? Even though it seems like the right thing to do at the time, does it not turn out that Captain Miller (Tom Hanks) makes the wrong decision by releasing "Steamboat Willie" (the German soldier captured at the radar station), since Steamboat Willie eventually kills him? It seems to most interpreters of this film that Spielberg wants us to consider whether or not the rightness of our actions really is determined by the way things turn out.

31. A cautionary note: because there are numerous varieties of consequentialism, my analysis of the difference between intrinsic and extrinsic goods will not be acceptable to all consequentialists; and even to those consequentialists who basically agree with me here, the analysis has probably moved too quickly. Nevertheless, I think this way of talking about consequentialism makes the most of the view's connections to "commonsense morality." That is really the point here.

32. A deductively valid argument is any argument such that the truth of the conclusion is guaranteed by the truth of the premises. In other words, if the premises of a deductively valid argument are true, the conclusion follows necessarily.

33. The utilitarian could respond this way, of course, but there are two reasons to think that this rejoinder does not work. The first is supported by the kinds of intuitions we have when watching a Spielberg movie and it has to do with the way "reasons to act" seem to work. Even if I believe that one ought to maximize utility or happiness, that is not *why* I want Ray to protect his kids, nor *why* an audience might be in favor of Anderton's protecting Agatha, and it is uniquely unsatisfying from the point of view of "matching up with common sense" to say that maximizing utility *should* be my reason even if it is not. This whole line of argument seems to beg the question against the special obligations objection, since what Ray's reasons should be is exactly what is called into question by the objection. The appeal to special obligation is, after all, an appeal to our commonsense intuitions, and if we can always set aside our perceived special obligations in favor of some maximizing principle, then the utilitarian obviously wins. But the dissonance between our perceived obligations and maximizing utility is precisely what is in dispute here, and no bald assertion from the consequentialist that our obligations are all agent-neutral will carry the day.

The second reason is that although it sometimes maximizes utility to protect the innocent, it does not *necessarily* do so. I can imagine, in fact, some kinds of felt special obligations that *usually do not* produce the greatest good for the greatest number. However, felt obligations to the innocent, at least the obligations I perceive Spielberg's characters to have, do not seem to vary with these circumstances. Even if you want to say that we ought to protect children, for example, because, being young, they have the potential of lots of pleasure for longer, the same does not apply in the case of Agatha, who is no longer a child—but we still feel as though Anderton ought to protect her. Our intuition that Anderton ought to protect Agatha remains, in other words, on whatever analysis of the utility of that course of action we end up with.

34. For discussion of *Poltergeist*, see note 28.

35. A consequentialist might, for example, read Spielberg's choices as reflecting the view that innocence is intrinsically valuable. If it is true that innocence is intrinsically valuable, then we may have a way to reconcile agent-neutral and agent-relative obligations—at least as far as innocence goes—within consequentialism.

The Recovery of Childhood and the Search for the Absent Father

Michel Le Gall and Charles Taliaferro

Spielberg's early films *Duel* (1971; made for ABC's *Movie of the Week* series), *Sugarland Express* (1974), and *Jaws* (1975) are the work of a driven young man taken with the power of the camera and its ability to create a sense of energy, obsession, and pending doom. His subsequent movies, however, advance a more sustained, subtle meditation on the responsibilities of fatherhood and the recovery of childhood. Many of Spielberg's later films could be mined for insights into the relationship between fathers and sons, but we intend to focus on *E.T.* (1982), *Hook* (1991), and the *Indiana Jones* movies (1981, 1984, 1989). By concentrating on these five films, we endeavor to give shape to a philosophy of sons and fathers or, more broadly, childhood and parenthood that may also be detected in his other work.

By taking on the potential harms of parenthood (especially the wound of growing up with an absent father), as well as the promise of recovering an integrated parent-child relationship, Spielberg's movies speak to a deep theme found at the beginning of Western mythology and philosophy. Greek mythology and early literature were haunted by the ways in which parent-child relations can go horrifically wrong: in Hesiod's *Works and Days* the god Chronus kills and eats his young; in Euripides' *Medea* a mother kills her children; and in Sophocles' *Oedipus Tyrannus* a son kills his father. Perhaps the most tender treatment of the father-son relationship, and the one that comes closest to bearing on Spielberg's themes, is Homer's *Odyssey*. When Odysseus is reunited with his son, Telemachus, they both weep, partly for joy at being together it seems, but also (arguably) for the loss of their twenty years apart, and thus the absence of a father-son relationship.

Although there is no unified philosophical response to these cultural narratives of fatherhood and childhood, there is a sense in which in Plato's work,

Socrates (who eventually came to be known as the father of philosophy) functions as the father of his interlocutors, pointing them in the direction of a new home or habitat. Especially in the *Republic*, Socrates eventually seems to dismiss the aged man Cephalus who is near death and has lost all erotic desire for fulfillment, and he concentrates instead on the younger men who are seeking guidance on understanding justice, women, and family. At the end of the *Republic*, Socrates presents the Myth of Er, according to which souls in a world beyond this one can choose which kind of life they would like to live; this is like a case of reincarnation in which you get to choose what kind of birth and life you will have. Many choose the life of a tyrant, but the one whom Socrates favors chooses the life of an ordinary person (10.620c). Here, Socrates' fatherly advice is to shun the life of worldly glory through fame or the love of money (which he condemns in books 8 and 9), or a retreat to a self-conscious "old age" that has no semblance of youth; Socrates instead counsels us to find youthful pleasure in the ordinary pacific affairs of life, beginning with the rebirth of the soul as a child.

We believe that Spielberg's films speak to a Socratic ideal of rebirth and wisdom: the *Indiana Jones* movies ultimately locate the restoration of a father and son in the setting aside of a quest for glory; *E.T.* underscores how sons sometimes have to act as fathers; and *Hook* shows us that sometimes fathers need to recover their childhood in order to restore their own parent-child relationships. These films bring to light the problems facing broken or dysfunctional families, while also suggesting a Socratic remedy: the way home is by way of the ever renewing (or continuous rebirth) of domestic tenderness and the beauty of hospitality rather than the pursuit of glory.

The Prodigal Son: *Indiana Jones*

For Indiana Jones (Harrison Ford), the absent father has here and there left traces—both emotionally and figuratively. On the face of it, Jones is a straight swashbuckling hero. He defies death and twice thwarts the Nazis: once in their effort to find the lost Ark, and once to find the Holy Grail. In between these adventures, he frees the children of an Indian village from the scourge of the "thuggees," a bloodthirsty cult devoted to the tantric goddess Kali.[1] All that in a day's work. And yet, despite the brown fedora, leather jacket, and whip, Indiana is not a typical hero.[2] Although Spielberg does not belabor this point in the first two films of the series, perhaps out of fear that cheap psychology will somehow debase the currency of his hero, there are signs that not all is well.

When Indiana is first approached at his college by two army intelligence officials, he is queried about his relationship with Dr. Abner Ravenwood, a leading archeologist and expert on the Ark of the Covenant who has gone missing. Indiana defends Abner from the implied charge of being a traitor, but admits to a falling out between them some ten years earlier. As he packs for his quest to find the Ark (a dangerous obsession and a pursuit that will kill many—mostly Nazis), a note of foreboding sounds in the score when Indiana's curator friend, Dr. Marcus Brody (Denholm Elliot), warns him not to worry about Abner's daughter Marion (Karen Allen), but instead to worry about the powers of the Ark.[3] When Indiana goes looking for Marion Ravenwood in Nepal to begin his search for the headpiece that will help him locate the Ark, their first encounter is anything but pleasant. He has to face Marion's scorn:

> MARION: I've learned to hate you in the last ten years.
> INDIANA: I never meant to hurt you.
> MARION: I was a child. I was in love. It was wrong and you knew it.
> INDIANA: You knew what you were doing.
> MARION: Now I do. This is my place. Get out.

Speaking of her late father's opinion of the young Jones, the two continue:

> MARION: He said you were a bum.
> INDIANA: Aw, he's being generous.
> MARION: The most gifted bum he ever trained. You know, he loved you like a son. Took a hell of a lot for you to alienate him.
> INDIANA: Not much, just you.

This exchange makes it clear that Indiana betrayed the trust of his mentor and adoptive father through his relationship (or tryst?) with the then young and naive Marion. Humbled by her anger and in need of her help, Indiana inevitably ties his search for the Ark to his effort to restore his relationship with Marion, and by proxy her late father.

Fortunately for the audience, Spielberg casts this theme in a broader framework. He offers up Indiana as the swashbuckling prodigal son: a young archeologist of great potential who has turned his back on his father and mother, as well as his mentor, in order to pursue archeological treasure. Although he is not given to drunken and disorderly conduct, Indy's behavior is nevertheless reckless (a far cry from the calculating and dispassionate heroes of standard-fare action movies) and, on occasion, cavalier and unheroic. The manner in which he disposes of the Arab swordsman he stumbles upon as he desperately tries to find Marion in a marketplace filled with wicker baskets is typical of Spielberg's depiction of his lovable hero: he does not engage in any Errol Flynn–style swordsmanship, but simply pulls out his pistol and shoots the black-turbaned giant dead. Funny, but not classically heroic.[4]

Being a prodigal son—alone and without a family anchor—is in the end a rather tiring, if not tiresome, predicament. Indiana Jones continues to hint at this throughout the movie. He is constantly on the road, in search of something, away from home and hearth and the comforts of family life. As he saddles up to return to Cairo, where the Nazis transported the Ark after Jones unearthed it, he yells in response to his friend Sallah's (John Rhys-Davies) inquiry about his plan, "I don't know, I am making this up as I go!" On board Mr. Kantaga's (George Harris) ship before being turned over to the Nazis, Marion notes, "You're not the man I knew ten years ago"—to which he responds, "It's not the years, honey, it's the mileage." By the end of *Raiders of the Lost Ark* (1981), Indiana has saved Marion from certain death—"Don't look!" he yells as the Nazis unleash the angry souls entrapped in the Ark. And their uneasy and uncertain relationship is cemented by Marion's invitation to her rogue lover, who is despondent at the fact that the government officials do not appreciate the full powers of the Ark. She counters, "Well, I know what I've got here. Come on. I'll buy you a drink. You know, a drink?" Off to the bar is hardly off into the sunset. Indeed, the last shot of the movie—an homage to the final panorama shot of *Citizen Kane* (1941) with all Kane's loot in the great hall—is anticlimactic. The hero has not come to terms with the declared object of his search. Instead, he has won the girl he once hurt and indirectly patched things up with his late mentor: a happy but unintended consequence of his prodigal behavior. The problem with his own father, however, persists.

Temple of Doom (1984) sees Indy return to fight in a darker and bloodier story—that of disappearing children in an Indian village haunted and terrified by the thuggees. In the course of his adventures with harebrained Willie Scott (Kate Capshaw) and child prodigy Short Round (Jonathan Ke Quan), Indiana learns the perils and rewards of being a parent, albeit an adoptive and spiritual parent, to the thousands of children he frees; and, of course, to Short Round. But Short Round is no helpless child. *Temple of Doom* hints at several themes—including Indy as the adoptive father and the child as parent—but resolves very few of them. This may be why many critics found the movie to be dark and violent: it offers so little thematic light.

By contrast, *Indiana Jones and the Last Crusade* (1989) resurrects and resolves several of Indy's quandaries as prodigal son. In the opening se-

Indiana Jones and the Last Crusade, Paramount Pictures/Lucas Film, 1989. The (eventual) restoration of the relationship between Indy (Harrison Ford, *right*) and his father (Sean Connery) after decades of neglect and resentment speaks to a Socratic ideal of rebirth and wisdom. (Jerry Ohlinger's Movie Material Store)

quence, a flashback, we are introduced to his father, Professor Henry Jones (Sean Connery), who is more concerned with deciphering an ancient text than with his out-of-breath son (who has just escaped with the Coronado Cross from a band of graverobbers). In the scenes that explain Indy's efforts to free his father from the Nazis, Spielberg serves up a full dish of humor through the contrasting characters of Henry Jones, the absent father and absent-minded archeologist, and his son, Indiana, whose love of adventure far exceeds his love of pure scholarly pursuits. Henry continues to call his son "Junior," suggests that the name "Indiana" came from the family dog, and addresses him with condescension.[5] The father's indifference to his adventurer son is made abundantly clear in one scene where the father, not the son, acts as the hero. After saving them from an incoming Nazi fighter by provoking a flock of seagulls, Jones senior strolls away, noting nonchalantly, "I suddenly remembered my Charlemagne: 'Let my armies be the rocks and the trees and the birds in the sky.'" Probably a spurious quotation—not to be found in Einhard's *Life of Charlemagne*—but one that indirectly serves to distinguish father from son, the scholar from the adventurer, the absent father from the prodigal son.

It is only in the face of death that the father and son are reconciled and the missed ritual of the father-son relationship is let go. First, Indiana is forced to retrieve the grail from a booby-trapped room in order to save his father, who has been shot by the Nazis. When water from the grail is poured on the wound, Professor Jones is miraculously healed. An attempt by Dr. Elsa Schneider (Allison Doody)—a Nazi agent who we learn has slept with both Jones senior and Jones junior—to escape with the grail leads to disaster. As the temple housing the grail begins to collapse, Indy slips and nearly falls into the abyss, but his father grabs his hand.

> PROFESSOR HENRY JONES: Junior, give me your other hand! I can't hold on!
> INDIANA JONES: [*reaching for the grail*] I can get it. I can almost reach it, Dad . . .
> PROFESSOR HENRY JONES: Indiana.
> [*Surprised, Indy looks up at his father*]
> PROFESSOR HENRY JONES: Indiana . . . let it go.

From the simple act of calling his son by his preferred name and not "Junior," the final moment of reconciliation takes place. The father and son have respectively saved each other. But more important, the father extends to the son the respect he deserves as a man. That, for Spielberg, is perhaps the more important aspect of the relationship. It is only fitting, then, that Indy, Professor Henry Jones, and Brody saddle up and ride off into the sunset this time—the final shot of *Last Crusade*—in contrast to *Raiders,* where Indy and Marion are off to the bar. The ending is romantic and playful, largely because their quest was not one of improper glory.

In Plato's dialogues, Socrates does not repudiate the life of a warrior, but he does offer an alternative to the deeply embedded Greek pursuit of worldly praise and awe known as glory (*kleos*) through war and martial victory. On this point, Socrates seems to side with one set of Homeric virtues rather than another. In the *Iliad,* glory dominates, but it seems to lead nowhere (the death of friend and self) except for memorial praise. But at the end of the *Odyssey,* Odysseus is reunited with his wife Penelope. Odysseus has put aside the possibility of living forever in martial or erotic glory on an island with a beautiful goddess (Calypso promises him everlasting eros but he turns this down to return to his wife). When his true name and identity are revealed to his wife, he and Penelope do the three things any lovers would want to do after a long time apart: they share their stories, make love, and then sleep together. This embracing of domestic love in the marriage bed is the Socratic ideal bed, because it seeks restoration of persons through renewed enjoyment of beauty. In place of Achilles and Hector's competition for glory before the city of Troy, Socrates points to the superabundant, restorative power of beauty. In the *Symposium* and the *Republic,* the ideals of beauty and goodness are seen as the true guiding principles in life; the goal of the most important adventure of the soul is to arrive at a life that participates in the good and the beautiful. Beauty rather than glory is the key to fecundity. For subsequent followers of Plato such as Plotinus, this end point was thought of as the true home of the soul.

Although Indiana's adventures in *Raiders* and *Crusade* involve religious artifacts that might be thought of as objects of beauty, they are more often seen as objects of sublime power, and the quest for them as a quest for glory. When Indiana lets go of this pursuit at the request of the restored father, he has arrived home. The notion that the point of an adventure is to arrive home is hinted at in the word itself—"adventure"—which is derived from the Latin *advenire,* meaning "arrive." True, Indiana arrives at the sites of the Ark and the grail, but he does not truly arrive in the full sense and complete his adventure until he is reconciled and rejoined with his father (who has learned to say the preferred name of his son) at the end.

Missing Fathers and Adult Children: *E.T.*

Both *Hook* and *E.T.,* more than any other Spielberg pieces save *Empire of the Sun* (1987), are a tribute to the resilience of fatherless children. To some degree, one might argue that *E.T.* is the sequel to *Close Encounters,* or life without father, and a prequel to the themes of *Indiana Jones and the Temple of Doom.* In *E.T.,* released between *Raiders* and *Temple of Doom,* Spielberg turned to one of his favorite haunts, suburbia—a bleak terrain he also examined as writer, producer, and off-the-record director of *Poltergeist* (1982).

In this land of dead-end, treeless streets and cookie-cutter houses, Spielberg casts a happily dysfunctional family that is strong but constantly arguing—especially Elliott (Henry Thomas) and his bigger brother Michael (Robert MacNaughton). Their father has deserted the family to go to Mexico with a certain Sally, and very quickly Spielberg establishes that the two boys, not the mother, are in charge. When E.T. is first heard banging around in the small back yard, Michael and his friends grab kitchen knives. "Nobody go out there!" Elliott warns; his mother echoes (ineffectively), "Stop you guys, stay right here! . . . And put those knives back!"

After Elliott discovers E.T. and hides him in his room, the plot launches into a story of the relationship between the alien—lost and separated from his family by accident after a landing on earth—and the young, lost, fatherless boy. In time, both E.T. and Elliott become, on different occasions, the father and the son. In his role as father and protector of E.T., Elliott internalizes the fears and discoveries of the lost extraterrestrial. Spielberg works this theme in a playful manner when E.T. explores the refrigerator and, in the course of dumping its contents on the floor, consumes several beers. At school, Elliott, overcome by the effects of the beer, begins to hiccup unexplainably in front of his classmates. The theme of Elliott as father also plays itself out as the young boy teaches his companion his first words of English, takes him out for Halloween dressed as a ghost, and plays with him as any good father would with his son. As Elliott remarks to E.T., "You could be happy here, I could take care of you. I wouldn't let anybody hurt you. We could grow up together, E.T." After all, that is what fathers hope for in an ideal world: to grow old in the company of their children and grandchildren. Likewise, that is the dream of childhood friends: never to part, but always to be together, safe from the threats and harsh realities of the adult world.

However, Elliott's brush with fatherhood goes further. When government agents invade the house in an effort to seize and study this unknown life-form, Elliott is confronted with the most serious challenge to his role as father: he must save the young alien from certain captivity and misery. In one exchange between Elliott and "Keys" (Peter Coyote), Elliott tries to explain that E.T. came to him but that now—like every child since Dorothy Gale in *The Wizard of Oz* (1939)—E.T. wants to go home.[6]

ELLIOTT: I really shouldn't tell. He came to me, he came to me.
KEYS: Elliott, he came to me too. I've been wishing for this since I was ten years old; I don't want him to die. What can we do that we're not already doing?
ELLIOTT: He needs to go home, he's calling his people, and I don't know where they are, and he needs to go home.
KEYS: Elliott, I don't think he was left here intentionally, but his being here is a miracle, Elliott. It's a miracle, and you did the best that anybody could do. I'm glad he met you first.

The final line delivered by Keys is the affirmation of Elliott's success as a father—he did the best anybody could do.

Conversely, E.T. teaches Elliott, the child, the hard lessons of life. The young boy has to watch his friend die (at least it appears that way for a while), learns to love for purely altruistic reasons, and ultimately must say good-bye. The now famous ending of the film (however schmaltzy) drives home one of the central ideas of the movie: a strong and appropriately protective relationship between father and son, and ultimately between friends, gives meaning to life, even if it is painful and requires separation.

Socrates similarly seemed to prize protective parent relations, even when the parent-child relationship is bad. In the *Crito,* Socrates claims that he should obey the laws of the state as a child obeys a parent, and in the *Euthyphro* he uses his dialectical power to try to prevent a son from rashly prosecuting his father. We do not have advice in Plato's corpus of how to treat an extraterrestrial, but Plato's dialogues celebrate hospitality (in Greek, *xenia,* a practice that was believed to be under the patronage of Zeus) as an essential precondition and setting for philosophy. Only when knives and threats are put away (in *xenia* a guest is asked to put aside all weapons) can there be fraternal exchange. And not just fraternal, for in the *Symposium* Socrates brings in Diotema, a philosopher-priestess who instructs the guests about the most important adventure of the soul: the love and pursuit of beauty.

Father and Son Reconciled Again: *Hook*

It should be no surprise to anyone the least bit familiar with Steven Spielberg that he would direct a film based on the Peter Pan story. In Spielberg's sequel to the original Pan story, *Hook,* Peter has grown up to be Peter Banning (Robin Williams), a tough merger and acquisitions lawyer. In a sleight of cinematic hand, Captain Hook (Dustin Hoffman) kidnaps Peter's children, and Peter returns to Neverland for a showdown. With the help of Tinkerbell (Julia Roberts) and the Lost Boys, Peter Banning must remember how to be Peter Pan once again in order to save his children.

Although the story line and the themes are perhaps less compelling than in other Spielberg films, the script has some rare moments of wit and quality writing. Spielberg recreates the Indy–Professor Jones exchanges in a refreshing way: this time, the child, Jack (Charlie Korsmo), challenges his father from the very beginning. On the way to London, they have the following brief exchange:

PETER BANNING: Jack, my word is my bond.
JACK: Yeah, junk bond. [*He hits the ceiling in the plane with his ball and causes the oxygen masks to drop down and scare Peter half to death.*]

Hook, TriStar Pictures/Amblin Entertainment, 1991. *Hook* explores the Spielbergian theme that parents—even of the likes of Peter Pan (Robin Williams, *left*)—must strive to recapture the joys and wonders of youth for both parents and children to flourish. (MovieGoods, Inc.)

PETER BANNING: What in the hell's the matter with you? When will you stop acting like a child?
JACK: I am a child.
PETER BANNING: Grow up!

In Neverland, when Banning encounters the Lost Boys he asks, "What is this? Some sort of Lord of the Flies preschool? Where are your parents? Who's in charge here?" After Banning insists on speaking with an adult ("Nooo Mr. Skunkhead with too much mousse, you are just a punk kid. I want to speak to a grown-up!") Rufio tells him, "All grown-ups are pirates. . . . We kill pirates." If adults are pirates, then Banning must recover his childhood to be able to save his children. He does this by returning to his Peter Pan state—as Tinkerbell explains it, "that place between sleep and awake, the place where you can still remember dreaming." By recovering his dreams and forgoing the accumulated years of cynicism and neglect for his children, Peter once again learns to fly and successfully defeats Captain Hook.

For all that it is mired in a feel-good emotionalism fueled by Robin Williams's hip humor combined with pathos, *Hook* brings together a number of important themes for Spielberg, notably the importance of childhood and the need for parents to engage in fantasy and cultivate the imagination with their children. *Hook* further suggests that, in the absence of parents, children are deprived of the joys and fantasies of childhood—something we all need for our sanity and happiness. Peter's wife warns him, "Your children love you, they want to play with you. How long do you think that lasts? Soon Jack might not even want you to come to his games. We have a few special years with our children, when they're the ones that want us around. After that you're going to be running after them for a bit of attention. It's so fast Peter. Just a few years, and it's over. And you are not being careful. And you are missing it."

From *Hook* to a Philosophy of Eternal Youth

We end our chapter with *Hook* in order to bring to light a vital respect in which Spielberg's work is very much in accord with a profound theme in Socratic inquiry. As we noted earlier, in the *Republic* Socrates' partner in dialogue is not the old man who has given up an eros or desire; his interlocutors are the young, the impetuous, those eager to challenge Socrates, those who are constantly asking questions, wanting to retrace arguments to see if they hold up. And this matches Socrates' method in virtually all the dialogues. He meets different people with settled convictions and asks them to think anew about their beliefs and actions. This is more of a mark of youth than a conventional portrait of old age. In a sense, Socrates may be read as warning us against the tired, settled habits that take hold with middle and old age.

From a Socratic point of view, why should one have reverence for those who are older? We suggest that one of the reasons lies behind the lesson Peter learns in *Hook*: Peter recovers his youth. In a sense, then, one reason for a young person to respect an older philosopher (and this can cover "all lovers of wisdom") is that he or she has been younger longer.

We are not suggesting that Spielberg has explicitly followed Socrates' repudiation of glory, his endorsement of the good and beautiful, the welcoming establishment of a protected forum (*xenia*) for wisdom, and the idea that philosophy involves the perpetuation of the virtues of youth. But we do suggest that all of these factors are in play as Spielberg wrestles with the problems of growing up with an absent father and points the way toward a resolution or restoration of father and son, parent and child.

Notes

1. Spielberg gets Kali's sex wrong and makes her a him.

2. [Lester Friedman in *Citizen Spielberg* (Urbana: University of Illinois Press, 2006) has also recognized this.—ed.]

3. Brody cautions, "Marion's the least of your worries right now, believe me, Indy. . . . For nearly three thousand years man has been searching for the lost Ark. It's not something to be taken lightly. No one knows its secrets. It's like nothing you've ever gone after before." Laughing, Indiana responds, "Oh, Marcus. What are you trying to do, scare me? You sound like my mother."

4. The scene is an homage to Alfred Hitchcock's *Foreign Correspondent* (1940; the umbrella/murder scene) and *North by Northwest* (1959; the sea of red caps at Chicago's LaSalle Street station).

5. The exchange goes:

SALLAH: Please, what does it always mean, this . . . this "Junior"?
PROFESSOR HENRY JONES: That's his name. Henry Jones . . . Junior.
INDIANA JONES: I like "Indiana."
PROFESSOR HENRY JONES: We named the dog "Indiana."
MARCUS BRODY: May we go home now, please?
SALLAH: The dog? You are named after the dog?
INDIANA JONES: I've got a lot of fond memories of that dog.

6. In the opening sequences of·the movie, keys sound an ominous note in a series of shots that show them on the belt of a government agent who is pursuing E.T.

Levinasian Ethics of Alterity

The Face of the Other in Spielberg's Cinematic Language

John W. Wright

All too often, the cinematic work of Steven Spielberg is viewed primarily through the lens of its commercial appeal, or through an examination of its historical accuracy, to ascertain its place in the popular culture of American film. Discussions of *Jaws* (1975), *Jurassic Park* (1993), and the *Indiana Jones* films (1981, 1984, 1989) commonly center on their use of melodramatic tropes (overt elicitation of emotional response and use of stereotypical characters) to produce commercially successful adventures and fantasies. Explorations of his "serious" work (e.g., *The Color Purple* [1985], *Schindler's List* [1993], *Saving Private Ryan* [1998]) usually revolve around an analysis of how successfully Spielberg manipulates historical reenactment to elicit emotional response.[1] Cinematic examinations of *The Color Purple*, for instance, often reduce the historical narrative of the "black" experience as Spielberg constructed it into the most simplistic images of "oppression" versus "freedom." This form of analysis has also pointed to such iconic images as the American flag (at both start and end of *Saving Private Ryan*) as semiotic representations of overt patriotism. When, however, one looks more closely at the films of Spielberg, it is possible to see how these surface judgments are too simplistic in comprehensively evaluating his use of cinematic language, especially in exploring human behavior and philosophical questions of ethics.

From a philosophical point of view, several of Spielberg's films engage the concept of ethical responsibility toward alterity (the difference of otherness). Although films such as *Raiders of the Lost Ark* (1981) and *Jaws* oversimplify or erase completely our need to respond to difference, other cinematic works, such as *Close Encounters of the Third Kind* (1977) and *Schindler's List,* diverge into more complex images of behavior and relationships that, however subtly, force the audience to reexamine its own ethical responses.[2] To this purpose, we will look first to the work of Emmanuel Levinas as a philosophical base from which these select films operate, then explore how Spielberg's use of cinematic language (the aesthetics of shot, editing, and mise-en-scène) are employed in creating images that challenge our views of "responsibility to the other."

Levinas and Ethical Responsibility: The Face of the Other

Emmanuel Levinas turned away from traditional metaphysical understandings of existence to posit that "ethics," the relationship of one (the "I") to the "other," is the first and central philosophical domain of human existence. In the work of Levinas (most notably in *Existence and Existents* in 1947 and *Totality and Infinity* in 1961), the other is unknowable, not tied within the bounds of subject or object. Man's existence, therefore, is primarily and most importantly a function of one's "ethical responsibility" to the "face" of the other.[3] The face is the presence of the other before us, at any time and in whatever form, that we are compelled to engage and take responsibility for.[4] Thus, the ultimate understanding of mankind, according to Levinas, is found in alterity, the sublime differences that exist between the "I" and the other. Within this philosophical argument, Levinas sought to turn human understanding from "knowledge as wisdom" to that of "love as wisdom."

It is important here to understand briefly what Levinas is really saying in terms of ethics. The concept of the Levinasian ethical response relies on his assertion that the other truly is "unknowable" in terms of its true self—that no matter how recognizable the other is to us, we can never comprehend its "self" as we do ourselves. To Levinas, the mere notion of a need for ethics in the first place arises from the interaction of the "I" (self) with the other. In other words, if one could truly "know" the other then one would not need to take ethical responsibility for that difference at all. Likewise, Levinas posits the concept of the "face" as being that part of the other that we can engage, that we can see and therefore "know," and thus his ethical philosophy suggests that it is only through interaction with this face that human existence finds its meaning. To Levinas, then, the danger of engaging the face of the other resides in trying to breach the unknowable part of the other behind the face, whereas responsibility occurs when one accepts the unknowable nature of the other and engages it merely through "love."[5]

The Levinasian approach to ethical responsibility lies at the heart of much of the cinematic work of Steven Spielberg. Film as an art form is particularly responsive to the philosophy of Levinas, for it not only presents images that come face-to-face with alterity on the screen, but also presents these faces directly to the audiences that view them. The "aesthetics" of cinematic language are often built on the construction of the "shot," or rather the specific image within each frame of a scene. Analysis of the evolution and use of shots to construct film has (within film studies) been mostly concerned with how these shots affect the structure of the film's narrative. Yet, the nature of moving from long shot to medium, from medium to close-up, and back again in sequence also immediately connects the aesthetics of these choices to the ethical questions of otherness that Levinas is most concerned with. As Louis Giannetti writes, "because our eyes identify with the camera's lens, in effect we are placed within [multiple] ranges vis-à-vis the subject matter. When we are offered a close-up of a character, for example, in a sense we feel we're in an intimate relationship with that character."[6] Here the word "intimate" is key, for it is essentially an encapsulation in more common language of the concept of ethical response to the other. What is intimacy but "coming to the face" of the other, as Levinas posits in his work?[7] Cinematic shots create this intimacy, this connection to the other, on two distinct levels: between the characters onscreen with each other and between the imaged characters and the audience members who encounter them.

The mise-en-scène and editing of film also enhance the Levinasian engagement of alterity through film as an art form. (Mise-en-scène, literally meaning "placing on a stage," refers to the way in which objects and characters are arranged within the frame onscreen.) From the beginning of twentieth-century filmmaking, these cinematic aesthetics have been linked with a dialectical understanding. Sergei Eisenstein's innovations of montage editing were specifically built on the idea of oppositional images placed in rapid counterpoint to create dialectical meaning.[8] As with the intimacy created by choice of shots, editing thus forces an encounter of "difference," spread over multiple others. Likewise, the placement of characters within a scene, the mise-en-scène in classical cinematic studies, provides contrasts between open and closed arrangements that either free the cinematic characters from their relationships with others or bind them visually within the structure of the frame.[9]

Steven Spielberg utilizes these aesthetics of cinema to "reveal" the face of otherness, both to his characters within the film and to each of us who engage his work. In his earlier endeavors, Spielberg explored alterity through genre, reaching for an ethical responsibility to that which might be considered the most completely "other": the alien (or extraterrestrial). In *Close Encounters of the Third Kind* and *E.T.* (1982), Spielberg created the image of the alien as an other that demands an ethical response (including sacrifice) from mankind as it first encounters extraterrestrials. Through the lens of Spielberg, the face of the alien other is one that inevitably must coexist in its difference from us, thus calling upon our taking responsibility for it—the "wisdom through love" of Levinas. The individual "I" that encounters otherness can never truly know it or understand it, which is the essence of being "alien." Thus, according to Levinas, we have only the choice to assimilate, thereby (in effect) destroying the other, or to accept the other and its difference from us.

In his later work, Spielberg not only continued this approach to his filmmaking, but also used the groundwork of images he began in genre pictures and returned them to more realistic human narratives: a historical understanding of alterity and ethical responsibility in the face of the Jew. With *Schindler's List,* Spielberg turned his aesthetic talents to reinvesting well-known human characters of otherness with the same images of responsibility and sacrifice as he did the alien in his earlier films. This cinematic connection is a powerful philosophical statement, for it ultimately forces the audience to reexamine their own relationships to the face of the other, and to engage difference through their own ethical responsibility—just as the characters onscreen must when they, too, encounter alterity.

The "Alien" Other: Changing Close Encounters from Fear to Responsibility

Critics of Spielberg have often maligned an overuse of childlike innocence, from *E.T.* to *Hook,* as the center of his cinematic narratives.[10] This "innocence," however, is really an appeal to a less cynical response when humankind encounters otherness. For decades, film had portrayed human interaction with otherworldliness (the alien) as a cause for horror and fear, as epitomized by Howard Hawks's 1951 *The Thing from Another World.*[11] The nature of the alien as other in Hawks's film and in the multitude of science fiction and horror B-movies of the 1950s and 1960s was presented nearly continuously as a face of destruction and mindless evil. The reasoning behind this was fairly simplistic: these genre pictures identified "otherness" with the dialectic of the Cold War, with the unknown reflecting the fear of the nation and thus its cinema toward any and all "threats" from beyond, whether that nebulous beyond was found merely across the ocean in the Soviet Union or across the stars in the guise of the alien onscreen. Indeed, the only notable exception to alien representation came with Robert Wise's 1951 counterpoint to *The Thing, The Day the Earth Stood Still.*[12] Even in Wise's film, however, where the alien Klaatu is identified as "good" and not simply as a monster, there remains the potential of destruction—Klaatu has come to Earth to demand the nations of this planet put aside their militaristic ways, with the incentive being the alien's use of similarly destructive power to eradicate Earth.

Steven Spielberg's first major success, *Jaws*, has a thematic focus similar to these earlier genre films. Fear is the defining factor, and here the most simplistic other (monster) is presented: a terrorizing shark. There is no need to ask for ethical responsibility to this particular other, because its existence is merely as an agent of destruction.[13] The choices in shots, editing, and mise-en-scène Spielberg employed in this film enhance the violent sense of horror experienced by both the central characters and the audience, much as the same aesthetics had been previously employed in reference to the alien. In both *The Thing* and *Jaws*, the camera remains aloof and distant from the object of otherness, separating it from the possibility of empathy or connective responsibility. Shots are rarely, if ever, closer than medium and are more often long shots. In fact, in both films the alien/shark is largely obscured from the camera's eye for the majority of the film, only being revealed in focused detail near the end.[14] Thus, the otherness presented here resists any claim of or call for recognition of difference. Instead, the choices made reinforce difference as a source of danger, of repulsion and horror only.

It was away from this standardization of genre films that Spielberg turned in 1977 when he made *Close Encounters of the Third Kind*. Whereas in *Jaws* he had followed the simplicity of fear, when he sought to engage the idea of the alien he chose instead to redefine the nature of extraterrestrial difference. Rather than constructing his "encounters" from the perspective of potential destruction, Spielberg decided in this film to reenvision the onscreen alien as an "other" to be embraced, to learn about. It is here that Spielberg adopts cinematically the philosophy of Emmanuel Levinas. Although the alien is "unknowable," it is through the mere *striving* for knowledge and understanding that both the characters and the audience gain wisdom; and from wisdom, in the philosophy of Levinas, comes "love"—or rather the acceptance of ethical responsibility in the face of the other regardless of the other's unknowable difference.[15] There are strong reasons that Levinasian ethics are at play in Spielberg's shift from fear- and horror-based genre ideologies: Levinas himself developed his theories primarily in response to the atrocities of World War II and the extremist horror of the Holocaust perpetrated on the Jews.[16] The postwar fears of "communist evil" that permeated the cinematic choices of the next several decades, especially in the science fiction of the day, mirrored the hatred and fear that Levinas sought to deconstruct.

Close Encounters of the Third Kind, Columbia Pictures, 1977. Roy Neary (Richard Drey-fuss) and a team of scientists atop Devil's Tower embody Spielberg's landmark cinematic decision to celebrate what Levinas might call "extraterrestrial alterity." (MovieGoods, Inc.)

According to Levinas, difference is bridged in the face-to-face encounter, when we come to the unknowable face of the other with the wisdom that the possibility of "knowing" that other is beyond our grasp. Interaction with the face of the other "cuts across the vision of forms," and thereby removes speech and the dialectic and requires only our *response*—the ethics of sacrifice and responsibility.[17] When Spielberg shifts his cinematic view of the alien other to this frame, he asks us as the audience to see our own prejudices and fears and to sacrifice them, to lay them aside. Cinematically this occurs when Roy Neary (Richard Dreyfuss), Lacombe (François Truffaut), et al. finally see the face of the physical alien other, rather than its mere representation as mystical "lights in the night sky."

For Levinas, we are always "I" to the other, and it is no coincidence that Robert Kolker states in *Film, Form, and Culture* that, in reference to film aesthetics, "the 'I' in cinema becomes, almost literally, the 'eye.'"[18] First we witness the characters in Spielberg's narratives undergo their encounters with the face of the alien other, and subsequently we as the audience must experience this same encounter. It is noteworthy that the very term "close encounter" was popularized by Spielberg's film, replacing genre jargon such as "invasion" and "abduction." At its most basic level, *Close Encounters* reverses the negative fears of otherworldliness and presents the alien other as a being to be engaged merely for the sake of that engagement.

Cinematically, the alien other resembles earlier genre incarnations only in one significant way: it is absent from the frame for most of the movie. Through the course of the first two acts, the aliens are encountered only externally as UFOs, colorful lights that occasionally fill the sky and the camera frame. The composition of these shots is predominantly open, representing the night sky as an endless vista. Long shots and extreme long shots are used, and the pace of editing is lyrical and slow. All of these aesthetic choices continually reinforce the unknowable aspects of the alien other, refusing both Neary and the audience the Levinasian encounter with the face of the alien. As the film reaches its last act, however, Spielberg alters the composition of shots, editing, and mise-en-scène to achieve the redefinition of his alien(s).

As filming progressed, Spielberg and his crew came to refer to the final act as "the experience."[19] It is an elaborate finale, built around the narrative of a quasi-governmental group led by Lacombe establishing a "landing field" at the base of Devil's Tower in Wyoming at the behest of messages sent from the aliens. Neary and others have been drawn to this time and place psychically, a different form of communication from the alien other(s). At the beginning of "the experience," the cinematic aesthetics are similar to those of the earlier portions of the film. The "field" is framed openly against the night sky, the editing remains lyrically paced, and the shots are primarily long, from the point of view of Neary and Gillian (Melinda Dillon) as they watch from their hiding place in the hills above. The "messages" sent non-telepathically to the scientists have come in the form of music (the famous five-toned theme composed by John Williams), a device that has also served to forestall the encountering of the face. As the sequence proceeds, several alien craft appear. The human scientists begin communicating via pulses, tones, and music that are reciprocated by the aliens via the technology of their crafts. The separation of this technology—its otherworldliness and its incomprehensibleness—from that of the human characters is one final reminder of the unknowable nature of the alien(s).

However, as "the experience" unfolds, the shots begin to change. Long shots are jettisoned first in favor of medium shots as Neary leaves his hiding place and moves closer. The initial craft depart, seemingly ending the sequence, only to have the camera reveal the enormity of the "mother ship" as it approaches. Its immensity changes the nature of the mise-en-scène, removing the night sky from the camera frame and closing the composition, thus forcing the characters and audience into a tight space that awaits the intimacy of the face-to-face. Here, Spielberg ingeniously reversed the meaning of the mise-en-scène, for in earlier sci-fi and horror films the closed frame was used to complete the sense of claustrophobia and fear, as with the darkened and threatening Antarctic research station hallways in *The Thing*. The editing of the sequence quickly changes, increasing rapidly and employing Eisensteinian montage techniques.[20] The scientists on the ground begin again to communicate via sound and music, although as the speed of this exchange increases geometrically one character asks, "Does anyone have a clue what we're saying here?" Gillian also moves closer; previously held back because she had not yet seen evidence of her missing son, she is drawn now to the immediacy of the mother ship.

As the final sonic exchange ends, the bottom of the mother ship opens. White light, epitomizing otherness in counterpoint to the darkness of the night around the field, fills the frame. Beings begin to emerge; but this, too, is a forestalling of the face, because these first emergent figures turn out to be humans, taken by the aliens over several decades and now returned. Among these is Gillian's son, and on her reunion with him her engagement with the aliens ends. Neary, on the other hand, has no personal reason to desire this encounter, no "payoff" beyond wisdom. When Lacombe asks him, "Monsieur Neary, what do you want?" he responds simply, "I just want to know that this is happening."

By this time, Spielberg has switched the framing almost exclusively to medium shots and close-ups. Now, with an almost casual suddenness, alien figures begin to emerge. They are childlike and small, and at first are blurred into the whiteness of the light behind them. Gillian's last act of purpose is to pull out her camera and begin snapping photographs of the aliens, at which Spielberg cuts to a sequence of extreme close-ups as if through her camera's lens, revealing quick snapshots of the aliens. This is our first encounter with the face of the alien, and Spielberg ensures it is an intimate one. Ultimately, a larger alien emerges (presumably a "leader") and communicates through hand gestures with the scientists.[21] In the final aesthetics of this alien Spielberg focuses on its eyes, in close-up, revealing the expressiveness of its face simultaneously to Neary, Lacombe, the scientists, and the audience. The alien, simply, smiles at Neary and Lacombe. They respond with their own smiles, and their facial reactions demonstrate their wonder. Language is nonexistent; there is only the response of the humans who come before it. Here, Spielberg does not destroy the moment with unnecessary dialogue or exposition; there are no trite or obvious translations of alien speech stating,

"We come in peace." Rather, he focuses solely on the faces of the alien and of those who are present acting "as witness to the other."[22]

The "experience" of *Close Encounters* ends when the aliens select Neary rather than the highly trained team of scientists to come with them into their ship and into the stars. The ending of the film returns to a final, lyrical sequence of long shots as Neary disappears into the ship and the ship lifts into the stars and the sky above. With this denouement, Spielberg reminds us that the alien other remains outside our full understanding. The "encounter" witnessed in the film gives no resolution to the characters' specific needs (Gillian's regaining of her son being the exception) or material desires.[23] Neary, in the end, has sacrificed his own life and desires (house, family, job, etc.) to come to this place and ultimately to leave behind his own world to join the aliens. The monstrosity of the alien other of previous cinematic images is thus changed, not only for the characters in the film but also for audiences of the late 1970s, mirroring a cultural period in which the simplistic othering of communism and non-American ideologies that occurred in the 1950s and 1960s was blurring.

Spielberg further evolves Levinas's concept of ethical responsibility in 1982's *E.T.: The Extra-Terrestrial*. Ostensibly a "sequel" to *Close Encounters*, the tale of a single alien left behind on Earth and befriended by a small boy named Elliott (Henry Thomas) reduces the encounter from the elaborate and massive scale of the earlier film to the intimacy of a small house in the suburbs of California.[24] Here, Spielberg only postpones the face-to-face encounter with the alien other for the briefest of times. He uses extreme close-ups to show hands, feet, and oblique parts of the alien E.T. as it wanders in the forest in search of plants to sample. When the ship leaves, Spielberg uses fast-paced editing to "humanize" the still faceless E.T. as it tries in a panic to make it back to the ship. The alien E.T. may be "unknowable," but Spielberg allows us this time to presage our engagement with its face through cinematic actions that seem familiar: a sense of helplessness, the ability to lose track of time and place, and the immediacy of the alien's loneliness at being isolated from that which it knows and is familiar with. As E.T. wanders alone, it comes across the suburb that is home to Elliott and his family.

For only a few short scenes, E.T. remains a faceless other to Elliott (and thus the audience), until Elliott lures the alien with candy. From this point on, the face of E.T. is revealed with very little fanfare, and Spielberg composes most of the film around the intimacy of the close-up. When Elliott introduces E.T. to his brother and sister, Spielberg tightens the frame, using the intimate space of Elliott's room to bind all three children with E.T. Spielberg chooses extreme close-ups on the faces of each to reveal their encounter, editing between increasingly close shots of E.T.'s face.[25] From that moment, Elliott and his siblings accept an ethical responsibility to the alien other that is E.T., ultimately providing the means for E.T. to return home.

One significant difference between the encounter of the alien face in *E.T.* as compared to *Close Encounters* is the reintroduction of "language" as central to a Levinasian ethics. "It is . . . by way of language that the relationship with the personal other is realized. This, Levinas holds, is what is essential to the social domain."[26] Whereas *Close Encounters* relegated language to the nonverbal, in *E.T.* Spielberg reinvests language through speech, as E.T. learns bits and pieces of English that he uses to communicate with Elliott. This process, of course, culminates with the ubiquitous phrase, "E.T. phone home," a plea from this being to those who have accepted responsibility for him to help him return to the otherness of his own world, his own kind. Most significantly, Spielberg does not allow E.T.'s ability to gain language to erase this particular alien's unknowable self. Elliott cannot truly "know" E.T., nor can his brother and sister, yet they can "love" him—once again returning the central thematic core of the film to a Levinasian ideal that wisdom comes through "love," not through "knowledge."

As in *Close Encounters* there is a nebulous, quasi-governmental group interested in the alien, but here it seems more clandestine and dangerous, attempting to "capture" E.T. for scientific knowledge (the opposite of true wisdom). The final act of the film centers on a chase to deliver E.T. from the hands of these scientists and to return him to his ship. In the end, Elliott realizes he must sacrifice his own desires (to keep E.T.) and let him go to fulfill his ethical responsibility. The spaceship itself is imaged as almost mundane, far less mystical or technologically impressive than those in *Close Encounters,* because Spielberg wishes the audience to focus solely on the face of E.T. The final moments of the film utilize (again) extreme close-ups alternating between E.T. and Elliott and the others gathered at his departure, and extremely closed framing provided by the forest and the ship itself. Peter Sedgewick notes that the Levinasian face-to-face encounter is at once "both pleasurable and painful," and this moment is clarified for the audience of *E.T.* through the simple word "Ouch," which encapsulates both the joy of Elliott and E.T.'s meeting and the pain of their final, yet necessary, separation.[27]

Both *Close Encounters* and *E.T.* changed the predominant nature of the sci-fi alien genre film. Although many films have continued to fall back on the standard fear and horror in the face of the alien (most notably Roland Emmerich's 1996 *Independence Day*), Spielberg's two pictures opened the way for myriad other cinematic stories that embrace rather than reject the alien other—James Cameron's *The Abyss* (1989) is a prime example. Most

E.T.: The Extra-Terrestrial, Universal Pictures/Amblin Entertainment, 1982. The ethical responsibilities incurred by embracing the other reach a symbolic crescendo in this tearful goodbye between Elliott (Henry Thomas) and E.T. (MovieGoods, Inc.)

importantly for the audience, Spielberg's films allow for the *celebration* of alterity, rejoicing in the encounter of the absolute difference represented in the alien other rather than fearing it. The era in which these two films were produced is important: the shift in image onscreen, in many respects, signified the changing nature of American attitudes toward otherness following the traumatic events of Vietnam, the civil rights movement, and the first era of détente with the previously archetypical "evil" of communism in the Soviet Union and China.[28] Significantly as well, the use of cinema to change this particular other would later allow Spielberg to turn the same dynamics back from the genre of science fiction and onto the more immediate of human endeavors, replacing the alien other with the engagement of very real human difference in modern history.

Finding Responsibility through Cinematic History: *Schindler's List*

In many respects it would seem that a Levinasian ethical approach would have asked Spielberg to begin with a cinematic exploration of historical events rather than finding them in the realm of science fiction. It was an engagement of history, after all, that Levinas wrote his philosophy for: an explanation of the events and actions of mankind during the mid-twentieth century.[29] Yet it is precisely because he first examined the alien as other that Spielberg was able to shift his audience's attention back from the genre encounters of *Close Encounters* and *E.T.* to the human story of the Holocaust. By first changing the perspective of our relationship to such a sharply distinctive other, Spielberg established for us the precedent of acceptance of alterity that may not otherwise have been so easily navigable when encountering difference so starkly amidst the mistakes of mankind's past.

In *Schindler's List*, Spielberg takes on a monumental moment in history, one that immediately reconnects his work once again with the ethics of Levinas: the Holocaust. Levinas's concept of the face as the central encounter with otherness derives directly from what he sees as the negative "othering" of Jews by the Nazis during World War II, a violent encounter with difference that ended in mass murder. Indeed, Levinas viewed violence against the face of the other as the central failure of human moral endeavors: "Humans can resort to murder as a means of annihilating the other. But the annihilation of murder is not the same as possession. . . . A person can want to murder the other, nothing else—one does not want to murder a tree. And this very fact pays testimony to the other's transcendence. 'Killing,' in this sense, is an act that negates the other as a sensible being."[30] The possession Sedgewick discusses here is central to the concept that otherness is something that can be *owned* through knowledge and understanding, and it is here that Levinas's argument again makes its central claim—that only through love, through ethical responses and sacrifice, can wisdom exist. To attempt wisdom through knowledge inevitably leads to a demand for possession of the other, and, according to Levinas, only results in the violent negation of the other, as in the Holocaust.

With this in mind, we can turn to how Spielberg evokes these same positions cinematically in *Schindler's List*. The film tells the story of one man, Oskar Schindler (Liam Neeson), a Nazi and war profiteer who ultimately saves more than a thousand Jews from extermination. Within the film, there are several sequences in which Spielberg's choice of aesthetics enforces a Levinasian philosophy: the opening list-taking in Poland; the ghetto massacre; the compilation of Schindler's list; and, finally, the coda at the end of the film. It should be noted here that one major initial directorial decision connects the film as a whole to Levinas—the use of black-and-white cinematography. Although Spielberg's choice was more a cinematic decision to frame his movie as a "documentary," with the starkness of black and white evocative both of this genre and of the "good versus evil" dialectic in the film, it also serves to reinforce the otherness of the characters onscreen by placing them in a disconnected world of no color. Indeed, there are only three moments of color photography, and each serves as a momentary bridge between the "I" of Schindler and the audience and the Jewish characters. The first occurs at the outset, with the lighting of candles during prayer. The second is the image of a single red coat, worn by a small girl during the ghetto massacre, which Schindler later sees on her body as it is burned. Finally, the coda shifts to color as the real Schindler Jews are introduced alongside the actors portraying them. In all three moments, the slippage of color into the frame breaks the distance of alterity otherwise enhanced throughout the film by the use of black and white.

At the beginning of the film, the Jewish prayer ends with a candle being snuffed out. The smoke dissolves into the smoke of a train, arriving with Jews in Krakow. They are numerous, and we see them in close-up as they approach the Nazi list-takers. Shots alternate between extreme close-ups on the typewriters recording names and the faces of the Jews. The names are given quickly and are seemingly irrelevant at this point. The shots offer the audience the immediate face of the Holocaust victims, yet the juxtaposition against the names being typed reminds us at once that the Nazis are uncaring toward these people; to them, they are merely possessions as others, not "sensible beings" whose encounter demands ethical responsibility. As the sequence progresses, the shots become tighter and the pace quickens, presaging the urgency of the Jews' situation at the hands of the Nazis. As the sequence ends, we hear music; this leads us away from this scene to Schindler's apartment, where the face of Schindler is obscured and close-ups and medium shots reveal only his attention to money, to dress, to decoration—the material desires that the central figure of Schindler is so attached to as a character at the start of the film.

Perhaps the most memorable expression of brutality in the film occurs during the ghetto massacre and clearing sequence. The Jews who had been, until this point, forced to live in squalid ghettos in Krakow are to be sorted, purging the elderly and infirm, with the remaining to be sent to concentration camps. Spielberg introduces the sequence with a series of shots edited in parallel between the Nazi commandant Amon Goeth (Ralph Fiennes) giving orders to his troops to carry out this brutality and images of the faces of the Jewish characters eating, praying, and simply living in their meager conditions. The shots of Goeth are framed openly, and are mostly medium and long, reinforcing the Nazis' disconnection from responsibility for the Jewish other. The shots of the Jews are closed within their homes and in close-up, forcing the audience to engage them in the Levinasian face-to-face encounter that the Nazis refuse. The trucks carrying the storm troopers arrive, and we again see list-takers setting up in the streets. Spielberg rapidly increases the pace of editing, crosscutting between wide and medium shots of the Nazi storm troopers spreading out and increasingly close views of the Jews trying to hide, concealing valuables, and showing fear at the impending event.

At this point, Schindler and his mistress, on a morning horse ride, approach the hill overlooking the ghetto. Their perspective of the event remains from a distance, and images showing their view of the ghetto events are always in extreme long-shot; this evokes the distance that Schindler begins with, but also a change in Schindler himself as he witnesses the brutal violence perpetrated on the Jewish others from this vantage point. As the sequence progresses and the Nazis perform acts of random murder and horror, the camera closes in increasingly on Schindler, ending in extreme close-up on his face as he realizes he has given nothing of himself to alter these events, that he himself has not yet accepted a responsibility for the Jews he has employed (to make money from the war). It is here that Spielberg makes the oft-discussed cinematic choice to use one simple reinsertion of color—the red coat of a lone young girl. By doing so, Spielberg aesthetically establishes the moment of individual responsibility for Schindler. The red coat becomes, for Schindler, the "face" of the Holocaust victim, pulling him from his distanced position astride the hilltop into the horror of the Nazi atrocities. Throughout the ghetto sequence, Spielberg yet again reverses his mise-en-scène construction, returning the closed frame to the purpose of claustrophobia and fear: the binding nature of this screen composition instantly switches from one of relations between Jews at the start of the sequence to one of inescapable oppression and subjugation thereafter. The Nazis strip the face from their victims, removing any and all sense of ethics from their actions. Alterity, or difference, only serves as their excuse for this brutality.

It is interesting to note here that Spielberg's films are often criticized for overreliance on archetypal evil in the presentation of villains, especially Nazis. In the *Indiana Jones* trilogy, for example, Nazis are near automatons of violence; and although films such as *Schindler's List* and *Saving Private Ryan* attempt to give more historical depth to the Nazis (Goeth is presented as a psychologically complex individual while still "evil" and cruel), their position as uncaring possessors of the Jews and subjugators of human otherness is seemingly reinforced. Yet critics miss one important point: Schindler himself *is* a Nazi. His transformation in the film is the crux of the philosophical call for responsibility, for an ethical response to the horror of the Holocaust. The reason that most critics miss this salient point resides in the ease with which Schindler's status as a Nazi is forgotten as he takes responsibility for the Jews who work for him. By taking an ethical stance, Schindler no longer resembles the archetypal evil of Nazism, yet he remains a Nazi until the end.[31]

Later in the film, Schindler has come to the realization of his own ethical responsibility to the Jewish other. He has come face-to-face with every one of his employees, and so seeks to save them by building his own camp and paying Goeth for each employee, thus sacrificing his own monetary desires and material needs.[32] This is especially revealed in sequences involving Schindler's interaction with his accountant, Itzhak Stern (Ben Kingsley), which are almost always presented in the classical editing style of alternating close-ups between the two in conversation. Their relationship culminates when, after Goeth has given in to Schindler's bribes, Stern and Schindler begin to compile the list of those they will save. Here, Spielberg counterpoints the unethical response of the Nazis by cutting from close-ups of Schindler and Stern to extreme close-ups of the names being typed, sometimes so close we witness the ink dots and paper imperfections. Schindler's face is sometimes placed in the same frame as Stern, closed off and with the typewriter. The meaning of these names is now different than it was for the Nazi list-takers at the outset of the film: for Schindler, they now represent each Jewish other to whom he is responsible. Spielberg makes sure to evoke this difference by waiting until *after* this sequence to show the faces of these Jews, now identifiable as individuals from the narrative of the film, as they present themselves not to be annihilated but to be saved by Schindler.

Finally, Spielberg uses the coda of the film to place a closing exclamation point on what Schindler's ethical sacrifice meant. The denouement occurs in the present day, at the burial site of Schindler, and in color. Each actor walks with the living Jew to the grave, the camera revealing the face of both the actor and the person he or she played in medium and close-up. Schindler is dead, and we see him only as the actor Liam Neeson standing in long shot in the final moment of the film. This technique specifically moves all focus of the "I" from the characters onscreen onto the audience—for this coda is *our* ultimate encounter with the face of the Schindler Jews.[33]

Spielberg's Work as Plea for Sacrifice to Alterity

In all the films examined here, one constant that Spielberg reinforces through his cinematic aesthetics is the Levinasian concept of sacrifice in the face of the other. Richard Rorty, whose work builds somewhat on Levinas, says that, ultimately, the self as "I" must come to a place of contingent sacrifice: "At the heart of the self lies the 'conscience,' which has the capacity to make the right moral choices—such choices lock on to the moral principles or laws that rise above the ravages of time."[34] Conscience, then, is the recognition of our response to the face of the other, and the need for each of us to sacrifice our needs to this face—not because we gain knowledge or material return from this, but merely because our presence before this face of otherness calls for our sacrifice. In each Spielberg film explored here, the characters onscreen that are "I" to otherness make a sacrifice: Roy Neary gives his material life (family, home, possessions, job) to encounter the alien other; Elliott sacrifices his own need for E.T.; and Schindler sacrifices his material desires.

Ultimately, the work of Spielberg specifically, and of cinema as an art form, serves as a powerful proclamation of Levinas's philosophy, for the audience as "I" is forced through the aesthetics of the film image to engage the face of the other. Certainly an audience or individual may turn from the screen or leave a theater, but the way in which Spielberg constructs his films compels the eye ("I") of the audience to respond to these images. The evolution of his choices also moves us as audience to a greater engagement; his early work selected the absolute other of the alien, and only in his later work does Spielberg turn the cinematic focus on the face onto our own historical human encounters. Although Spielberg probably did not consciously choose Levinas as a philosophical basis for these choices, he nevertheless succeeds in promoting it.[35]

For us as an audience, the impact of these films is critical at our own historical moment when otherness is constantly pushed to the violent reaction of possession and subjugation. All of these films predate the events of 9/11, the aftermath of which has certainly seen the distinctive return to engaging the other as destructive or threatening. The increased numbers of horror films and science fiction films that return to the idea of the other as monster or dangerous invader have, in recent years, shifted the cinema backward to the era of the Cold War. Even Spielberg has fallen prey to this trend with his 2005 remake of *War of the Worlds*. Yet these films from before that event remain, and each calls to us to set aside, to sacrifice our own fears and desires, in the continual encounter with the differences that exist between us and the other, whether it be in the image of an alien, a Jew, or a slave, or in the faces of Africans in Darfur, Arabs and Palestinians in the Middle East, or any form of alterity we engage.

Notes

1. See Darren Slade, "Different Views of Spielberg," *Talking Pictures,* http://www
.talkingpix.co.uk/Article_Spielberg.html (accessed September 20, 2007). Here, Slade
comments on how Spielberg's work is often criticized for being "sentimental, calculated
and devoid of ideas."

2. For the oversimplification of our need to respond to difference, see again Slade's
discussion in "Different Views of Spielberg."

3. Emmanuel Levinas, *Totality and Infinity: An Essay on Exteriority,* trans. Alphonso
Lingis (Pittsburgh: Duquesne University Press, 1969).

4. Levinas, *Totality and Infinity,* 8–10.

5. His concept of wisdom through "love" rather than through "knowledge" is
posited as a result of his belief that attempts to "know" otherness ultimately can only
fail, and that such attempts historically result in one group attempting to "own" knowledge of the other, ending in the vilification and subjugation of difference rather than
in celebration of it. Thus, it is through "love," the acknowledgment of the unknowable
difference of the other, that true wisdom is found.

6. Louis Giannetti, *Understanding Movies* (Upper Saddle River, NJ: Pearson,
2005), 85.

7. Levinas, *Totality and Infinity,* 22.

8. The use of Eisenstein's development of the montage form of editing as a creation
of dialectical construction is well covered in most basic cinema studies texts, including Robert Kolker, *Film, Form, and Culture* (Boston: McGraw-Hill, 1999), 44–47, and
Giannetti, *Understanding Movies,* 163–83.

9. Kolker, *Film, Form, and Culture,* 50–58.

10. I here use no specific citation for this general claim against Spielberg, although
Slade ("Different Views of Spielberg") references it, but certainly it is reflected in commentary by numerous film critics (Rex Reed, for example) and in scholarly reactions
to his films as "artistic." The protection of "childhood" is evidenced clearly through
images such as the ubiquitous "ouch" between Elliott and E.T., clearly symbolizing
the playful and childlike view of "pain" as more representative of a children's band-aid
commercial. The presentation of "modern" childlike accessories such as skateboards
and Nickelodeon-TV–style colorful food-fights are commonly seen as signifiers that
Spielberg's work panders to the simplistic desire to remain blissfully ignorant and detached from the adult world.

11. I credit Hawks here even though Christian Nyby is the officially credited director;
it is now common knowledge that Hawks directed the picture mostly by himself.

12. The influence of the "dangerous" alien other as opposed to the "good" Klaatu
in *The Day the Earth Stood Still* is reflected in the box office success of *The Thing* against
the relatively small return of *Day,* despite *Day*'s positive critical reviews at the time.

13. Lester Friedman makes much the same argument in *Citizen Spielberg* (Urbana:
University of Illinois Press, 2006).

14. Much has been made of the "happy accident" in the production of *Jaws* in which the mechanical effects for the shark did not work properly and Spielberg was forced to "obscure" the beast, ultimately leading him to the aesthetics of fear discussed.

15. Levinas, *Totality and Infinity*, 193.

16. Richard Beardsworth, "Modernity in French Thought: Excess in Jacques Derrida, Emmanuel Levinas and Jean-François Lyotard," *Telos* 137 (2006): 75–76.

17. Levinas, *Totality and Infinity*, 193.

18. Kolker, *Film, Form, and Culture*, 58.

19. Much information on the production of *Close Encounters* can be found in Julia Phillips, *You'll Never Eat Lunch in This Town Again* (New York: Random House, 1989). Although this is ostensibly a Hollywood "tell-all" book, Phillips was a primary producer on the film and her accounts offer much insight into the choices Spielberg made.

20. Kolker, *Film, Form, and Culture*, 45–46.

21. The film crew nicknamed the pneumatic puppet used for this alien "Puck" after the mischievous fairy in Shakespeare's *A Midsummer Night's Dream*.

22. Emmanuel Levinas, *Existence and Existents*, trans. R. Bernasconi and A. Lingis (Pittsburgh: Duquesne, 2001), 37.

23. Discussions on the use and importance of language to express material desire in the work of Levinas can be found in Peter Sedgewick, *Descartes to Derrida: An Introduction to European Philosophy* (Malden, MA: Blackwell, 2001), 182–89.

24. The working title for *E.T.* was "Watch the Skies."

25. Elliot's sister (Drew Barrymore) at first screams and runs, scaring E.T., but this response is quickly remedied and changed to acceptance.

26. Sedgewick, *Descartes to Derrida*, 185.

27. Sedgewick, *Descartes to Derrida*, 183–84.

28. It was, of course, a short-lived détente, as the Reagan era saw the reemergence of imaging communism as "the evil empire," reflected in film images of the alien other in movies such as *Alien* (Ridley Scott, 1979), *Aliens* (James Cameron, 1985), and *Predator* (John McTiernan, 1987). These and other films would return to the classic representation of the alien as "monster," yet the impact of *Close Encounters* and *E.T.*, which are essentially companion works, opened a window of difference that at least allowed for the acceptability of the alien as something other than monstrous.

29. Beardsworth, "Modernity in French Thought," 74–76.

30. Sedgewick, *Descartes to Derrida*, 183.

31. During his "breakdown" scene as he flees, he still has his Nazi party pin, even remarking, "Why didn't I sell this? Two people . . . this would have gotten me two more people."

32. Other "historical" Spielberg films strive to create similar face-to-face interaction: in *Amistad* (1997) the "breakthrough" of the film comes in the face-to-face conversation between Baldwin and Cinque, while in *Empire of the Sun* (1987) the young Jamie finds ethical responsibility in the face of the Japanese boy who also dreams of flying, and who is shot by Americans (John Malkovich and Joe Pantoliano).

33. Not all the Schindler Jews were still alive at the time of filming. In a few cases the actors appear with widows (of Stern, for example) or children.

34. Alan Malachowski, *Richard Rorty* (Princeton: Princeton University Press, 2002), 103.

35. In researching this article I found no record of any interview or discussion in which Spielberg indicated he was aware of or influenced by Levinas; I have therefore assumed that Spielberg's intentions were not specifically related to Levinas's work, but merely reflected the ideas of the philosophy.

The Paradox of Fictional Belief and Its Moral Implications in *Jaws*

Christopher R. Trogan and Dean A. Kowalski

A small troop of Boy Scouts frolic in the water just a few yards from shore. It is a bright, warm summer day; you hear the gulls in the distance. As you scan the horizon, appreciating the vast stillness of the ocean, you spy a white, triangular fin rising out of the water. Is it a shark? Is it bearing down on the boys? You scream, "Oh, no, not the Boy Scouts!" But no one hears you because the television does not have ears (or a central nervous system). You are watching *Jaws* (1975) again. No matter how many times you see the film you cannot help but feel anxious for the Boy Scouts. But they are not *actually* in danger. They are not even Boy Scouts, they are child actors. And, on some level, you *know* all of this, but you feel alarmed nevertheless.

This is just one example of film's enormous power to affect our emotions. Sometimes, as in documentary, our emotions are targeted via the intellect. More often than not, however, our emotions are provoked directly through the fictional presentation of characters and events. As the Boy Scout scene reminds us, Spielberg's first summer blockbuster effectively demonstrates the ways in which film as an aesthetic medium can induce a plethora of feeling and emotions—from anxiety and fright to relief and accomplishment—in order to put forth a series of propositions for intellectual consideration. Spielberg's vision of Peter Benchley's novel gives viewers an opportunity to enter into the lives of those on Amity Island and to suspend disbelief through emotional identification. We somehow experience the terror and loneliness of Chrissie Watkins (Susan Backlinie) as she is violently pulled under the dark water during the movie's unforgettable opening sequence (aided by John Williams's haunting score).[1] We are moved by the seething but remorseful indignation of Mrs. Kintner (Lee Fierro) as she slaps Chief Brody (Roy Scheider) across the face. We are shocked at Mayor Larry Vaughn's (Murray Hamilton) disregard for public safety in the face of the pending tourist season. We are terrified and thrilled by the dangerous, open-sea shark hunt of Chief Brody, Quint (Robert Shaw), and Matt Hooper (Richard Dreyfuss) and by the challenges they face. Although we experience these emotions, it cannot be overlooked that these events and the characters living them are fictional. None of these people are actually grief-stricken or in any danger, yet we feel their physical and mental pain. This rather surprising feature of human nature is the focus of this essay.

Films like *Jaws*, depicting fictional characters and events, make our emotional responses puzzling. It may be that some part of us does not quite "know" that the film is fictional. However, this would only partially explain our emotional reactions to it. We know that Chief Brody and Matt Hooper and the events they encounter in the film are the deliberate creations of Spielberg and Benchley. Yet we experience some of the same emotions we would if they were real people and events. The film poses interesting aesthetic issues about the connection between beliefs, judgments, and emotional responses. The nature of this connection forms the core of an intense aesthetic debate. Regarding this debate, it will be argued here that, although our beliefs, judgments, and emotional responses to *Jaws* (and to other fictional works) may *seem* unjustified because the events depicted are not "real," a proper appreciation of the imagination will allow for a rationally justified and even ethically advantageous response. In short, it will be argued that our appreciation of *Jaws* is more than an enjoyable pastime: it allows us to enhance our capacity for empathy and understanding of other people in general—in effect, to become more "human."

Real Responses, Fictional Characters

The film takes place on Amity Island, a small, summer tourist haven on the East Coast. Martin Brody is its new police chief. He, along with his wife and two young sons, has left the hustle and bustle of New York City behind. Now Brody's most pressing cases are parking violations and kids karate-chopping a man's white picket fence. But his first summer is fast approaching, and with it thousands of tourists to crowd the tiny island town. Summer also signals beach parties. One partygoer, Chrissie, runs off toward the water—well ahead of her new suitor—for a late-night swim. Nearing a buoy, she is jerked under water. We do not see her attacker, only her panicked face emerging from the black, still water. From beneath, her body is swung in a circle; she disappears, and we never see her again.

Chrissie's suitor alerts Brody's office the next morning. Her body is found and identified and subjected to a postmortem examination. The coroner determines that Chrissie died from a shark attack. Brody immediately sets to closing the beaches. The mayor and members of the business community complain that Brody has overreacted. They inform him that the coroner has revised his report. It is now claimed that Chrissie died from a terrible boating accident; her body was ripped apart by an outboard motor, not a man-eating shark. Brody—with grave professional reservation—decides to keep the beaches open. Unfortunately, young Alex Kintner (Jeffrey Voorhees) is the shark's next victim. He paddles out on his air mattress, never to be seen again.

Matt Hooper arrives from the oceanography institute. A shark expert, he helps Brody reassess the situation. Hooper believes that the situation is dire, but the town board remains skeptical. The board authorizes additional police and coastguard support, but the beaches remain open for the July 4 rush. When another young man is swiftly and brutally attacked very near shore, the beaches are finally closed. The town hires Quint, a grizzled local fisherman, to hunt down the man-eating great white. Brody, who hates the open water, and Hooper, who immediately clashes with Quint's "old-school" ways, join Quint on the expedition. Both Quint's traditional "sharking" ways and Hooper's reliance on new technology ultimately fail to stop the great white. Brody, however, eventually succeeds in destroying the shark.

What role do our beliefs and judgments play in our emotional responses to the events of the movie? Does the experience of these emotions indicate that we believe these events to be "true"? Moreover, these questions are significant in relation to our emotional reactions as the film continues: we experience anxiety and confusion as we watch Chrissie pulled under, dread as we see Brody study the water between attacks, frustration with the town board as it prioritizes economics over public safety, and regret and pity that Brody was the focal point of Mrs. Kintner's angry grief even though the town board was more to blame for Alex's death.

In everyday circumstances, beliefs and judgments clearly play a crucial role in our emotional responses. If you are afraid of someone chasing you, you must first judge and believe that someone is (actually) chasing you. If you feel sorry for your friend Chris because he is experiencing hardship, you must believe that Chris exists and that he is, in fact, having difficulty. Is it any different in film? If we feel sorrow at the loss of young Alex Kintner, do we believe that Alex and the attacking shark exist and that this event actually occurred?

On the one hand, it seems that in many circumstances an emotional response is in one way or another dependent on belief in the existence of what we are responding to: you cannot feel sorry for Chris unless Chris and the reasons for feeling sorry for him exist. On the other hand, it seems that—as in the case of Chrissie, the Kintners, and the great white—we are moved by what happens to fictional characters and events knowing full well that they do not and never did exist. So, it seems that we must choose between concluding that our emotional responses to fiction are unjustified because they are irrational, and holding that our justified emotional responses, at least sometimes, need not be grounded in truth.

Aestheticians (philosophers who debate issues in the arts) are divided in their approach to resolving this apparent dilemma. One approach is to analyze the rationality of our responses to films in which fictional characters and events are portrayed. These philosophers argue that our emotional experiences are inconsistent and irrational since we *know* that these characters and events do not exist. A second and quite different approach is to argue that certain emotions depend on the adoption of a certain sort of perspective—that is, on "seeing things from another point of view" by focusing on the power of the imagination. Perhaps films even demand such a response from their viewers.

The Paradox of Being Moved and "Being Moved"

Before undertaking an analysis of what it means to "be moved" by this, or any, film, it would be well to consider emotions and how they differ from other affective states, such as feelings, moods, and desires. Many philosophers subscribe to a "cognitive" theory of emotion, in which emotions are defined by having cognitive components. A "cognitive component" is a mental proposition, what one contemporary philosopher calls an "unasserted thought"—a thought tentatively considered, but not believed (i.e., not thought *actually* to correspond to facts in the world).[2] The cognitive theory of emotion, then, maintains that to experience an emotion such as fear or anger requires that (1) you have a certain kind of belief, for example that you are in danger or that you have been wronged (and that there is sufficient cause in the external world to warrant this belief), and (2) you have certain corresponding values or desires (e.g., that you want to stay out of danger so that you can survive, that you should not be held responsible for something you have not done).

When thinking about "feelings" in light of the cognitive theory of emotion, it might be concluded that they are unlike emotions in that they have no cognitive import and are not linked to a particular external object (we may "feel" one way or another regardless of what we believe to be the case externally). Desires, unlike feelings, *are* cognitive because they require a belief that what we desire is (for lack of a better term) somehow to our advantage—whether physically, psychologically, or otherwise. In fact, it may be only because of that belief that we have the desire to do something in the first place (e.g., we desire to go swimming because we know that exercising is beneficial). But it cannot be overlooked that some desires are desires to do things whether or not we believe it is good for us (e.g., our desire to take a walk in Central Park). You might even have the belief that something is good simply because you want to do it rather than the other way around. In addition, it must be mentioned that some desires are completely irrational. These are the kinds of desires we have even though we know full well that fulfilling them will be bad for us (e.g., deliberately becoming intoxicated). As can be seen, arriving at clear definitions of emotion, feeling, and desire is no easy feat, and the relationship between these is even more complicated; yet thinking about these issues is crucial for understanding the relationship between our affective responses to film and our responses to real-life situations.

If our friend Jones sits us down to tell us a story about how her son was the victim of a horrific, fatal shark attack the day before, and if we react to that story with sadness—perhaps even with tears—only to find out that the story is false, we would feel quite embarrassed for behaving the way we did and would probably become angry (and somewhat perplexed) at her for lying to us about something so serious. Yet, when we sit down to watch *Jaws* and see Alex's blood stain the water surrounding his air mattress (as Williams's all-too-familiar theme sounds in the background), we might also have emotions of dread, sadness, and anger even though the events depicted are clearly fictional (after all, "it's just a movie"). In the first case, our reaction to Jones's deception is justified, even expected, once we find out the truth. In the second case, the same reaction would be ridiculous since the success of the film hinges upon its ability to deceive us even though we are never *unaware* that we are, in fact, being deceived. How do we reconcile these two scenarios?

Some philosophers argue that we simply cannot. Jerome Shaffer has argued that emotions are irrational and indefensible. Here and there an emotion might be beneficial because it is pleasant or has some practical advantage, but as a whole there is no good reason to have emotions and we would be better off without them.[3] But the argument can be made that, under the right circumstances, emotions need not be irrational; rather than being contrary to reason, perhaps they arise apart from rational processes. They are thus nonrational or arational in the way that moving your foot is when you drop something heavy. Less extreme in his view, but still skeptical, Colin Radford challenges philosophers to explain how it is possible and desirable for us to have emotional reactions to fictional works.[4] Radford offers several "solutions" to this dilemma. Although Radford's analysis is focused on fiction and drama, it would be useful to apply some of his proposals to our cinematic case study.

First, Radford proposes that when we read a book or watch a play we are "caught up" in it such that we "forget" we are being deceived. Analogously, as we watch *Jaws*, we are "taken in" to such an extent that, among other things, we "believe" that a great white is attacking innocent people. We forget that "it's just a movie" and that the so-called shark in question is actually mechanical (and often did not function properly).[5] Our emotional reactions are excused because the intensity of the film cajoles us into losing ourselves in the narrative. In fact, one way to interpret what people mean when they say a film is "good" is just that it is powerful enough to get us "caught up." However, Radford argues that this is not a real solution to the problem because it "turns adults into children." After all, we are adults and we know that what is happening on the screen is fictional, that the characters are actors, and that the events are not real.

Perhaps, Radford continues, we can explain our emotional reactions to fictional events as occurring because we "suspend our disbelief" in the reality of these events. After all, millions of dollars are spent to create a world that makes it easier for us to do this. There are directors, writers, cinematographers, and producers who dedicate their lives to enabling the suspension of disbelief. Those of us who went to the theater to watch the events on Amity Island in the summer of 1975 would have been quite upset if there had been a baby crying in the seat behind us, or if the picture had been out of focus. That is, we would have been annoyed if we had paid admission to the illusion of the film and not gotten what we paid for. We consciously and voluntarily went in to be deceived, to enter into the minds and worlds of Spielberg and Benchley. So, Radford maintains, because we are fully aware of the deception, we cannot be fully justified in our emotional reactions, since these reactions are, again, predicated upon fictional characters and events.

Could it be that when we see Quint eaten by the shark (infamous blood capsule and all) and (nevertheless) feel pain and sorrow for him, we are actually experiencing the pain and sorrow we would feel for a real person in a similar *situation?* Radford agrees that there is something to this explanation, but holds that it is not enough. He maintains that we feel for the *character,*

Jaws, Universal Pictures, 1975. The interactions of fictional characters (*left to right*) Chief Brody (Roy Scheider), Quint (Robert Shaw), and Matt Hooper (Richard Dreyfuss) provide the viewer various opportunities to examine the ways in which each of us interacts with others. (Jerry Ohlinger's Movie Material Store)

not for someone like him in a similar situation. Radford's comments are here focused on the fictional character of Anna Karenina, but they apply just as well to Chrissie, the Kintners, or Quint: "We are moved by what happens to her, by the situation she gets into, and which is a pitiful one, but we do not feel pity for her state or fate, or her history or her situation, or even for others, i.e. for real persons who might have or even have had such a history."[6] In other words, Radford discounts the possibility that our emotional reaction is directed toward someone else in a similar situation. Instead, he argues that we are emotionally invested in *this* character and *this* situation.

So, we are sad for Mrs. Kintner because of the situation *she* faces. But because Mrs. Kintner is not an actual person, feeling sorry for her is analogous to feeling sorry for a child's imaginary friend (even if the "friend" is referred to by name). The problem, for Radford, would be that since Mrs. Kintner does not actually exist, our emotional reaction is based on a false belief. Because our emotions in everyday situations are based on true beliefs

(I feel angry at Smith because Smith stole my wallet; in order for Smith to steal my wallet, there must *really* be a Smith and a wallet), Radford holds that it is "inconsistent and so incoherent" that we would apply one standard to life and another standard to art. Radford proposes that our emotional reactions to any fictional character or event mirror the kind of fear one might have toward death. To feel sad for a fictional character like Mrs. Kintner is similar to fearing death in that, according to Radford, there is no true *belief.* Just as it is inconsistent and incoherent to base our emotional reaction to Mrs. Kintner's situation on a belief in her existence (since she does not exist), it is equally inconsistent and incoherent to be fearful of death, since, in Radford's estimation, fearing death is, literally, fearing nothing. To fear death is to experience an emotion not based on true belief: "there is, literally, nothing to fear."[7]

Accordingly, Radford does not accept that one could justifiably experience an emotion based on a *fictional* belief. But others would argue that entertaining this possibility would explain away the apparent experiential, epistemological, and—by extension—aesthetic paradox that so confounds him. Perhaps the kinds of beliefs we have when watching *Jaws* or reading a novel are fundamentally different from those we have when experiencing real people and events. If so, then it might not be incoherent to have two different standards for beliefs regarding fictional and actual scenarios.

The Ethical Significance of Imagination

In order to resolve this seeming paradox we might adopt a less narrow view of "belief" than Radford does. Perhaps the beliefs involved are of a more general sort than he lets on. Perhaps I (justifiably) believe that the events of the sort presented in *Jaws* have occurred, or that they are likely to occur, or even that they might possibly occur even if I do not believe in the existence of the particular people, situations, and events described in the film. So, perhaps my response to the film results from my more general beliefs about what the world is like.

We might also question Radford's assumption that belief in the truth of what one reads or sees is necessary for having an emotional response. It could be that the "cognitive component" of an emotion could be an unasserted thought, rather than an actual belief; we would then avoid the charge of irrationality (i.e., that the emotion is irrational because the belief is irrational). To generate an emotional response, it might be enough simply to think of Amity Island and the events of the film and *imagine* that they are real. However, the question remains as to whether an unasserted thought is potent enough to get us as emotionally "worked up" as a belief can. If we believed that Jones's son was eaten by a great white, we would feel intense despair for her. Once Jones admitted that she was lying and that her son was safe at boarding school, we would no longer feel intense despair for her (although we probably would be angry at her deception).

It is also the case that many unasserted thoughts pass through our heads. Some unasserted thoughts are emotionally affecting while many others are not. How could this be? Something else besides simply having the thought and the relevant desires and values is necessary to explain why watching a film that generates such thoughts can be emotionally affecting. Perhaps it is a mark of a "good" film that it can present characters and events in such a way that they are emotionally affecting (that they "stick"). A film that affects us emotionally must contain convincing actors, an engrossing plot line, a rousing musical score, and perhaps even some special effects. All of these features, of course, are hallmarks of Spielberg's films.

In truth, the problem Radford poses is actually broader than even he acknowledges. We respond to fictional works—including film—not only with emotions but also with feelings, moods, and desires. Feelings and moods are not generally held to have cognitive components in the form of beliefs or unasserted thoughts. So, it is unclear how beliefs or unasserted thoughts could help to explain nonemotion affective responses, such as feelings and moods that do not have cognitive components. How does one explain such responses?

Kendall Walton, for one, attempts an explanation by developing a systematic account of imagination.[8] He argues that responding to fiction is an extension of ordinary games of make-believe similar to but more sophisticated than those that children play. So, in responding to fictional events we are using a book (or in our case, the film) as a prop in a game of make-believe, and within the game, we believe what happens to Brody and Hooper and the world they inhabit. It becomes provisionally "true" in this game of make-believe that they are faced with great challenges to keep Amity safe from the shark (among other things). On this view, just as it may be true in the game of make-believe that I feel sorry for Quint or admire Brody, it is not true of me (qua *me*) that I "really" have these emotions. Contrary to Radford's view that a response like this would transform an adult into a child, it is important to note that Walton argues for an *extension* of the game of make-believe that children play. Far from changing an adult into a child who is a "victim" of a game's logic and emotional effect, we adults willingly and self-consciously enter into the "game" of the film and are aware—on some level—that we are playing the game. Unlike children who are often (though not always) unable to detach themselves from make-believe, we can make this conceptual separation. It may take some effort to make the transition, but it can be done. Radford's view does not take this into consideration.

However, if emotional responses to film are not mere child's play, then how we respond may be important. It certainly seems that anyone who cheers on the mayor's poor choices and laughs when Quint recounts for us the horrors of treading water overnight in shark-infested ocean after the sinking of the USS *Indianapolis* is responding inappropriately to the film. What makes these cheers and laughter inappropriate? Little work has been done explaining how to make any such assessments of our responses, but clearly these responses are of the greatest import. If I laugh when Hooper finds the severed head in the hull of the capsized boat, when Ellen Brody (Lorraine Gary) helplessly watches her husband sail out to sea, or when the great white traps Hooper in his own shark cage, I seem to have missed a very important part of the point of the film. Those events are created to move us to fright and sorrow. If we do not experience these feelings, it seems fair to conclude that we have failed to get some of the most important value from the film.

Assessments of responses as appropriate or inappropriate are intimately connected with questions about why it is important to respond at all to fiction of any kind. So what if the events in the film do not have the intended emotional effect upon you? Is anything lost? Why bother watching the film at all? It seems that the value and importance of film, literature, or any other kind of fiction is wrapped up with our responses to it, and a failure to respond is (to that extent) a failure to appreciate the work. And this helps us to understand why it is so important to have not just any response to a work, but to have appropriate responses (conceding that several responses may be equally appropriate, revealing different qualities or aspects of a work). Rather than settling the issue, however, this solution merely raises another question.

Appropriate affective responses to a film are part of what it means to appreciate it, but why is it important to appreciate a film in the first place? To put this another way, why is it good to have around things like films that are supposed to (and presumably do) move us in all sorts of ways? A very old idea is that the function of the arts is to delight and instruct. Suppose we say that the function of a film is solely to please or delight us. It would then appear that we should respond with emotions and feelings that provide the most delight or pleasure; this would remove the need for an exclusively objective standard for the responses (i.e., a standard that resides in the properties of the object, the film, to which we respond) and would accept the preferences of each viewer. On the other hand, some ways of responding to a film may be more likely to produce richer and more fulfilling pleasures than others. If so, the approach with the richest potential overall in the long run could provide a basis for judgment of the appropriateness of the responses.

Furthermore, delight might not be separate from instruction. Aristotle pointed out that learning can be pleasurable. How can emotions and other affective responses instruct? Martha Nussbaum has argued persuasively that literature teaches us to "see," where seeing not merely involves a cognitive or sensory dimension, but is broadly experiential and affective as well.[9] Perhaps something like this kind of "seeing" connects to Walton's notion of experiencing something like sophisticated "make-believe." Far from turning us into children, as Radford claims, temporarily allowing ourselves to accept propositional content and the resulting emotional states may hone our ethical sensitivities. This is not small change: these sensitivities are affective as well as cognitive and influence how we experience the world and how we relate to other people. We can learn in a very straightforward way what it is like to be another sort of person, or to be in a situation other than our own. We can certainly imagine how this would apply to empathizing with Mrs. Kintner. By watching this film and "seeing" it in the way Nussbaum suggests, we might enhance our capacity for empathy and understanding of other people in general. And contrary to Radford's notion that responding emotionally to film "turns adults into children," an emotional response to film may help us as adults better deal with other adults. Perhaps by developing the cognitive and affective skills required to appreciate *Jaws,* by expanding the capacities of the human mind, by genuinely experiencing what this film—or any "good" film—can do *to* us, we are put on the road toward awareness of our own choices and what leads to them in order that we can begin to understand the choices of others. We can then appreciate what film can do *for* us.

What can *Jaws* do for us in this way? We suspect that multiple plausible answers exist. Ethical insights are gleaned from Brody's decision to kowtow to economic and social pressures rather than standing his ground in keeping the beaches closed. But rather than focus on Brody's failures, we suggest that one profitable approach begins by asking why Brody succeeds in killing the shark. First, note that he is Spielberg's iconic Everyman thrust into extreme circumstances. He must act heroically, putting aside his fear of open water. (When the Brodys take the ferry to the mainland, he does not even get out of his car.) He must cooperate with Quint, whom he knows but does not trust, and Hooper, whom he trusts but does not really know. He is also caught between their two divergent worldviews. Quint is skeptical of anything except methodologies that have proved successful; he resists all technological or even social change. Hooper relies heavily on technology and new research to better understand and control his environment. Brody is more of a pragmatist (among other things). He succeeds in killing the shark by fusing the worldviews of his comrades: he uses Quint's old rifle to pierce and explode one of Hooper's oxygen tanks, which has fallen into the shark's mouth. Perhaps the moral of the story is that we, too, should be mindful of well-tested paths without disparaging new ideas. Respecting the old and embracing the new just might prove to be a most successful approach.[10]

Notes

1. Music powerfully aids our aesthetic responses to film. Of Williams's Academy Award–winning efforts on *Jaws,* Lester Friedman writes, "His pulsating cello theme for the shark still sends shivers up the spine of the most jaded viewers brought up on far more grisly movie fare. As [Spielberg] put it in 1995, on the twentieth anniversary of the film, 'the music became the soul of *Jaws.* John Williams rediscovered my vision through his *Jaws* theme. And gave *Jaws* an identity, a personality, a soul'"; see Lester Friedman, *Citizen Spielberg* (Urbana: University of Illinois Press, 2006), 174.

2. Roger Scruton, *The Aesthetic Understanding: Essays in the Philosophy of Art and Culture* (London: Methuen, 1983).

3. Jerome A. Shaffer, *Philosophy of Mind* (Englewood Cliffs, NJ: Prentice Hall, 1968).

4. Colin Radford, "How Can We Be Moved by the Fate of Anna Karenina?" *Proceedings of the Aristotelian Society* supplementary vol. 49 (1975): 67–80.

5. The received view is that Spielberg generated additional aesthetic tension and suspense by not allowing us to see the shark until well into the film. We see the end of the dock being dragged toward Charlie (Robert Chambers) as he frantically swims toward safety, and Quint's orange barrels slicing through the sea, but rarely the shark itself. However, this cinematic choice was forced on Spielberg because the mechanical shark often did not work properly.

6. Radford, "How Can We Be Moved by the Fate of Anna Karenina?" 72.

7. Radford, "How Can We Be Moved by the Fate of Anna Karenina?" 78.

8. Kendall L. Walton, *Mimesis as Make-Believe: On the Foundations of the Representational Arts* (Cambridge, MA: Harvard University Press, 1990).

9. Martha Nussbaum, "'Finely Aware and Richly Responsible': Moral Attention and the Moral Task of Literature," *Journal of Philosophy* 82:10 (October 1985): 516–29.

10. Admittedly, the points raised in this paragraph may trade between ethical and pragmatic considerations, but not (we would argue) in objectionable ways. For more on

understanding Brody's character, as well as competing theories that attempt to interpret the interactions of Brody, Quint, and Hooper, see Lester Friedman's *Citizen Spielberg* (pp. 163–68). Friedman also catalogues a myriad of competing interpretations of the film (pp. 163–65). For a more in-depth study of the Brody character from a virtue ethics perspective, see Joseph Kupfer's *Visions of Virtue in Popular Film* (Boulder, CO: Westview Press, 1999).

A.I.: Artificial Intelligence and the Tragic Sense of Life

Timothy Dunn

A.I.: Artificial Intelligence (2001) is undoubtedly one of Steven Spielberg's most philosophically ambitious films. A visual and emotional tour de force, *A.I.* resists easy categorization. It is considerably darker than most Spielberg films, reflecting, in part, the somewhat misanthropic influence of the late Stanley Kubrick, with whom Spielberg collaborated before Kubrick's death in 1999. Yet it remains a distinctly humanistic work, pessimistic perhaps, but not without empathy and hope. And despite its flaws, which include some clumsy exposition and occasional sentimentality, *A.I.* is a profound meditation on the human condition.

My aim in this essay is to offer an interpretation of *A.I.* while defending the film against various critical charges. In particular, I focus on the much-maligned final sequence, arguing that it is not the gratuitous, sentimental tack-on that many critics accuse it of being.[1] The essay is structured in five sections. In the first section, I explain why I assume that David (Haley Joel Osment) is, in any sense that matters, a person. In the second section, I briefly sketch *A.I.*'s interpretation of the human condition. My contention is that *A.I.* offers a "tragic" interpretation of human life (which I explain). In the third and fourth sections, I discuss two possible solutions to the problems raised in section two; and in the fifth section, I discuss whether these two solutions can, in some sense, be synthesized or transcended.

Is David a Person?

Although the question whether, and in what sense, David, Gigolo Joe (Jude Law), and the other mecha are persons is an extremely important and difficult one, it is not the primary focus of this essay. Nevertheless, any interpretation of *A.I.* must say something about it. For my purposes, I assume that at least David, and probably Gigolo Joe as well, are persons in any sense that matters. I make this assumption for two main reasons.[2]

First, such an assumption is consistent with the events of the film. At least after his "imprinting" David certainly appears to feel genuine human emotions. His apparently jealous behavior toward Henry (Sam Robards) and Martin (Jake Thomas), for example, seems behaviorally indistinguishable from real human jealousy. His fear of rejection and loss, his desire for uniqueness and love, his feelings of betrayal by Monica (Frances O'Connor) and Professor Hobby (William Hurt) all suggest that he is, in any sense that matters, a person.

Moreover, he is clearly so regarded, at least eventually, by both Monica and Professor Hobby. After Martin manipulates David into snipping off a lock of Monica's hair, thereby accidentally endangering her, Monica dismisses the whole episode as a simple case of sibling rivalry. Her growing fear, soon to be confirmed, that David might pose a threat to her biological son implies that she fears losing him—a fear that is best explained by her regarding David as a "real" son. In fact, the film quite subtly hints that her anguish at having to return David to Cybertronics is partly caused by the fact that she has come to love him even more than she loves Martin. And when David finally arrives in Manhattan, he meets a jubilant Professor Hobby, who informs David that he is real, or at least as real as any robot he has ever made. Despite this caveat, Hobby seems to regard David's desire to "chase down his dreams," to become real, as itself proof that he was real all along (one of several allusions to *The Wizard of Oz* [1939]).

Second, the assumption that David is a person, or nearly a person, makes it easier to identify with him. That such an identification is intended is clear. The entire "Flesh Fair" sequence, for example, relies on our feeling at least some empathy for the persecuted machines. Otherwise, why all the fuss about their destruction? The obvious visual references to lynchings and concentration camps seem wildly misplaced unless we regard the mecha as, at the very least, something like persons. When the rabble-rouser Lord Johnson-Johnson (Brendan Gleeson) says to the crowd, "Don't be fooled by the artistry of the creations," we recognize his admonition for what it is—a rationalization. It is certainly not an excuse for such cruel behavior, even if we also understand the legitimate (though innocent) threat that the mecha pose to human beings.

For these and similar reasons, I propose to regard David as a person.

Doing so allows us to identify more readily both with his emotions and with his search for love and meaning, a search that seems destined to end in tragedy. It is to this tragic sense of life that we now turn.

The Tragic Sense of Life

Most of us would readily acknowledge that individual events or lives can be tragic. A child's premature death from leukemia, a soldier's loss of a limb in combat, Othello's murdering Desdemona only to discover that she had been faithful all along—these are clearly examples of tragedies, not only for the individuals themselves but also for those who love them. But in its normal sense, the term "tragedy" is relative in at least two respects: the magnitude of the loss or suffering must be great, and its occurrence must be at least somewhat rare. A person's suffering a bloody nose or a mild beating at the hands of the schoolyard bully is clearly not a tragedy. And death itself, when not premature or unusually horrific, is not normally regarded as a tragedy, for the simple reason that, as bad as it is, it is a fate we all share. But then if tragedy is relative in this way, in what sense can human life *in general* be tragic? If tragedies are relative to the norm, how can the norm itself be tragic?

There are at least two ways in which we can regard human life in general, or the human condition, as tragic. The first is simply to drop the requirement that tragedies be relatively rare: any death, any sufficiently grave suffering or loss is, in this sense, tragic. Alternatively, we can retain the essentially comparative nature of the term but allow comparisons not only with other actual persons, but also with possible states of affairs. In other words, we can say that, relative to how things might have been, the fact that human beings in general die on average after only seventy years or so when we could imagine living much longer (even indefinitely), the fact that even the happiest lives are filled with sorrow and pain, and so on, makes human life in general tragic. Either way, the claim that human life or the human condition is itself tragic is simply a modest departure from the ordinary sense.

Nevertheless, to qualify as a tragedy in either sense, an event must involve a significant degree of suffering or threat of loss. As an essay on the tragedy of the human condition, *A.I.* abounds with examples of such threats, not only to individuals, but to humanity as a whole. Three kinds of desires, the frustration of which threatens to create tragedy, are singled out in *A.I.* for special treatment: our desires for love, uniqueness, and immortality. Let us look briefly at each of these in turn.

Our desire for love needs little explication or defense. Nearly all of us

A.I.: Artificial Intelligence, Warner Bros. Pictures/Amblin Entertainment, 2001. Monica's (Frances O'Connor) decision to imprint David (Haley Joel Osment)—a "mecha" child who will neither age nor stop loving her until he is destroyed—plays an integral role in Spielberg's depiction of tragedy and the human condition. (MovieGoods, Inc.)

desire some degree of love and acceptance by others. David's desire to be loved by Monica is the narrative device that drives much of the film. Once he is imprinted, he becomes obsessed with this desire. Interestingly, despite its initial awkward purity, David's love soon becomes tainted with jealousy and envy (witness, for example, his early drawings, which seem to indicate that he wants his mother to himself), making it far more realistic and emotionally recognizable.

Spielberg's realism about children's love for their parents applies equally to parents' love for their children. Monica's love for David, for example, is clearly at least partially driven by selfish concerns, some benign, some not so benign. During the imprinting process, she neglects to include Henry as an object of David's love, thus keeping his singular devotion for herself (this might be partially excused by the fact that, from the outset, Henry seems largely indifferent to David—for him David is merely a supertoy). That David should remain forever a child, forever loving her, is itself a rather selfish desire, though unfortunately perhaps not uncommon. As critic Rick Groen asks, "what parents haven't entertained the selfish wish that their child remain a child, suspended in a single sublime frame—'always perfect, never changing'?"[3]

A second pervasive human desire is the desire for uniqueness. Nearly all of us strongly desire to preserve our unique identity, to be one of a kind, to be irreplaceable. Or perhaps more accurately, we fear the loss of our identity, our uniqueness, or whatever makes us irreplaceable. One illustration of this fear can be found in some common objections to human cloning, even if some of the metaphysical assumptions on which such objections are based are erroneous. More commonly, such fear is reflected in more mundane concerns. But whatever its cause, and whether or not such a fear is rational, it is certainly deeply rooted.

This fear is also prominently on display in *A.I.* Consider Martin's evolving attitude toward David. At first, he seems to regard David as a potential playmate—a superior, more interesting version of Teddy (voice of Jack Angel). But gradually David inadvertently begins to challenge Martin for Monica's affections. This becomes clear in the scene in which the technicians at Cybertronics are removing spinach from David's electronic "stomach." As Monica dutifully holds David's reassuring hand, the camera shows Martin's face in the background fuming with jealousy. Lord Johnson-Johnson's later assertion that David is the first step in the eventual replacement of our children is an understandable fear.

Ironically, the fear of replacement also plagues artificial persons. As David arrives in Manhattan expecting to meet the Blue Fairy, he comes face to face with his double. Initially confused, David quickly becomes enraged and brutally destroys him, as if he himself were a Flesh Fair executioner. And when he discovers that he is merely a successful prototype, the first in a long line of future Davids, his despair drives him to attempt suicide—he is not only replaceable, he is in fact being replaced.[4]

Finally, we fear death and desire immortality, both for ourselves and for others. I do not mean, of course, that we are preoccupied with these things—on the contrary, most of us live much of our lives without giving our own deaths too much thought. Although we do not typically dwell on our mortality, the thought that our lives will come to an end, that all our accomplishments, relationships, knowledge, loved ones, and so on, will disappear forever, fills us with dread and anxiety. At least for those of us who do not believe in an afterlife, death is viewed under normal circumstances as the greatest of evils: the complete and permanent cessation of all conscious experience.[5]

The fear of death, whether one's own or that of others, is a recurring theme in *A.I.* Early in the film, David asks Monica if she is going to die.

When she somewhat absentmindedly answers yes, David begins to realize that he will someday be alone. As viewers, we are keenly aware of something David may not understand—that eventually David's love will tragically be left without a possible object, his imprinting guaranteeing the impossibility of loving others. When this happens, David's own death at Cybertronics will presumably be the inevitable result. Worse, in a carefully executed scene, Monica's expression reveals the glimmering, guilty realization of what she has done: created a child destined always to love her but never to age. And recall Gigolo Joe's enigmatic comment as he is being hauled up by the police, facing imminent destruction: "I am, I was . . ." Joe's life is about to come to an end, and his dying words reinforce this fear, not only of dying, but of the loss of his identity.

In our more contemplative moments we despair not only at our own deaths and the deaths of our loved ones but also at the eventual and inevitable termination of humanity itself. The powerful imagery of a partially submerged, crumbling Manhattan is not simply an illustration of the potentially devastating effects of global warming—it is a reminder of the transience of human civilization. This feeling rightly belongs to the tragic sense of human life, for in the ordinary, comparative sense, there is nothing tragic about the mortality of human beings.

In sum, what makes the human condition tragic is that the things that we desire most, that give our lives meaning (such as the desire for love), are bound ultimately to be destroyed; that what we value most will soon be lost; and that all our striving and progress will be wiped out forever. Our mortality seems objectively inescapable, and with that realization often comes a sense of grief. I am not arguing that, because all things perish eventually, our lives now are somehow meaningless or lacking in value. This view (a non sequitur) is opposed to the view I have in mind: our condition would not be tragic unless the things we value the most retain their full subjective value despite their impermanence. It is not that a thing must last forever to be valuable, it is rather that a valuable thing's impermanence makes its loss tragic.

If there is a recognizable and meaningful sense in which life itself is tragic, it is natural to look for some form of escaping this condition. Although numerous potential forms of escape seem possible, including some questionable ones (suicide comes to mind), *A.I.* singles out two for careful scrutiny: the development of science and technology on the one hand, and religious faith and practice on the other. Both endeavors offer at least some promise of escape from or transcendence of the conditions that give rise to the general sense of human tragedy. But in each case, the film's verdict, at least until the final sequence, is negative: both of these putative solutions turn out to be at best ineffective and at worst fraudulent. The final sequence, however, raises the possibility of a deeper form of escape or transcendence.

The Scientific Solution

One way in which one might attempt to transcend the tragic nature of the human condition is to use science and technology as a means of allaying our fear of loss and fulfilling our desire for love. And that is precisely what many of the characters in *A.I.* attempt to do. But from the very beginning of the film, there are signs that science and technology are not the answer to our problems. Start with the opening narration: We learn that global warming has caused the destruction of coastal cities, the starvation of hundreds of millions of people, and the forced migration of millions of others. This in turn has led to the introduction of policies limiting the number of children couples can have, policies that in part prompt Professor Hobby to develop an artificial person. Not only has science failed to alleviate misery on a massive scale, but also the greenhouse gases that presumably contributed to the catastrophe are themselves partly the result of technological innovation. Far from being a solution, science and technology are portrayed as part of the problem.

Another interesting example of the failure of science and technology is provided by the Flesh Fair sequence. The angry mob is composed of latter-day Luddites, who are fearful not of being put out of work, but rather of being replaced entirely. Consequently, they seek the only remedy possible: the destruction of the perceived cause of their persecution. That their response is barbaric and cruel does not delegitimize their fear.

In fact, *A.I.* is full of signs that the technologically marvelous mecha, whether built for work or pleasure, are a real threat to human beings. For example, Patricia (Paula Malcolmson), the woman who hires Gigolo Joe, wants not merely a good time, but love and companionship—something she clearly is not getting from her abusive (the abuse is implied) lover. Gigolo Joe offers her the kind of rapturous attention that is analogous to the unconditional love Monica apparently desires. Unfortunately, Patricia's gain is our loss, as we contemplate the possibility that our own services, whether as lovers or as friends, will one day no longer be required. We can accordingly understand (but of course not condone) the point of view of the nameless killer who frames Joe for the murder of his lover: he clearly regarded her liaisons with Joe as equivalent to real infidelity.[6]

However, by far the strongest critique of science and technology is provided through the character of Professor Hobby. His monologue in the opening scene sets the stage for the major themes of the film. At first, he appears to be a rather kindly, benevolent scientist, motivated by humanitarian concerns to develop artificial children for childless couples. His company, Cybertronics, uses technology to suspend terminally ill children in cryogenic freeze until a cure can be found, presumably a noble endeavor. Yet his arrogance is present from the beginning. When a colleague asks him whether creating robots who love does not generate a corresponding obligation to love in return, he responds by suggesting that God made human beings in order that they should love him—a response that shows not only hubris in its implicit comparison but also a disturbing willingness to absolve both himself and God of moral responsibilities for their creations.

Hobby does not acknowledge any responsibilities to the mecha he helps create, even as he later pronounces his "experiment" a success. In fact, one gets the impression that, for Hobby, David's destruction of his double is a necessary final rite of passage into personhood—never mind what happens to the other David, who presumably has the same emotional complexity as David, at least potentially. That Hobby seems more interested in his own accomplishments than in David's welfare indicates that he has little understanding of the implications of his own technological marvels, making him a kind of Dr. Frankenstein. Little wonder, then, that upon seeing his numerous duplicates hanging like cattle in a slaughterhouse, David feels despair. He climbs to the ledge of the building and jumps off—his attempted suicide an indictment on the hubris of science. Admittedly, Hobby's moral failings are his own. Yet the tendency of science to objectify persons is clearly being indicted here.

David's falling to his presumed death reinforces the tragic interpretation of the human condition: Science is not our salvation. It is, in a sense, self-defeating. As a means of overcoming death or fulfilling our desire for love, science and technology threaten to undermine the very sense of uniqueness that makes the desire for love and immortality meaningful.[7]

Religious Faith

Religious analyses of the human condition, together with putative solutions to problems that arise from it, are familiar. Nearly all religions hold out the promise of transcendence of some sort, if not immortality. Christianity, for example, emphasizes our uniqueness, our irreplaceability, and the eventual triumph of love over death. Whatever tragedy befalls us in this world is merely temporary, and in that sense, our lot is not tragic at all. All losses will be restored, all tears wiped away. The eventual eradication of the conditions that make human life tragic is secured not by technology but by an omnipotent, all-loving god. Such is the solution (extremely oversimplified, of course) offered by the perspective of religious faith.

The most obviously religious/mythical imagery in *A.I.* is that of the Blue Fairy. The Blue Fairy represents the desire that our deepest wishes be fulfilled—in Freud's view, the core of all religion. Her physical resemblance to the Virgin Mary is obvious. David's odyssey to find the Blue Fairy is a kind of religious quest. If Professor Hobby has let David down, perhaps the Blue Fairy will not. Perhaps she can succeed where Hobby has failed. Alas, the Blue Fairy turns out to be an even bigger fraud than Hobby—in a stunning image, David is left praying to a statue of the Blue Fairy belonging to the submerged theme park of Coney Island (the tawdriness of Coney Island making her seem that much more phony). Trapped by a falling Ferris wheel, he remains frozen for all eternity, his pathetic prayers destined never to be heard. For those who have struggled with the apparent deafness of an inscrutable god, this moment serves as a painful and even comic reminder of the futility of wishful thinking (identified by the scientist Hobby as humankind's great flaw).

Another scene in which religion is addressed more overtly occurs during the Rouge City sequence. Witnessing a distraught believer leaving a chapel (itself a lonely outpost amidst a sea of hedonism), Joe wryly comments on the emptiness of religious promises. Believers enter the chapel and, after prayer and supplication, the only thing they usually find is him. Some of Joe's commentary we can probably do without (as, for example, the somewhat clunky line, "Those who made us are always looking for those who made them"). But Joe's comments are made more credible by his demonstrated understanding of human needs and vulnerabilities. If we disagree with Joe, we ought at least to take his comments seriously.

A.I.'s verdict seems clear: religious faith fares no better than science as a solution to the tragic nature of the human condition, for the simple reason that the necessary means of transcendence—a personal god—either does not exist or does not care about human welfare. In his indictment of religious faith, Spielberg appears not to pull any punches. The film's message seems to be "Let David's fate not be our own."

Synthesis and Transcendence

Many critics thought that the film should have ended here, if not earlier. The Blue Fairy is a fraud, human beings are selfish and vain, and David is left suspended in eternal uncertainty and futile longing—a pessimistic and dark conclusion fitting for a film inspired by Stanley Kubrick. The final sequence, however, seems to take back the pessimism and replace it with something that no serious movie can supposedly ever have: a "happy ending." As Rick Groen complained, the final sequence "undermine[s] the central theme, replacing the human condition with the Hollywood condition."[8] Rob Vaux was even more critical: "[The final sequence] gushes with the shameless sentiment that Spielberg is notorious for, spilling over with pretentious speeches and weepy-eyed actors. The dramatic impetus slows to a crawl, and the complexities suddenly descend into movie-of-the-week territory."[9]

In my view, whatever its aesthetic drawbacks, the final sequence is a philosophically fascinating addition to the narrative. The stage is set in the "Dr. Know" (voice of Robin Williams) sequence, in which David's questions are answered only after Gigolo Joe suggests combining two seemingly contradictory categories of information: flat fact and fairy tale. This in itself raises an interesting question: how can something be both a "flat fact" and a fairy tale? Are not fairy tales make-believe, while facts are "real"? Spielberg may simply be making the point that when interpreted metaphorically, fairy tales, like other forms of myth, often express important truths (or facts). But I do not think that is all he intends to say here. For there is at least another way in which one might resolve a contradiction: demonstrate that the assumptions on which it allegedly rests are themselves suspect, and that the alleged contradiction is in an important sense not actually a contradiction.

To see this, let us continue our examination of the final sequence. Once the seemingly contradictory categories are combined, Dr. Know provides David with the clue (drawn from a W. B. Yeats poem) that leads him back to Professor Hobby. Eventually David is frozen for thousands of years until highly advanced androids extract him from the frozen sea. There he finds himself face to face with the very statue of the Blue Fairy to which he had been praying. As he reaches to touch it, to see if it is real, it shatters like glass, its physical composition compromised by its being frozen for so long.

At first this seems like an unnecessary continuation of themes already developed: we already know that the Blue Fairy is a sham. But wait—perhaps not after all. In an attempt to fulfill David's deepest desires, the androids who rescue him from the frozen sea simulate the Blue Fairy as a hologram. For David, the Blue Fairy becomes, in an important sense, real. He accepts her reality without question, despite the many false Blue Fairies he has encountered so far. The alleged contradiction is somehow transcended: the fairy tale comes true.

This account might strike us as too easy: she is not *really* real, we might say, she is merely a simulation, and therefore this is not a real resolution.

But this response is too dismissive. The shattered statue of the Blue Fairy from Coney Island, along with whatever she represents, is a fraud. But the simulated Blue Fairy, the representation of the androids' desire to make David happy, to love him the way Monica did not, is real. Or if it is not real in the ordinary sense, then it is real in any sense that matters.[10]

This theme is developed further as the final sequence unfolds. When a lock of Monica's hair, preserved by Teddy, makes it possible for the androids to "resurrect" her, she is arguably as real as her flesh-and-bone ancestor. Some might object that she is a mere simulation, a clever copy or duplicate, and not the real Monica. Such a view cannot be ruled out, of course. But it is also entirely possible that the simulated Monica is indeed real, in any sense that matters, at least for David.[11] David allows the realistic fantasy to play out in the hope of experiencing his mother's true love—the "fairy tale" is synthesized with "flat fact." Thus, the final sequence nicely illustrates some challenging philosophical questions: Can a perfect simulation of love suffice for true love? When might simulations be real, or at least real enough? The complexity of such questions makes it difficult to conclude that the finale is simplistically added to pander to the audience's need for a happy ending.

Aesthetically, the final sequence may seem marred by an extraordinary contrivance: David's mother can be "resurrected" only for twenty-four hours. Why this should be so is not well explained, and even allowing for the fact that this is a science fiction film, it at first seems to be a rather implausible or gratuitous plot twist. On one level, we can see it as a reminder of the limitations of science. The advanced androids of the future presumably descend from the mecha of David's world, which, in turn, were created by human beings. They thus represent the pinnacle of scientific achievement. And yet even they are unable to satisfy David's wishes fully.

Or are they? When confronted with the choice, David opts to have his mother "resurrected" for one day. Assuming that David understands the literal significance of this limitation (that his mother can live for only one more day, a fact that the androids clearly stress), there are at least two ways to understand his decision. On the first interpretation, David accepts the terms of this bargain, reaffirming his love for his mother and his uniqueness (she and he are the only inhabitants of their simulated world) and conquering, at least, his fear of loss. Exactly what happens next is somewhat unclear, but it is reasonable to assume that, after she goes to sleep, David, too, goes to sleep, never to awaken. David achieves the only form of transcendence that is possible: acceptance of the tragic conditions of life, while simultaneously affirming it. Once he does this, death becomes no longer something to be feared, and he is free to enjoy a single day of his mother's company as if it were an eternity. On this interpretation, David embodies a kind of sober humanism.[12]

But there is another interpretation. One could argue that the final sequence makes the film that much more tragic, if not for David, then at least for us. As Monica lies down to go to sleep, *we* know that it is forever. This may be a happy ending for David, but for this viewer at least, it is disturbing, perhaps even more tragic. For as David lies down with his mother he is witnessing her death—her resurrection is only temporary, and she, like all of us, will be lost forever, surviving if at all only as a memory in the mind of a robot. The threatened happy ending dissolves as quickly as the Blue Fairy herself, leaving us with only empty promises and irredeemable longing. On this view, a temporary reprieve from the human condition is a poor consolation and in no way reduces its tragic nature.

If any of these interpretations is even remotely correct, then I do not see how one could reasonably dismiss the final sequence as a gratuitous coda, unworthy of the late Stanley Kubrick. None of the above interpretations is particularly optimistic or happy. In each case, the prospects for genuine escape from the tragic sense of life are limited. I therefore urge critics who despised the finale to consider giving it, and *A.I.*, a second chance.

Notes

I thank Dean Kowalski for helpful comments on earlier drafts of this essay.

1. See, for example, Brian McKay, "A.I.: Artificial Intelligence," *eFilmCritic*, http://efilmcritic.com/review.php?movie=4734&reviewer=258 (accessed May 2, 2008), and Jeffrey M. Anderson, "A.I.: Artificial Intelligence (2001)," *Combustible Celluloid*, http://www.combustiblecelluloid.com/ai.shtml (accessed May 2, 2008). McKay writes that "what could have been a dark but brilliant film drags on until it finally finds some kind of happy ending"; Anderson writes that "Spielberg doesn't know when to quit, and the final twenty minutes of *A.I. Artificial Intelligence* turn sickeningly sweet."

2. For careful analysis of the question of whether David is a person, see V. Alan White's "*A.I.: Artificial Intelligence*: Artistic Indulgence or Advanced Inquiry?" in this volume.

3. Rick Groen, "Artificial Sweetener," *Globe and Mail* (Canada), June 29, 2001, R1. Groen does not, of course, endorse such an attitude.

4. Fyodor Dostoyevsky's short story "The Double" (1846) captures this fear well. Yakov Golyadkin, a minor civil servant, arrives at work one day to find to his astonishment that his desk is being occupied by a person who looks and acts exactly like him. Gradually, his double begins insinuating himself into his life, taking over his assignments,

reporting to his boss, and so on. Golyadkin's attempts to prevent his life from being taken over prove futile; eventually the double completely assumes his identity. The story ends with Golyadkin being sold into the anonymity of serfdom.

5. In George Orwell's *1984* (1949), the Party does not merely eliminate its enemies, it wipes out all trace of them—anything that could testify to their existence. It does this in part to control information, but also to utterly defeat its enemies, inflicting the worst possible punishment on those who would defy it: complete annihilation.

6. As an interesting extension of this point, some critics have noted the sexual nature of the relationship between Monica and David, especially in the final sequence. See, for example, Lester Friedman, *Citizen Spielberg* (Urbana: University of Illinois Press, 2006), 38–39.

7. Another indirect critique of science is provided by the "Dr. Know" sequence. Dr. Know, a kind of cartoonish Einstein, can presumably answer any question for a fee. But as long as David's questions remain in the "factual" category, Dr. Know's answers are totally irrelevant. This is not a critique of science as such, but rather points out its limitations: science cannot provide the answers to some of our deepest questions.

8. Groen, "Artificial Sweetener."

9. Rob Vaux, "A.I. Artificial Intelligence," *Flipside Movie Emporium*, July 2, 2001, http://www.flipsidemovies.com/ai.html (accessed September 29, 2007).

10. I am indebted to Lester Friedman for his discussion of David's accidental shattering of the Blue Fairy; see Friedman, *Citizen Spielberg*, 43–45.

11. Whether this Monica is, indeed, identical to the woman who "imprinted" David is a rather difficult metaphysical question.

12. [In this way, Hobby's allusion to David as the *Wizard of Oz*'s Tin Man is vindicated, albeit in a way that Hobby did not realize. It is not that David's humanity is expressed by the fact that he makes choices and conducts himself with goal-oriented behavior. Rather, David's humanity is affirmed by his deep appreciation for the importance of love, regardless of how long we have to enjoy it, and the choice to lead his life according to *that*. This interpretation is bolstered by recalling the prominent role distant fathers and especially familial relationships play in Spielberg's corpus.—ed.]

Part II

Values, Virtue, and Justice

What Is Wrong with Cloning a Dinosaur?

Jurassic Park and Nature as a Source of Moral Authority

James H. Spence

Jurassic Park (1993) has at its heart a familiar problem: our limited capacity to control our own technological innovations. It begins with the premise that scientists have recreated dinosaurs from ancient genetic material, and both the opening sequence, in which a newly created dinosaur gets loose and must be killed, and the second scene, which graphically depicts what a velociraptor can do to a human being, foreshadow the chaos that is about to result. The movie also presents a familiar analysis of the problem: there is an important line between the natural world and all else, and to ignore this line is to behave wrongly and suffer the consequences. In short, the moral of the story appears to be that we should leave the natural world alone.

In this essay I aim to clarify the debate that occurs within the movie and to distinguish the practical arguments against cloning dinosaurs from the moral arguments offered. The question I ultimately examine is whether the popular notion that nature provides us with moral guidelines can withstand careful scrutiny. Can nature serve as a source of moral standards? Is it wrong to tamper with nature? I argue that it is a mistake to maintain that a distinction between the natural and unnatural can provide a basis of moral argument. Although tampering with nature may be unwise and have dire consequences, it is not inherently immoral.

Building Jurassic Park

At the beginning of *Jurassic Park,* wealthy John Hammond (Richard Attenborough) is completing a new theme park filled with living dinosaurs that have been cloned from fossilized dinosaur blood. There is a problem, though. An employee has been killed by a dinosaur, and the insurance company is now requiring that two experts certify the park is safe. Two paleontologists, Dr. Alan Grant (Sam Neill) and Dr. Ellie Sattler (Laura Dern), as well as a mathematician who specializes in chaos theory, Dr. Ian Malcolm (Jeff Goldblum), are brought in to help analyze this problem and determine how great a risk the park presents.

Much of the tension in the early part of the movie concerns whether or not it is wise to pursue the park project. Hammond, the entrepreneur, is enthusiastic. He is fully confident in the ability of science to control his new creations and puzzled by worries about things getting out of control. In his view, there is nothing mysterious about the natural world, and there are in principle no limits to human knowledge or our ability to control our environment. The question of safety is a purely technical one, and he believes that he possesses the technical means to ensure the safety of park guests. When confronted with concerns about his actions, he responds, "I don't understand this Luddite attitude."[1] Hammond believes that we have sufficient knowledge to limit the risks involved in cloning, and therefore that we have moral permission to use it.

Grant and Sattler are intrigued by the park; their lives, after all, have been spent trying to understand dinosaur species. They are less confident that Hammond can make the park safe. Sattler asks, "How much can you know about an extinct ecosystem, and therefore, how could you assume you can control it? You have plants right here in this building, for example, that are poisonous. You picked them because they look pretty, but these are aggressive living things that have no idea what century they're living in and will defend themselves. Violently, if necessary." Grant is "elated and frightened" by what is happening in the park, and expresses his concern: "Dinosaurs and man—two species separated by 65 million years of evolution—have just been suddenly thrown back into the mix together. How can we have the faintest idea of what to expect?" For our pair of paleontologists the problem is that our knowledge is limited. This implies that there are risks involved in developing the park, and at best some moral uncertainty about the situation.

Any moral disagreement between Hammond and the paleontologists, then, stems from differences regarding the ability to minimize risks. Hammond believes that any problems can be foreseen and contained. Grant and Sattler are more skeptical about our ability to foresee all complications, and consequently more willing to entertain the possibility of tragic results. They

Jurassic Park, Universal Pictures/Amblin Entertainment, 1993. Young Tim Murphy (Joseph Mazzello) becomes the prey of two velociraptors, highlighting the ethical ramifications of building a cloned dinosaur theme park. (Jerry Ohlinger's Movie Material Store)

have the same concern—to avoid causing harm—but disagree about certain facts related to the probability of that harm occurring.

Malcolm also has practical worries, and it would be surprising if he did not. But his concerns seem to go further. If the only problem were the practical one of managing risks, then Malcolm would be more open to hearing what Hammond has to say about the precautions that have been taken. He would advocate taking great care with the project, perhaps to the point that the project would need to be abandoned. Instead, he tells Hammond, "You wield it [genetics] like a kid who's found his dad's gun." This is a moral charge: Malcolm has determined that Hammond is irresponsible, which is to say that his actions are *morally* wrong. It is possible Malcolm merely has the same epistemological concerns as Grant and Sattler, and he has already concluded that the risks involved are so serious that there is no responsible way to proceed with the park. A different interpretation, however, is that Malcolm has a second, primarily moral concern that is independent of the morality of managing risks. Nature, he seems to believe, *deserves* to be respected.

An exchange between Malcolm and Hammond illustrates the moral aspects of the disagreement:

> MALCOLM: Your scientists were so preoccupied with whether or not they could that they didn't stop to think if they should. [An earlier version of the script continues: "Science can create pesticides, but it can't tell us not to use them. Science can make a nuclear reactor, but it can't tell us not to build it!"[2]]
>
> HAMMOND: But this is nature! Why not give an extinct species a second chance?! I mean, condors. Condors are on the verge of extinction—if I'd created a flock of them on the island, you wouldn't be saying any of this!
>
> MALCOLM: Hold on—this is no species that was obliterated by de-forestation or the building of a dam. Dinosaurs had their shot. Nature selected them for extinction.

Here, both Hammond and Malcolm seem to be in agreement that there is something good about nature. Hammond sees himself as, in some sense, preserving it. Malcolm, on the other hand, seems to have a more complicated view. Nature is to be respected, and if nature selects dinosaurs for extinction, then dinosaurs should remain extinct.

The disagreement is framed in terms of what is natural, and the underlying assumption is that what is natural is good. Hammond believes that no one would object if he were cloning an endangered species, and that there is no moral difference between cloning an endangered species and cloning an extinct one. Malcolm denies this, and his denial involves drawing a line between the natural world and human activity. He points out that many endangered species are endangered because of human activity, such as deforestation or building a dam. The implication seems to be that saving an endangered (and perhaps even an extinct) species is acceptable if the danger to the species was created by our interference with the natural world. On the other hand, he maintains that nature, not human beings, caused the extinction of the dinosaurs. Therefore, to bring back the dinosaurs would be tampering with nature in a way that preserving condors would not.

Should they build Jurassic Park? The question has both practical and moral dimensions, and these are interrelated. As a practical matter, we can agree that it is wrong to impose large or needless risks on others. When we do, our actions may be immoral. If nature deserves the sort of respect that Malcolm seems to believe that it does, then there may be distinctly moral objections to the park, independent of any practical concern. This would involve making a distinction between human activity and the natural world, and avoiding anything that, in a sense, contradicted nature.

Let us return to the debate between Hammond and Malcolm. Hammond sees no moral problem with the interaction between human technology and the natural world. The only issue for him is whether or not sufficient safeguards have been put in place to prevent any accidents. He believes that his interference with the natural world is as much a part of nature as any nonhuman event. Malcolm, on the other hand, draws a sharp distinction between the natural world and human actions. He believes that he can distinguish good uses of cloning from bad, and the principle he uses to do this requires him to draw a line between what is natural and what is not.

Malcolm's position seems to me the more difficult position to defend. First, he will need to make the distinction between natural extinctions and nonnatural extinctions plausible; he should also provide us with principled means of determining the issue for ourselves and of resolving disagreement. Perhaps I agree with him that it is permissible to clone condors, because I agree with him that their extinction would not occur naturally; but perhaps I also believe the same about dinosaurs. Dinosaurs' extinction, I might assert, occurred because an asteroid hit the earth, and not as a result of any natural ecological factors. Whether an asteroid caused the extinction of dinosaurs is a factual question; however, whether this should be considered a natural cause of extinction is a theoretical question that Malcolm will need to resolve. Finally, once we have resolved these theoretical issues, Malcolm will need to defend the moral significance of the distinction. Perhaps the extinction of the dinosaurs was natural and the potential extinction of condors is not. So what? Tooth decay is natural but we fight against it twice a day. Consider the following list of actions and try to draw a line between those that are natural and those that are not:

> Putting on a coat when it is cold
> Turning on a light when it is dark
> Turning on the air conditioner when it is hot
> Having a blood transfusion (perhaps with artificial blood)
> Fertilizing a human egg with human sperm outside of a human
>   body
> Using a pacemaker to regulate a heartbeat

Growing a human heart inside a pig for purposes of transplantation[3]

Transplanting flounder genes into a tomato to help it survive a frost[4]

Mixing human sperm with hamster eggs to test the sperm's health[5]

Cloning condors to preserve them from extinction

Cloning dinosaurs to entertain and educate ourselves

My guess is that many people when reading this list will think some of these actions wrong, and perhaps unnatural.

Deriving Norms from Nature

It is tempting to think that nature can provide us with some moral guidance. The morality of sexual activity, for example, has often been approached in this way. The natural purpose of sex was thought to be the creation of children, and therefore any nonreproductive sexual activity was considered immoral. Consequently, there were many laws regulating sexual activity. The sale and advertisement of contraceptives were for many years illegal. Until fairly recently, many states in the United States prohibited homosexual activity, and statutes often explicitly referred to all forms of sodomy as a "crime against nature." Even sexual activity within marriage was regulated by law—oral sex could result in a long prison sentence. Although these activities may appear to be importantly different to us today, the logic of the argument, whether directed at homosexual or heterosexual activity (or masturbation), remains the same: nonreproductive sex defies the natural purpose of sexual activity and is incompatible with the natural goal of creating children.[6] These arguments have been called "perverted faculty" arguments, and I discuss them in more detail below.

The idea that we can look to nature for moral guidance has a long history. More than two thousand years ago Aristotle distinguished between natural justice and conventional justice, and asserted that natural justice was the same in all places, for all people.[7] The Stoics believed that there is a natural order in the universe, that human beings as rational creatures can understand that order, and that we ought to live in accordance with it. Cicero explained things this way: "True law is right reason conformable to nature, universal, unchangeable, eternal, whose commands urge us to duty, and whose prohibitions restrain us from evil."[8] Christianity adopted the idea that there is a natural moral law knowable through reason. According to this view, there are objective moral rules or laws that apply in all times and places; this natural moral law is somehow embedded in and an essential part of the natural order; and human laws ought to reflect, or at least be compatible with, this natural moral law. Perhaps the most famous of these natural law theorists is Thomas Aquinas. Aquinas maintained that God made the world according to a plan, and that some aspects of this plan—the natural law—could be determined using our ability to reason. Human beings, as a part of God's plan, are inclined toward the good even if they are often mistaken about what is good and what is not. When we think clearly and choose soundly, we are assuming our appropriate place in God's creation, and things will go well.

Aquinas developed this theory many centuries ago, but it is still influential. The perverted faculty arguments I have mentioned come from this theoretical perspective and depend on the natural law idea that there is a moral order and moral necessity built into the natural world. There are certain natural and divinely ordained goals for some human activities, and to engage in these activities for reasons other than the intended goal is to pervert that aspect of human conduct. Any activity contrary to that proper function and goal is unnatural and contrary to God's will. That is why, on this view, sodomy, contraception, and masturbation are perversions of the natural act of sexual reproduction: they are incompatible with reproduction. The analysis can be applied to more than sexual conduct. The natural purpose of eating is to nourish the body, and therefore gluttony—excessive eating for sheer pleasure—is a sin. It is easy to see how these arguments are appropriately viewed as religious, even though they can be made without any mention of God. "Natural" and "God's will" refer to the same thing, since God made all of nature.

David Hume

Malcolm is a mathematician, not a theologian, but his view resembles the natural law tradition in several ways. First, he tends to personify nature. Second, he believes that nature has goals and acts to achieve them ("Life," he says, "finds a way"), and that it establishes boundaries (he opposes cloning dinosaurs because "it's anti-nature"[9]). Finally, this personified nature infuses the world with morality. That Malcolm equates God and nature, and that he sees the park as intervening in the natural/divinely ordained order, is strongly suggested in a scene in which he thinks aloud, "God creates dinosaurs. God destroys dinosaurs. God creates man. Man destroys God. Man creates dinosaurs."[10] Like natural lawyers, he also seems to believe the natural world teaches us that there are some actions that should be avoided, even though our intellectual powers are limited and we will never fully understand the natural world's workings.

This general perspective provides the grounds for Malcolm's specific moral claims. That nature deserves to be respected suggests that some of our actions are respectful of and compatible with the natural order and other actions are not. In other words, there is a significant moral difference between what happens naturally and what happens as a result of human interference with nature. The park, he thinks, is an example of human interference with nature rather than an activity compatible with the natural order, and for that reason it is a mistake, in both moral and practical terms. He accuses Hammond of thinking only of what we *can* do, and ignoring what we *ought* to do.[11] In these arguments, Malcolm is touching upon issues discussed by the philosopher David Hume.

Hume was known as a great skeptic, and he was particularly skeptical about our ability to use our factual knowledge of the world to guide our actions. He made a sharp distinction between facts and values, arguing that facts about the world and moral principles about what we ought to do seem to be different sorts of things. This is a logical problem that we encounter when we try to read moral norms from the natural world; it has become known as the "is/ought problem."[12] A second problem involves the difficulty of drawing a line between the natural world and the unnatural. Both of these are issues for anyone sympathetic to Malcolm's position.

Hume, of course, was unaware of DNA and the possibilities of cloning. He was, however, aware that in the past people had appealed to a natural order to support their moral objections to suicide, inoculation, and diverting rivers to irrigate crops. In his essay "On Suicide" he writes, "'Tis impious says the old Roman superstition to divert rivers from their course, or invade the prerogatives of nature. 'Tis impious says the French superstition to inoculate for the small-pox, or usurp the business of providence by voluntarily producing distempers and maladies. 'Tis impious says the modern *European* superstition, to put a period to our own life, and thereby rebel against our Creator."[13] Today, few people would object to diverting a river or inoculating against a disease on the grounds that these actions are unnatural and contrary to God's will. Similarly, Hume seemed to believe that moral objections to suicide were unfounded and would disappear over time.

The problem Hume identifies in his essay is that there is no principled way to distinguish between the natural, God-intended order of things and actions that are unnatural and contrary to God's will.[14] God governs the

material world with general, unchanging laws. God also created living creatures. "To govern the animal world," Hume says, "he [God] has endowed
all living creatures with bodily and mental powers; with senses, passions,
appetites, memory, and judgment, by which they are impelled or regulated
in that course of life to which they are destined. These two distinct principles of the material and animal world, continually encroach upon each
other." In other words, the universe (or at least our part of it) consists of an
ongoing interaction between the natural laws of the physical world (such as
gravity) and the actions of living creatures. Every time we stand up, we are
fighting with the law of gravity. Moreover, Hume argues, there is nothing
unnatural about any of this. There is nothing unnatural when the material
world disrupts the human world, as when a hurricane destroys a city, and
there is nothing unnatural when human beings inject themselves into the
natural world. There is nothing unnatural about animals huddling together
when they are cold, or eating when they are hungry, or running to avoid
being crushed in an avalanche. "All events," according to Hume, "in one
sense, may be pronounced the action of the Almighty. . . . A house which
falls by its own weight, is not brought to ruin by his providence, more than
one destroyed by the hands of men; nor are the human faculties less his
workmanship, than the laws of motion and gravitation." All of our actions,
or none, are natural.

Hume's argument is not intended to justify a particular moral conclusion
about suicide, or inoculation, or diverting a river—at least not directly. His
reasoning is directed against the type of argument that attempts to draw a
line between actions that are natural and actions that are unnatural. Hume
thinks we should abandon all such arguments. If we agree, then we cannot
hold moral objections to contraception, homosexual activity, masturbation,
diverting a river, or cloning dinosaurs on the grounds that they are unnatural.
If these actions are wrong, it must be for another reason. We cannot sensi-
bly assert that some of our doings are natural and others not—either all we
do is natural or none of it is.[15] There is no line in nature to provide us with
moral guidance. By this reasoning, Malcolm's moral objections to building
the park are seriously flawed.

Malcolm's view seems to be that the scientific knowledge involved in
learning how to do something is insufficient to provide us with the wisdom
to know *what* to do. The moral wisdom needed is something greater than a
knowledge of the scientific facts. It is unclear whether Malcolm believes that
factual knowledge is insufficient for moral wisdom, or that it is necessary to
be intimately involved in the scientific process of discovery to acquire this
wisdom (a stronger, less plausible claim). He seems to believe that *he* has this

sort of moral wisdom, although he was not involved in the discovery of the process of cloning. On his view, then, there is a gap between the scientific fact of the matter and knowledge of what we ought to do about it. This raises a problem. How do we reconcile the claim that science (which, after all, is the study of the natural world) cannot tell us how to act with the belief that we ought to live in accordance with nature, that nature somehow informs us how we ought to behave? How can we know what nature requires without taking a scientific stance toward it? This goes back to Hume's more widely known argument, the "is/ought problem." This argument, if successful, also undermines "perverted faculty" type arguments.

As I have said, the problem Hume saw is that descriptive claims about how the world *is* seem to be fundamentally different from moral claims about how we *ought* to behave. Hume believed that too many moral arguments involve a sort of "bait and switch" tactic, beginning with assertions about the natural world (what *is*), and from these concluding what our behavior ought to be. But, Hume objects, "this *ought*, or *ought not,* expresses some new relation or affirmation, 'tis necessary that it should be observed and explained; and at the same time that a reason should be given; for what seems altogether inconceivable, how this new relation can be a deduction from others, which are entirely different from it." In other words, such arguments need to explain the relationship between the natural fact and the moral ought, and more importantly, how it is possible to derive one from the other.

Logically speaking, the problem is this: you cannot assert something in your conclusion that you have not mentioned in your argument. If I am trying to argue that the United States is wealthier than Canada, I cannot support my conclusion by stating only that Canada is colder than the United States. Or consider making an argument that Aristotle was a better philosopher than Socrates in this way: "Aristotle was taller than Plato, and Plato was taller than Socrates. Therefore, Aristotle was a better philosopher than Socrates." In each case the conclusion introduces a relation ("wealthier than" in the first, "better philosopher than" in the second) that is not included in the premise. This makes them poor arguments.

Hume believes that the same is true when we are trying to support a moral claim. A list of natural facts, no matter how long, will never be sufficient to support a moral conclusion about how we ought to live simply because a moral "ought" establishes a new and different sort of relationship. Even if we determine that it *is* possible to drawn a line between natural and unnatural actions, it seems that we still cannot look to nature for *moral* guidance because the truths of the natural world do not carry any inherent moral significance. It may be true that pregnancy is caused by sex, or that a particular woman is my mother, or that inserting a knife into a person will cause them pain. However, the moral significance of these natural facts is another matter entirely.

Morality and Nature

Hume is a controversial figure in philosophy; but even traditional natural law theorists have had reservations about deriving moral norms from the natural world. They were, after all, Christian philosophers, and God was believed to be the ultimate source of moral law. They therefore worried that believing moral norms could be determined from the natural world undermined the importance of God for morality. If the world is made in such a way that certain activities are just morally wrong as a natural fact, then morality has little need for God or religion. All we need to do is understand the natural world, and we will know how to live.

A second concern addressed the nature of morality and the guidance it provides. If morality is simply a set of natural facts, how can it have any moral authority over us? Pain, for example, seems to be naturally bad, but that is not a moral reason to avoid the dentist. For this reason, some natural law theorists have argued that the lawlike, authoritative nature of morality implies that it must come not from the natural world, but instead from a superior being such as God. I think it is this sort of concern that leads Malcolm to personify nature and assume that nature somehow acts and makes decisions. However, I think even Malcolm would, if pressed, concede that nature is simply not the sort of thing that can make rules. So, if moral rules require a lawmaking authority, then the nature of things is not sufficient to place moral requirements on us.[16]

It is even debatable whether Aquinas, the most famous of natural law theorists, believed the natural/unnatural distinction was basic to morality.[17] A careful look at his moral philosophy seems to reveal that he did not endorse the idea that moral norms can be easily read from nature. Instead, his emphasis was on "right reason" and our rational nature. Contemporary natural law theorists tend to agree. The basic idea is this: Human nature allows us to intuitively recognize very basic general moral principles, such as "Do good and avoid evil." These self-evident "first principles" provide us with a place to start our moral reasoning. This helps us bridge the is/ought gap, and even to better understand the natural world. John Finnis, a contemporary natural law theorist, explains it this way: "Human nature is not the basis of ethics; rather, ethics is an indispensable preliminary to a full and soundly based knowledge of human nature."[18] In other words, he believes that we cannot begin to accurately understand human nature without first having some moral wisdom. If this is so, even natural law theory does not start with the natural world and derive basic moral principles from it. Instead, it posits we have an intuitive grasp of some basic moral requirements, and these are necessary to properly understand the natural world.

Once we think about it, this much seems obvious: we need something to help us sort out which aspects of the natural world matter morally and which do not. Both Hume and natural law theorists seem to agree on this point. For the natural law theorists, reason helps us not only to understand the natural world but also to further this understanding by seeing some basic moral truths. Hume would not agree that there are some basic moral truths we intuitively know. Instead, he believed that human nature provides us with certain natural sentiments and predispositions, and that these serve as the basis for morality.[19] Most people, in ordinary circumstances, respond positively to acts of generosity and kindness, and they respond negatively to acts of violence or selfishness. In unusual circumstances, though, such as when we are using new technology, we reach the limits of our natural sentiments and our reactions can be tainted by fear of the unknown and false belief (or, as Hume would have said, superstition). Despite this deep disagreement over the foundations of morality, these theorists would agree that we must bring something to our moral analysis of the natural world, either basic moral principles known by reason or natural human sentiments.

Can Moral Norms Be Derived from Nature?

Jurassic Park provides us with the opportunity to reflect on the relationship between morality and nature. It helps us think about the difference between practical risks, related moral concerns, and moral objections that are independent of any practical consideration. Facts about the natural world do, of course, matter. It is typically good to know how to prevent a disease, or irrigate crops, or avoid famine.[20] The point, though, is that this knowledge of the world is one thing, and what we ought to do is another. It is certainly true that interfering in nature can have terrible consequences. The question is whether that means that we ought to avoid interfering with nature at all, or only whether we should do so very carefully. I think Hume is correct. We cannot avoid interfering with nature—we do it all the time.

Malcolm may be correct in stating that there are great dangers involved in cloning dinosaurs. He may also be right to think that there would be no way to completely eliminate those dangers. But a better explanation for this seems to be that human knowledge is limited, not that "life finds a way." This is nothing more than a concession regarding the limits of human knowledge masquerading as wisdom. Knowledge of the natural world can help us live better, more satisfying lives. But nature will not tell us what we ought to do, nor how we ought to live. To the extent that Malcolm, Grant, Sattler, and even Hammond would agree that it would be wrong to open the park if doing so would risk serious harm, they are appealing to something other than the thought that "if we open the park now, people will get hurt." That extra something is a *moral* belief that we ought to refrain from causing harm to others. To argue that it is wrong to clone dinosaurs because doing so is contrary to nature, however, is an altogether different sort of moral argument. Rather than starting with an uncontroversial moral belief (that we ought to refrain from harming others) and debating the facts regarding the risks of harm, this objection hinges on the dubious moral claim that it is wrong to act in a way contrary to nature.

Moral appeals to nature and what is natural are undeniably popular, and the argument that something is unnatural is an easy way to criticize actions that seem foreign to us. When examined closely, though, these ideas seem to have little normative force. Often they are no more than the expression of a bias or prejudice against the unfamiliar. It may be true that we cannot control our own technologies, and that the result is sometimes tragic. But these tragedies are not punishment for improperly tampering with nature, and our inability to control our technologies provides no support for the familiar analysis offered by Malcolm. To deny that there are moral lines drawn in and by nature is perhaps less dramatic than the view that nature possesses some immutable patterns with which to guide our lives and an agency that enables it to punish those who ignore these patterns; but it is also one that seems better supported by reasoned argument. Progress (vaccinations, our understanding of diseases and mathematics) and man-made dinosaur disasters are two sides of the same coin. Sometimes we will take risks that we should not, and sometimes we will draw on moral standards to criticize changes made in the name of progress. Where these moral standards come from is open to debate, but "from nature" is unlikely to be the answer.

Notes

1. "Luddite" is a term used to describe someone strongly opposed to technological change and innovation.

2. See http://www.dailyscript.com/scripts/jurassicpark_script_final_12_92.html.

3. See, for example, "Grow Your Own Transplant Organ," *BBC News*, December 18, 2003, http://news.bbc.co.uk/2/hi/health/3328509.stm.

4. See "Lovers of Tomatoes Fear Dr. Frankenstein's Garden," *New York Times*, August 5, 1992, C1–2.

5. See "Q&A: Hybrid Embryos," *BBC News*, January 5, 2007, http://news.bbc .co.uk/2/hi/health/6233415.stm.

6. Although it is now somewhat dated, Norman St. John-Stevas provided a worldwide survey of some of these issues, including appendices with various statutes, in *Life, Death and the Law: Law and Christian Morals in England and the United States* (Bloomington: Indiana University Press, 1961).

7. See Aristotle's *Nicomachean Ethics*, ch. 5.

8. From *On the Republic*, quoted in Howard P. Kainz, *Natural Law: An Introduction and Re-examination* (Chicago: Open Court Press, 2004), 10.

9. Although it is in the script (http://www.dailyscript.com/scripts/jurassicpark _script_final_12_92.html), this line was not included in the movie.

10. Ellie completes his thought for him—"Dinosaur eats man"—and adds, "Woman inherits the earth," which is interesting given that one of their concerns is whether an all-female population of dinosaurs can reproduce. It does, and men are eaten.

11. In an earlier version of the script he claims much more than that. "Science," he says, "can create pesticides, but it can't tell us not to use them. Science can make a nuclear reactor, but it can't tell us not to build it." See http://www.dailyscript.com/scripts/ jurassicpark_script_final_12_92.html.

12. For Hume's moral philosophy, see his *Treatise of Human Nature*, book 3, and his *Enquiry Concerning the Principles of Morals*. His brief mention of the is/ought problem is in the *Treatise*, book 3, part 1, section 1, at the conclusion of his critique of rationalism in morals. The passage is highly controversial.

13. David Hume, *Essays on Suicide and the Immortality of the Soul: The Complete Unauthorized 1783 Edition*, Version 1.0, ed. James Fieser (Internet Release, 1995), http://18th.eserver.org/hume-suicide.txt.

14. We do not need to make that strong a claim. For the purposes of this essay, we need only claim that the natural world will not offer us a way to make this distinction, leaving open the possibility that some other source of knowledge, such as the Bible, offers us a way of understanding it.

15. John Hardwig makes a similar point in "Dying at the Right Time: Reflections on (Un)Assisted Suicide," in *Ethics in Practice*, ed. Hugh LaFollette, 2nd ed. (Oxford: Blackwell, 1997), 48–59.

16. For an interesting history of moral philosophy that attends to these issues, see J. B. Schneewind, *The Invention of Autonomy* (Cambridge: Cambridge University Press, 1998).

17. See Vernon Bourke, "Is Aquinas a Natural Law Ethicist?" *The Monist* 58:1 (1974): 6.

18. John Finnis, *Fundamentals of Ethics* (Washington, DC: Georgetown University Press, 1983), 21.

19. This is why, for Hume, morality at its most basic level is not something that can be known, but only felt. It is, in other words, a matter for the heart rather than the head. It is interesting that Hume and the natural law theorists retain the idea that morality is connected to the natural world by way of our human nature. Natural law theorists argue that what is essential about human nature is our rational capacity, which enables us to see the basics of morality. Hume (like several other British moral theorists of his time) argues that human nature is more or less uniform and that morality flows from our natural human sentiments. Bishop Butler can be seen as something of a midway point between these two traditions. Regarding the general argument of this essay, though, it should be noted that "following human nature," whether rational or sentimental, is far removed from the sorts of claims that Malcolm would need to make to distinguish between the morality of cloning endangered condors and the immorality of cloning extinct dinosaurs.

20. It might not be so good if, for example, doing so causes even greater problems in the future.

Is Oskar Schindler a Good Man?

Roger P. Ebertz

With *Schindler's List* (1993), Stephen Spielberg brought the name Oskar Schindler out of relative obscurity. Based on a "nonfiction novel" by Thomas Keneally, the film portrays the story of a Nazi, Schindler, who saved more than a thousand Jews from death.[1] Against a sickeningly realistic portrayal of the horrors of the Nazi treatment of Jews, the film seems to present Schindler (Liam Neeson) as a hero. But is he truly a "good man"? The film makes clear that Schindler is far from being a saint: He is unfaithful to his wife. He relishes his influence and fame. His modus operandi is deceit and bribery. Can a man such as this still be good?

In this essay, I explore Schindler's character from two ethical perspectives: first, through Kantian conceptual lenses, and second, through the ethics of virtue. After clarifying how Kantianism would evaluate the actions and character of Oskar Schindler, I argue that this perspective fails to account for all of our intuitions concerning Schindler's goodness. Virtue ethics also provides some interesting conceptual tools to better our understanding of Spielberg's Schindler; yet, I argue that, in a plausible virtue approach, Schindler falls short of living a "good life" in a complete sense. Finally, I posit that, despite his shortcomings, Schindler can still be seen as a moral exemplar from which others can learn and by which others can be inspired to live well. Although Schindler is not a good man, he exemplifies virtues that are appropriate for living a good life. In Schindler, Spielberg has given us the story of a broken man in whose life we can catch a glimpse of the good.

I should make clear that it is not my intention to analyze the film. I am a philosopher, not a film critic. Stories and "thought experiments" are the stock-in-trade of philosophers; they help us understand ideas and theories. I use *Schindler's List* as a well-developed thought experiment for considering what it means to be a good person, to live a good life, and to be morally exemplary.

The Story

Although a brief summary cannot do justice to the power of the film, I highlight some key scenes here to lay the groundwork for discussion. In the opening scene, Oskar Schindler is pinning a gold swastika to his lapel in preparation for a night at the club. It becomes clear that he is a Nazi businessman with powerful connections who has come to Krakow to make the most of the war. Taking advantage of the forced closure and sale of a Nazi enamelware factory, Schindler contacts the Jewish accountant, Itzhak Stern (Ben Kingsley), who has kept the factory's books. Schindler offers to let Stern manage the factory if Stern will convince Jewish investors to help Schindler purchase it. Since Jews are not allowed to earn money, Schindler will pay the investors in goods they can trade on the black market. Stern will manage the accounts; Schindler will add panache. "That's what I'm good at," he tells Stern; "not the work, the presentation."

Later, as Schindler and Stern are setting up the operation, Schindler insists on hiring Jews rather than Poles. He shows no regard for the fact that their salary will go straight to the Nazis; the Jews themselves will get nothing. "Poles cost more," he observes. "Why should I hire Poles?" Stern does produce Jewish investors, who have little choice but to give Schindler their money since if they do not it will be stolen by the Nazis or rendered worthless. Thus, Schindler is able to purchase the factory for a steal. Through black-market purchases and bribes, Schindler acquires the contacts and contracts to make the business functional.

After the factory has become operational, Schindler's estranged wife, Emilie (Caroline Goodall), arrives unexpectedly from Czechoslovakia to find Schindler with one of his many mistresses. The mistress is embarrassed, but Schindler shows neither embarrassment nor guilt. Emilie is obviously pained, but not surprised, by Oskar's infidelity. Later, in the club over dinner, Schindler tells Emilie of his new business. He has discovered the secret to success: war. Schindler is certainly not a man who delights in the law, or one who senses the compulsion of duty. It is wealth and glory that he has in his sights. And morality need not get in the way. He says to Emilie:

> Take a guess how many people are on my payroll? My father, at the height of his success, had fifty workers; I've got three hundred and fifty. Three hundred and fifty workers on the factory floor with one

purpose—to make money. . . for me! . . . They won't soon forget the name Schindler here, I'll tell you that. "Oskar Schindler," they'll say. "Everybody remembers him. He did something no one else did. He came here with nothing but a suitcase and built a bankrupt company into a major manufacturer. And left with a steamer trunk, two steamer trunks full of money, all the riches in the world."

Emilie's response is telling. "It's comforting to see that nothing's changed," she says. This is the Schindler she knows: unfaithful, a seeker of fame and fortune.

Stern, meanwhile, has been rounding up workers for the factory. Knowing how to work the system, he represents professors, musicians, and older and disabled Jews as "skilled metal workers," thereby hiring people whom the Nazis would otherwise ship out for extermination. One day, Stern brings one of the workers to Schindler's office. "There's a machinist outside who'd like to thank you personally for giving him a job," Stern tells Schindler. "He asks every day. It'll just take a minute. He's very grateful." Schindler's response is cold and hostile, but he allows Stern to bring the man in. Mr. Lowenstein (Henryk Bista), who has only one arm, enters the office. "I want to thank you, sir," he tells Schindler, "for giving me the opportunity to work." Trying to get the man out as quickly as possible, Schindler accepts his thanks and thanks him in return for the great job he is doing. But Lowenstein continues, "The SS beat me up. They would have killed me, but I'm 'essential to the war effort,' thanks to you. . . . You're a good man." As Stern leads Lowenstein from the room, the man continues to invoke God's blessing on Schindler. Rushing off to an appointment, Schindler turns to Stern and rebukes him: "Don't ever do that to me again!" He points out to Stern that this man has only one arm. How could he be useful? But he does not fire Lowenstein. Nevertheless, Lowenstein is not saved. When the Jewish workers are forced to shovel snow, Lowenstein is singled out, ridiculed as being old and useless, and shot on the spot. Schindler complains to the Nazi authorities that he has lost a good worker, a skilled machine operator. Forced to defend his practices before the Nazis, Schindler acquiesces in Stern's efforts to help Jews survive, although he has not yet made it his own project.

As the plot progresses, Spielberg effectively develops Schindler's character in contrast to an "opposite," the Nazi officer Amon Goeth (Ralph Fiennes). Goeth is sent to Krakow to establish a work camp, and ultimately to "clean" Krakow of its Jewish population. Schindler and Goeth are similar in age, position, and ambition. But the film artfully contrasts them, juxtaposing scenes in which Goeth displays total disregard for the lives of the Jews with scenes in which Schindler is moved to acts of kindness toward them.

A pivotal moment in the film takes place on the day Goeth and his men "liquidate" the Jewish ghetto, ridding Krakow of its entire Jewish population in one day. Systematically, the troops move through the ghetto, rounding up the inhabitants. From a bluff overlooking the ghetto, Schindler and his mistress, pausing during a horseback ride, watch the chaos and slaughter below. Gunshots ring out; men, women, and children fall dead in the chaotic streets; Jews are lined up and shot point-blank. While Schindler looks down and observes the massacre, Goeth walks the streets, laughing at the slaughter, taking pride in ridding the city of its Jews. Spielberg presents this scene as a turning point in Schindler's life. As he watches the murderous Nazi activity below, Schindler is transfixed by the sight of an innocent young girl in a red coat who wanders through the streets, unnoticed by the Nazi soldiers. Her red coat stands out in the frame, the only point of color amidst the black-and-white images of death. It is as though the sight of this little girl marks the beginning of a shift in Schindler's mind and heart.[2] Perhaps Schindler is recognizing the true worth of the Jewish people he is seeing and the true horror of the massacre. His goals and motivations change, beginning to move beyond wealth and glory.

To emphasize this point, Spielberg intensifies the contrast between Schindler and Goeth. In a scene following soon after the emptying of the ghetto, Schindler looks down at the empty floor of his factory. In a quick shift we move to the balcony of Goeth's villa, where Goeth stands looking down at the forced labor camp. He picks up his rifle and shoots a Jewish woman who walks below. Then, sitting down, he shoots another, as if for a kind of morning entertainment.

In spite of what seems to be a growing concern for the Jews, Schindler never rebukes Goeth or breaks off their "friendship." What he does, however, is use his relationship with Goeth, and with other Nazis, to work on behalf of the Jews. When Goeth is ready to bring all the factory workers into his labor camp, Schindler convinces Goeth to allow him to set up a work camp of his own for his Jews, in exchange for a cut of the profit. At the heart of the film, Spielberg highlights the contrast between Schindler and Goeth in a series of brief scenes lasting only a few minutes. In the first, Goeth accuses a Jewish worker of failing to make hinges fast enough, drags him outside, and attempts to shoot him. The worker is saved only because Goeth's guns fail to fire. In the next scene, Stern pleads with Schindler, who gives Stern a cigarette lighter to use as payment for bringing the man into the camp. We then see Goeth standing with a group of Jewish men, investigating a theft. When no one confesses to the crime, Goeth chooses a man at random and shoots him. A scared boy comes forward and says he knows who did it; he points at the dead man on the ground. The scene switches and we see Stern once again pleading with Schindler, who gives Stern a cigarette case. The boy is brought into Schindler's camp.

Building on the stark contrasts painted by these scenes—between Goeth and Schindler, death and salvation—Spielberg develops the next series of scenes in greater detail. A young woman comes to plead with Schindler to hire her parents, who she is sure will be sent to the death camp if they are not deemed "essential workers." "They say that no one dies here. They say your factory is a haven. They say you are good," she tells him. "Who says that?" he asks. "Everyone," she answers. "My parents . . . are old. They're killing old people in Plaszow now. . . . Will you bring them here?" Schindler turns on her in rage. "I don't do that. You have been misled. I ask one thing: whether or not a worker has certain skills. That's what I ask and that's what I care about. Get out of my office." In tears, the confused woman flees from his office as he threatens to have her arrested. When she is gone, Schindler rebukes Stern for spreading the word that Schindler will save Jews. "It is dangerous," he yells. But then Schindler reaches down to his wrist, removes his expensive watch, and hands it to Stern, telling him to go and request that Mr. and Mrs. Perlman be brought to the factory. The watch from his own wrist will be the "gratitude" that Stern is to use to save these Jews from death.

Another key event brings home to Schindler the horrors taking place around him. Goeth has received orders to exhume from mass graves and incinerate the bodies, clothing, and any remnants of the thousands of Jews who were killed in the Krakow massacre. The flames leap high into the sky as bodies are dumped into the fire and soldiers cover their faces, at least some horrified by what they are seeing. Goeth is annoyed by the trouble all these dead Jews are causing him. Schindler, on the other hand, is deeply moved. Among the bodies he witnesses being exhumed and cremated is that of the young girl in the red coat. Soon afterward, Schindler devises a plan. He will build a factory in his home town, Zwittau-Brinnlitz in Czechoslovakia, and have Jews transported to work there. As he dictates names, Stern types the list of workers. His Jewish investors, the Perlmans, the Jews who have been working in his factory, and other Jews with whom he has had dealings. Stern is confused as to how Schindler has convinced Goeth to let him have all these workers, but realizes even as he inquires that Schindler is paying for each one. The criteria no longer have anything to do with making money. Schindler is seeking to save people for whom he cares. "Schindler's list" is created, one name at a time, eleven hundred names in all. The list will save the lives of those it names. As Stern says, the list "is an absolute good. The list is life."

All along, Schindler makes clear that he wants "his Jews." Goeth offers him other workers, but Schindler insists that he needs these. Once he has made a deal, the Jews on the list are rounded up and transported to Zwittau-Brinnlitz, where Schindler's factory will make armaments for the war. The men and boys arrive, but Schindler discovers that the women and girls have been diverted to Auschwitz. Spielberg paints a grim picture as the women are stripped, shorn, humiliated, and herded into chambers. The smoke they see rising from the smokestack confirms the horrible rumors they have heard. In the nick of time, Schindler negotiates with the Nazi command, exchanging diamonds for the release of the women and girls. They are sent to Czechoslovakia to join the men and boys.

As Schindler's factory becomes operational, Spielberg uses an exchange between Schindler and Stern to make clear that Schindler is purposely making defective munitions, not wanting to produce anything that will help the Nazis kill the Jews. Buying munitions from other sources, he sells them to the Nazis, losing money until he is absolutely broke. Just as it looks as if the factory will be closed and the Jewish workers lost, the allied forces prevail and the Jews are liberated. Schindler, however, must flee, a condemned member of the defeated Nazi Party. Oskar Schindler, war criminal. Oskar Schindler, savior of Jews. As we are told at the end of the movie, "there are fewer than four thousand Jews left alive in Poland today. There are more than six thousand descendants of the Schindler Jews."

In *Schindler's List,* Spielberg has produced a film that is truly a vision of the worst of the human condition. It is a vision of a world we really do not want to remember, a world in which a race of people are reduced to nonpersons, in which power and cruelty are expressed in the senseless and insensitive slaughter of thousands of women, men, and children. Against this backdrop, Spielberg tells the story of one man who saved a multitude. Is it not ludicrous to ask whether this man, Oskar Schindler, was a good man? Surely he was. In contrast to the "devil" Goeth, Schindler appears all the more a "saint." And yet Schindler's goodness is clearly mixed with imperfections, his virtue mixed with vice. What does it mean to be a "good person"? In what sense might this label be applied to Oskar Schindler? These are the questions to which we now turn.

Schindler and the Ethics of Duty

What does it mean to be a good person? A natural response might be that to be a good person is to do one's duty, to follow proper principles of right. Ethical theories that focus on duty are called "deontological" theories; these theories ground principles of duty in various ways, such as in God's commands, in reason, or in intuition. The most influential philosophical theory of this type is Kantianism, the general approach inspired by the eighteenth-century enlightenment thinker Immanuel Kant. For the purposes of this essay, I stick closely to the ideas of Kant himself, although his general approach has been developed and refined by later ethicists. Kantianism can shed helpful light on the goodness of Schindler's actions.

Kant famously begins *Grounding for the Metaphysics of Morals* with this line: "There is no possibility of thinking of anything at all in the world, or even out of it, which can be regarded as good without qualification, except a good will." At the end of the same paragraph, he writes, "The sight of a being not graced by any touch of a pure and good will but who yet enjoys an uninterrupted prosperity can never delight a rational and impartial spectator."[3] To understand whether Schindler is a good man from a Kantian perspective, we need a grasp of Kant's concept of the will and its role in moral goodness. For Kant, prosperity and happiness alone are not enough to make a "good and admirable" life. For a life to be good and admirable it must be "graced by . . . a pure and good will." It is this aspect of the passage that is particularly relevant for us. We have no delusion that Schindler's life is marked by "uninterrupted prosperity"; he dies a poor man. But we might still think that his life is good and admirable. According to Kant, however, Schindler's life is only good if Schindler can be characterized as having and acting from a good will.

What does it mean to have a good will? For Kant, the faculty he calls the will is closely connected to human rationality. As he explains, the will is a faculty that determines "itself to action in accordance with the representation of certain laws, and such a faculty can only be found in rational beings."[4] This faculty can set laws for actions in two ways, according to Kant. First, it can determine action based on "subjective grounds." These grounds depend upon the situation of the agent and apply only if the agent has certain inclinations and desires. Schindler wants to make money. Since hiring Jews will help him make more money, he has subjective grounds to hire Jews. But if he should no longer have the desire to make more profit, he no longer has these grounds for hiring Jews. When the goodness of a thing is based on subjective grounds, it is only good *if* one has the appropriate inclinations and desires.

And since such goodness is based on an "if," Kant calls the commands that arise from such grounds "hypothetical imperatives."

Second, in contrast, the will can set laws for actions according to "objective grounds." Objective grounds are given by reason alone and are "equally valuable for all rational beings." Commands that arise from objective grounds are "categorical." They are not based on an "if," but apply to all rational beings no matter what their inclinations and desires. If Schindler has "objective grounds" for saving the lives of Jews, then these grounds are based not on his inclinations or desires, but on reason itself. According to Kant, if a command arises from reason and no other factors, then it must apply to all rational beings equally. Thus it is not hypothetical; it applies not to particular persons only, but to all persons.

Human rationality grounds not only categorical commands, but also human worth. Since human rationality, according to Kant, enables humans to set the will to determine actions freely or autonomously, it sets humans apart and gives them inherent value. Properly understood, human beings are not merely tools or means to be used to fulfill our desires. They are not valuable only *if* I am inclined to value them. They are valuable in themselves: intrinsically, not just instrumentally. In Schindler's context, Kant's reasoning would affirm that each Jew is valuable in himself or herself, not simply as a means to acquiring an end. At the beginning of the film, Schindler does not seem to appreciate this truth. He sees the Jews and their plight as the key to making money. Early in the film, Schindler hires Jews rather than Poles only because they cost less, reinforcing the idea that Schindler is rather self-ish (or self-serving). But as the story develops, Schindler seems to come to appreciate the Jews he relates to as persons with value in themselves.

To more fully understand how Kant applies this concept and how Kant's ideas apply to Schindler, we must consider what Kant takes to be the basic principle of morality, which he calls "the categorical imperative." Although he speaks of this imperative in the singular, he formulates his basic principle in several ways, two of which have become influential in philosophical ethics. The first formulation, the "Ends Formulation," goes like this: "Act in such a way that you treat humanity, whether in your own person or in the person of another, always at the same time as an end and never simply as a means."[5] Because of our reason, Kant is arguing, we have intrinsic value. And because of this, we should both act rationally and be treated rationally. This is based on reason, not on our inclinations, and is thus an objective ground for action. Reason commands that we respect the rationally grounded worth of all human beings. Thus, as we have seen, we have a rational obligation to treat Jews with respect, not to merely use them (or worse).

Since reason, and reason alone, is what grounds this moral value, there is a sense in which Kant equalizes all rational beings. This explains another of Kant's formulations of the categorical imperative, the "Universal Law Formulation." This goes something like the following: Act only in such a way that you could rationally will the rule or maxim that underlies your action to be true of all rational beings, that is to be a universal law. Roughly, he is arguing that one should not do something one could not rationally will for every rational being to do. The ground for this reasoning seems to be that if we are all equally rational, then rules (and exceptions to rules) that apply to me should apply to all other rational beings. When I act in a way I would not want others to act, I am setting myself apart, above the rules that apply to rational beings in general. But since we are all rational, to set myself above others is irrational. Therefore, such actions are forbidden by reason. Once again, it is clear that the categorical imperative, as long as the Jews are recognized as rational persons, makes the Nazis' actions morally wrong. The Jews are to be respected as rational beings. They are not things, they are persons.

For Kant, then, a right action is one that conforms to the categorical imperative. One might therefore think that, for Kant, a good person is a person who always performs actions that conform to this basic standard. But this is only a part of his story of what it means to be "good." Kant adds another factor: to be good, a person must not just perform right actions, but must be motivated by a good will. A good will is one that is moved by reason alone, by rational duty. We have seen that the will can determine actions according to subjective or objective grounds. To determine actions by subjective grounds is to choose according to one's desires and inclinations. Actions determined in this way may well conform to the categorical imperatives, but they are not performed out of duty. If Oskar Schindler is kind to his workers to increase their productivity and make more money, his actions may conform to the categorical imperative, but he does not perform them out of duty. A stark example of this occurs when Schindler saves Stern from deportation to Auschwitz. Schindler scolds him, "What if I'd gotten here five minutes later? You'd be gone; then where would I be!" Schindler does the right thing in saving Stern, but appears to act from self-interest and not from duty. In contrast, actions determined by objective grounds—that is, by rational duty—are performed because it is one's duty to perform them. The good will acts out of duty, not out of inclination. If Schindler is kind to his Jewish workers because they are rationally worthy of his respect, then his action has moral worth. Schindler's actions are good not simply in virtue of being the right actions; they are good when he performs these actions for the right reasons.

Is Oskar Schindler a good man? On a strict reading of the historical Kant, it is clear that many of Schindler's actions are not morally praiseworthy. They do not even conform to the categorical imperative. For example, Kant argues that it is always wrong to lie. When one lies to someone, one uses the other person as a means and does not treat that someone as an end in him- or herself. Similarly, when one lies, one acts on a rule that one could not rationally will everyone to act on. Schindler could not rationally will that all of the people he deals with hide their real activities, demand bribes, and engage in manipulative behavior. Therefore, these actions are wrong. He further violates the categorical imperative in his relationships with women, including his wife. He fails to treat them with respect, treating them as means, not ends.

In spite of this, we might be tempted to believe that Schindler is acting in a spirit that is consistent with Kant's ends-in-themselves formulations. The Nazis, it is clear, are not treating the Jews as ends-in-themselves. They place them in slave camps, exploit them for labor until they are too old, weak, or sick to be any more use, and then send them to be exterminated. In an illustrative scene, Goeth approaches his maid as if about to rape her. He tells her, "I would like so much to reach and touch you in your loneliness. . . . I mean, what would it be like? . . . I realize that you're not a person in the strictest sense of the word." He then moves as if to kiss her but changes his mind and beats her, throwing her onto a bed and pushing a shelf of jars over onto her. "No, I don't think so, you are a Jewish bitch!" The frequent, random slaughter of Jews on the streets and in the camp is another example of the clear and horrible failure to treat them with respect, as ends-in-themselves. In the course of the film, however, Schindler develops a respect for the Jews with whom he deals. When he looks down from the bluff at the slaughter in the streets of Krakow, he is horrified by what he sees in a way he would not be if he saw the Jews as mere things to be used.

Clearly there are times when Schindler performs actions that are in accord with Kantian duty. I would argue, however, that *Schindler's List* does not depict him as acting out of rational duty.[6] On Kant's view, duty is based in reason. Schindler's moral development in the film is not characterized by a growing realization of any rational duty to help the Jews, but a growing attachment toward the Jews, toward particular Jews, and an increasing desire to help them. The fact that his conviction develops in response to experience itself points away from Kant. But a variety of specific scenes point in the same direction. When, in Spielberg's depiction of the burning of the exhumed Jewish bodies, he highlights the young girl's red coat in the midst of blacks and grays, as if through the eyes of the watching Schindler, the emphasis is on passion, not on reason. Schindler *feels* the wrong that is being done around him and *wants* to prevent it. In a Kantian framework, these inclinations and desires are not rational grounds. He does not help the Jews because of a duty imposed by reason, or any other external force; he helps them because he cares about them and wants to help them.

Another indication that Schindler is not motivated by rational duty is his clear partiality toward "his Jews." If he were acting purely from reason, all persons would stand in a radically equal position. He would have no more duty to help *his* Jews than any other. His insistence that "his workers" be transported to Czechoslovakia gives evidence that it is not rational duty that motivates him, but a more partial concern. The film does not depict Schindler as a man increasingly moved by proper Kantian reasons, but as a man who increasingly cares about the people who have worked for him and whom he has seen around him. From a non-Kantian perspective we may judge this as worthy of praise, but not from a Kantian perspective.

Thus, as Kant portrays the notion of a good person, Schindler falls short. Although Kantianism helps us to see how Schindler's actions are in conformity to what is right, it does not explain our intuition that in some (if limited) sense he is a good person. Only by having a good will could Schindler truly be called a good person. And he does not live a life that demonstrates either conformity to rational duty or motivation by a truly good will.

Schindler and the Ethics of Virtue

Perhaps the most valuable contribution of the application of Kantianism to Oskar Schindler is the insight that the moral failing of many was the failure to treat the Jews as persons, as beings with value in themselves. However, Kantianism has not helped us to understand how Oskar Schindler could be a moral exemplar. On Kantian analysis he seems to be motivated by the wrong reasons, and thus his actions have very little moral worth. Yet, is not Oskar still a hero, or a moral example in some sense? With this question in mind, let us turn to the alternative moral framework of virtue ethics.

Virtue ethics—grounded in ancient Greek philosophy, especially in the thought of Aristotle—centers on the virtuous character. Discussion of virtue ethics has grown from a whisper to a roar over the past sixty years. Most ethical theories, if they claim to be complete in any sense of the word, include an account of virtue and virtues. To be virtuous is to have appropriate virtues. A virtue is a praiseworthy character trait; a vice, in contrast, is a blameworthy trait. Nonvirtue theories derive virtues from other elements of their theory. Kant, for example, derives virtues from the concept of duty. In contrast, Aristotle writes that the human good is "the soul's activity that expresses virtue."[7] To determine what is good for a human requires that we determine what is virtuous. Once we identify the proper human virtues, we can fill out what a good life would be, how a good person would live, and so forth. Concepts of right action are derived from the concept of virtue, not vice versa.[8]

A simplified virtue theory might define a "good person" and "right action" as follows: Virtue Approach to Goodness (VAG)—A person is virtuous if he or she exercises all of the virtues. A good person is a virtuous person. An action is right if it is what a virtuous individual would perform, wrong if it is not. The first thing to note is that according to VAG, "good person" and "right action" are defined in terms of the virtues. To be virtuous is not to act rightly; rather, to be right or good is to act virtuously. This raises the questions of just what the virtues are and how they can be known. In Greek thought, most clearly expressed by Aristotle, a virtue is seen as a character trait that promotes human flourishing or well-being. On this approach, one's understanding of what constitutes a virtuous person depends on what constitutes the good life, a question that different people answer differently. An alternative approach would not ground virtues in human flourishing, but simply argue that certain character traits are intuitively recognizable as virtues, that they are simply "basic."

For the sake of discussion, I will lay out a plausible list of some important virtues. (I will not argue for them here, but I suspect that these character traits contribute to human flourishing by many accounts of what that means.) A good human life, it would seem, requires self-respect. Further, I suggest self-control, or temperance. Concern for others, honesty or trustworthiness, faithfulness to promises, and justice in relationships with others also seem crucial to many concepts of a good life. Would it really be possible to flourish as a person if one were not in caring relationships with friends and family members? And would it be possible to have such relationships if one were not caring for, honest with, faithful to, and fair in one's dealings with others? Starting, then, with this list of plausible virtues, we can apply virtue ethics to Schindler.

One aspect of virtue ethics lends itself nicely to the Schindler story. Virtue theory seeks not just to identify the human virtues, but to account for how they are developed. Are some people simply born virtuous? Aristotle says no. He writes, "We become just by doing just actions, temperate by doing temperate actions, brave by doing brave actions."[9] Virtues are habits that develop in us as we act in ways that a virtuous person would act. Consider the moral development of Oskar Schindler. At the beginning of the film, there is very little in Schindler's life that one would point to as virtuous. But by the end of the story, Schindler does seem to exercise virtue, even if it is limited to a particular domain.

How does this transformation take place? This is the mystery of Schindler's life. While not dissolving the mystery, the film does suggest that the change was at least facilitated by several things. Itzhak Stern plays a key role. At first, Schindler wants only to make money. Stern, on the other hand, works the system so that Schindler begins, somewhat grudgingly, to help the Jews. Repeatedly, Stern tells Schindler stories of evils Goeth has performed. Slowly, as the relationship develops and as Stern presents Schindler with additional opportunities to be of help to Jews, Schindler grows to have true concern for "his Jews." By acting as a good person would, Schindler becomes a better person. But does he become a "good person"? Can his life as a whole be considered a good one?

Taking self-respect, self-control, concern for others, trustworthiness, faithfulness, and justice as some of the virtues of a good person, let us look at Schindler's life. Is he virtuous? This is still not an easy question to answer. VAG is vague. For example, when would we say that Schindler has adequately exercised all of the virtues? Must he exercise them all of the time? That would be a very high standard. On the other hand, it would not be adequate to be honest once in a while, but generally dishonest. At the very least such a person would be untrustworthy. Honesty, it would seem, must prevail to a significant degree. One could argue in similar ways for the other virtues.

Let us apply this to Schindler. Although he does some very good things, which benefit many people, he fails to consistently exercise important virtues. At times he is honest, but often he is not. Here one might argue that as a good person, he knows when to be honest and when not. He is, as it were, a real-life example of the thought experiment philosophers use about the Gestapo at the door. If you are asked whether you are hiding Jews, do you lie or tell the truth? The virtuous person, one might argue, would lie. She would have the wisdom to know when to lie and when to tell the truth. It is far from clear, however, that all of Schindler's lies are virtuous lies. Schindler is obviously unfaithful to his wife, Emilie, which causes her emotional pain. Does not this unfaithfulness also involve an element of dishonesty? It is difficult to see how either Schindler's unfaithfulness or the dishonesty that is linked with it could be called "virtuous." Finally, one might argue that Schindler is not a good person at the beginning of the film, but that he becomes one by the

Schindler's List, Universal Pictures/Amblin Entertainment, 1993. According to virtue ethicists like Aristotle, moral exemplars play a key role in the proper development of one's character. Arguably, the example set by Itzhak Stern (Ben Kingsley, *right*) helps Oskar Schindler (Liam Neeson) to become a better man. (Jerry Ohlinger's Movie Material Store)

end. He clearly grows to care for the Jews and to do some virtuous things. But it is not clear that his life as a whole can be characterized as good or virtuous.[10] In other words Schindler, if virtuous at all, is virtuous selectively. And as such, it would be inappropriate to label him as a "good person."

Schindler as Moral Exemplar

We have reached an interesting conclusion. On at least some readings of two influential theories of ethics, Oskar Schindler is in fact not a good man. This, however, is somewhat troubling. Schindler is not a perfect person, no one can doubt this. But is he not, as he is depicted in *Schindler's List,* a moral example or hero? Perhaps there is a lower standard. Consider Kantianism: here there are both possibilities and problems in applying a lesser standard to Schindler. We might point out that some, though not all, of his actions conform to the categorical imperative. However, I have argued that on Kantian grounds these actions are not morally praiseworthy because he does not perform them for the right reason, out of a sense of duty. Kantian tools do not enable us to say in what sense Schindler himself is praiseworthy, if not "good."

It is here that virtue language may provide more helpful conceptual tools. As we have seen, according to VAG, a person is good if he or she exercises all of the virtues. Clearly, Schindler does not exercise all of the virtues all of the time. But does he not at times exercise virtue? I would argue that he does. Let us take the virtue of "concern for others." In *Schindler's List* we see a man who comes to be concerned for the Jews, not impartially, but deeply. This concern is rooted not in universal reason, but in relationship. Out of this concern, Schindler risks his own life and loses all that he has to save those for whom he cares. This, it seems to me, is the exercise of virtue. I believe it is possible to praise virtue even if a person is not "good" in the stricter sense. Consider the following principle: Principle of Moral Exemplarity (PME)—A person is morally exemplary *in a particular way,* for a particular period of her life, if in one or more areas of her life she acts in such a way that following her example would promote human flourishing. PME depends on several plausible assumptions. First, that it is possible for a person to exercise virtues in a particular way, for a particular period, without doing so all of the time. Second, that when a person does so, it is appropriate to hold this virtue up as a moral example. Based on PME, we can affirm that Schindler is indeed a moral example.

This also enables us to continue to maintain a high standard of moral goodness. It is not at all clear that Oskar Schindler's life as a whole constitutes a good life. A high standard of human goodness explains why this is so. However, there is also a value in being able to recognize virtues in the lives of Schindler and others, even if they fall short of being "virtuous." This, I believe, is what the Principle of Moral Exemplarity enables us to do. Oskar Schindler was and is a significant moral example, whose concern for the Jews and the actions that grew out of that concern, if emulated by us, would significantly promote human flourishing.[11]

In *Schindler's List,* Steven Spielberg has given us both a moving portrayal of the Holocaust and the story of one person who did remarkable things to rescue Jews. The film was named Best Film of 1993 by the Los Angeles Film Critics Association, the New York Film Critics Circle, and the National Board of Review of Motion Pictures, and it won seven Academy Awards, including Best Director.[12] Yet, as I have discussed *Schindler's List* with friends, I have found a near universal consensus that this is not a film people want to see again. We do not want to see the horrors it portrays. We do not enjoy the ambiguity in the world it paints, where the evil Goeth has a human dimension and the hero is weak and flawed. It is a painful film to watch. It was painful for Spielberg to make.[13] Nevertheless, it is a film that can contribute to our understanding of our world and inspire us to act to make that world better. It is truly a vision of the human condition at its worst. But it is also a vision of how goodness can break out into human life, even through broken people such as Oskar Schindler, or through you and me.

Notes

1. Thomas Keneally, *Schindler's List: A Novel* (New York: Simon and Schuster, 1982). Several other accounts of Schindler's life have since been published. By far the most carefully researched, and presumably accurate, of these is David M. Crowe's *Oskar Schindler: The Untold Account of His Life, Wartime Activities, and the True Story behind the List* (Boulder, CO: Westview Press, 2004). Although the question regarding the historical accuracy of Keneally's book, and of the film itself, is an interesting one, this essay considers Spielberg's use of the story, and is primarily concerned with the Schindler of the film.

2. [John W. Wright makes a similar claim in his "Levinasian Ethics of Alterity: The Face of the Other in Spielberg's Cinematic Language," in this volume—ed.]

3. Immanuel Kant, *Grounding for the Metaphysics of Morals*, trans. James W. Ellington, 3rd ed. (Indianapolis: Hackett, 1993), 7 (standard pagination, 393).

4. Kant, *Grounding for the Metaphysics of Morals*, 35 (standard pagination, 427).

5. Kant, *Grounding for the Metaphysics of Morals*, 36 (standard pagination, 429).

6. See Kristen Renwick Monroe, "Morality and a Sense of Self: The Importance of Identity and Categorization for Moral Action," *American Journal of Political Science* 45:3 (July 2001): 491–507. In this fascinating discussion, Monroe points to empirical evidence that Schindler and others who aided Jews did not conceptualize their actions in terms of principles of duty. See also Lawrence A. Blum, "Moral Exemplars: Reflections of Schindler, the Trocmes, and Others," *Midwest Studies in Philosophy* 13 (1998): 196–217, and Steven Sverdlik, "Motives and Rightness," *Ethics* 106:2 (January 1996): 327–49.

7. Aristotle, *Nicomachean Ethics*, trans. Terence Irwin, 2nd ed. (Indianapolis: Hackett, 1999), 9 (standard pagination, 1098a17).

8. For introductory discussions of virtue theories, see Michael Slote, "Virtue Ethics," in *The Blackwell Guide to Ethical Theory*, ed. Hugh LaFollette (Oxford: Blackwell, 2000), 203–26; Christine McKinnon, *Character, Virtue Theories, and the Vices* (Peterborough, ON: Broadview, 1999); and Robert Solomon, *On Ethics and Living Well* (East Windsor, CT: Wadsworth, 2006).

9. Aristotle, *Nicomachean Ethics*, 19 (standard pagination, 1103b1)

10. Schindler appears to patch up his relationship with Emilie when he returns to

Czechoslovakia, which could indicate a more general change in his character. At the end of the film, however, we are told that after the war Schindler's marriage failed.

11. For additional discussion of characteristics of moral exemplars, see Blum, "Moral Exemplars," and Monroe, "Morality and a Sense of Self."

12. Joseph McBride, *Steven Spielberg: A Biography* (New York: Simon and Schuster, 1997), 436.

13. McBride, *Steven Spielberg*, 426.

A Spielbergian Ethics of the Family in *Saving Private Ryan* and *The Color Purple*

Robert R. Clewis

> This story shall the good man teach his son;
> And Crispin Crispian shall ne'er go by,
> From this day to the ending of the world,
> But we in it shall be rememberèd;
> We few, we happy few, we band of brothers;
> For he to-day that sheds his blood with me
> Shall be my brother; be he ne'er so vile,
> This day shall gentle his condition.
> —*Henry V* (Act IV, Scene 3)

Steven Spielberg's films *Saving Private Ryan* (1998) and *The Color Purple* (1985) can be useful in helping us to understand and evaluate certain ethical theories, in particular the ethics of care and the ethics of the family. Although the ethics of the family typically considers such issues as parent-child relations, parental responsibility, marriage and divorce, sex, and reproduction, I do not address these issues in the usual manner here.[1] Instead, I am interested in how the films can be interpreted in light of what I call a "Spielbergian ethics of the family."[2]

The Spielbergian ethics of the family maintains that a good, ethical life involves demonstrating care for family members, and that one has moral obligations to family members and close friends that are not owed to strangers and that are therefore unique. It is a type of virtue ethics; it holds that moral worth derives from having a good character, adopting certain virtues (above all, care), and habitually exercising good judgment. The Spielbergian ethics of the family maintains that personal identity, or who one is, is an important factor in determining how one should act and be treated.

It interprets personal identity in terms of familial relations such as sister-hood, brotherhood, fatherhood, and motherhood. Although fatherhood and motherhood are important themes in both films, *Saving Private Ryan* emphasizes brotherhood and *The Color Purple*, sisterhood.

I do not assess the films' aesthetic merits or demerits here; nor am I concerned with what the director intended.[3] Rather, I discuss the instances of an ethics of the family that can be found within the films (although these approaches are not necessarily mutually exclusive).[4]

Ethical Theories: An Overview

Since Spielberg's films can be viewed in light of recent criticisms of utilitarianism and Kantianism made by virtue ethicists, it is worth describing these leading approaches to ethics. Utilitarianism, articulated by David Hume, Jeremy Bentham, John Stuart Mill, and others, derives its name from its reliance on the concept of utility. Utility refers to an object's or action's usefulness. According to the utilitarian ethicist, the concept of utility allows one to make judgments of value and so to assess the moral worth of actions and events. Utility thus functions as a basic unit that enables one to determine right and wrong. Utilitarianism (in one form) maintains that an action is morally good if it promotes the greatest good for the greatest number. In one version, utilitarianism understands the "good" as the promotion of pleasure and the reduction of pain or suffering. It views "the greatest number" in terms of the number of human beings affected (although some utilitarians also include sensation-feeling animals). What is good is determined by an estimated calculation of what, consequent to a particular action, people (or creatures) would feel. Utilitarianism is thus called a "consequentialist" ethical theory. For example, vaccinating a certain population, according to utilitarianism, becomes a moral duty if the suffering caused by vaccinating that population is less than the benefits consequent to the vaccination (i.e., the prevention of disease and the promotion of health).

Kantian ethicists, by contrast, hold that the morally right action is the one in which the agent (the one acting) desires or intends to do what is good. A genuinely moral agent has a "good will": she desires to fulfill her obligation or duty. Kantianism is thus a form of "deontological" ethical theory (*deon* in Greek can be translated as "duty"). What counts as a moral duty is determined by Kant's "categorical imperative" test. Rather than estimating or projecting future pleasure or pain consequent to a certain action (as utilitarianism does), this procedure asks whether or not an agent's principles ("maxims") could be consistently adopted by other rational agents.

A "maxim" is a description of the guidelines that underlie one's actions. If the maxim or principle could be assented to by others, the act is morally permissible; if the principle cannot be consistently adopted by other rational agents, the act is morally forbidden. For example, studying hard to pass an exam would be morally permissible since no one would have a problem if everyone acted according to the principle "One should study hard for one's exams." Cheating, on the other hand, would be morally wrong since, if everyone in the class cheated, taking tests would be pointless and the assigned grades would be meaningless. (A similar argument can be made against grade inflation—i.e., giving out too many A's without good reasons.) Lying, too, would be morally forbidden, since if everyone lied communication would be very difficult and few people would take anyone seriously—we would all be on our guard.

Since the early 1980s in particular, virtue ethicists writing from within the Aristotelian tradition have criticized utilitarian and Kantian approaches. Virtue ethics focuses on the development of character and the promotion of the virtues—such as care, generosity, charity, compassion, trust, and courage—rather than on fulfilling duty (Kantianism) or maximizing a social good or benefit (utilitarianism). Virtues are excellent qualities of individuals. They are dispositions to feel, desire, think, and act in specifiable patterns that make the individuals who possess these excellent traits worthwhile or valuable. Like the golden mean, virtue is conceived as a median between extremes of excess on the one hand and deficiency on the other. These extremes are the vices that correspond to the virtue. For example, one virtue, courage, has both an extreme or vice of excess that we call recklessness (having too much courage) and a vice of deficiency known as cowardice (having too little courage). A second feature of virtue ethics is the focus on the community (although it is not always clear how large this group is) and the promotion of the common good. According to one virtue ethicist, Alasdair MacIntyre, the best communities are built on a shared conception of the good and an ideal of living.[5] The common good is understood as the flourishing of a particular community, which is made up of citizens who are seen not as atomistic or discrete individuals, but as essential elements in an organic whole. In *The Color Purple* and *Saving Private Ryan* the *family* counts as such a community, albeit a small one. Both films can be seen as illustrating that there are special obligations to family members and close friends that we do not owe to strangers.[6]

Finally, feminist ethics focuses on the issues that are typically associated with women, such as caring for loved ones, health care, and education (although some advocates suggest—plausibly—that even this way of thinking may be based on misconceptions about gender roles).[7] Feminist theories contend that such issues have been overlooked by the more "masculine" approaches associated with Kantianism and utilitarianism—masculine in the sense that these theories have neglected the unique and important perspectives of women. One type of feminist ethics is known as the ethics of care.[8]

Some advocates of the ethics of care resist calling it a normative ethical theory, preferring instead to see it as a mosaic of insights.[9] Other advocates hold that the ethics of care is a normative ethical theory—that is, a theory that offers a principle or concept that determines what makes actions, principles, relationships, or character traits desirable or undesirable (or right or wrong).[10] Since the ethics of care attempts to provide such a concept (i.e., care), in my view it qualifies as a normative ethical theory. A leading advocate of the ethics of care, Virginia Held, shares this view; she describes the theory as follows: "The central focus of the ethics of care is on the compelling moral salience of attending to and meeting the needs of the particular others for whom we take responsibility. . . . The ethics of care respects rather than removes itself from the claims of particular others with whom we share actual relationships. . . . The ethics of care recognizes the moral value and importance of relations of family and friendship and the need for moral guidance in these domains to understand how existing relations should often be changed and new ones developed."[11] Notice that Held mentions friendship as well as family. The ethics of care says that we do and should put the interests of those who are close to us (i.e., family and close friends) above the interests of strangers. Our interests, it claims, are intertwined with the people we care for. It holds that the well-being of a caring relationship involves the cooperative well-being of the persons in the relationship as well as the well-being of the relationship itself.[12]

According to some ethicists, with whom I agree, the ethics of care can be characterized as a type of virtue ethics.[13] In other words, care can be understood as a central virtue that agents should develop and promote. To whom does one demonstrate care? Care is typically exemplified in one's interactions with loved ones, close friends, and family members. Even if care might also be extended toward strangers and nonrelatives such as customers, clients, and patients, the typical case remains the care that is demonstrated toward and by family members and close friends.

I conceive of the Spielbergian ethics of the family as a type of ethics of care, which in turn is a type of virtue ethics.[14] Some of the key normative and descriptive claims that can be attributed to the Spielbergian ethics of the family are as follows:

1. The good and ethical life involves demonstrating care toward family members and close friends.
2. One has moral obligations to family members and close friends *because* they are family members and close friends; these duties are unique in that one does not owe them to strangers.
3. Moral worth derives from having a good character, exemplified by demonstrating care toward family members, or at least toward other human beings viewed as family members.
4. Ethical theory should consider personal identity, or who one is, to be an essential element in moral deliberation and action. Personal identity should play an important role in determining how one should act and be treated.[15]
5. Personal identity should be interpreted in terms of membership in a family; that is, in terms of brotherhood, sisterhood, fatherhood, motherhood, and so on.

The Spielbergian ethics of the family has some affinities with deontology since it emphasizes respect of persons and obligations to human beings. However, it also differs from deontology since it claims that we should give special treatment to certain persons (family members and close friends) and that such care is not required of us in our interactions with nonfamily and nonfriends. Not only do we have obligations to human beings, it maintains, but we also have unique obligations to family and friends. An ethics of the family interprets personal identity in terms of membership in a rather small community: one's circle of friends and family.

Saving Private Ryan

Saving Private Ryan revolves around the search for a single person, Private James Francis Ryan of Payton, Iowa (Matt Damon).[16] There are two distinct types of approaches to assessing the value of Ryan's life and thus the worthiness of the rescue mission. We can call these the utilitarian and the nonutilitarian. Sergeant Michael Horvath (Tom Sizemore), Private Richard Reiben (Edward Burns), and Private Daniel Jackson (Barry Pepper) each at one point defend the utilitarian position, according to which the greatest good for the greatest number is what counts or is morally salient. Before disembarking on Omaha Beach, Sergeant Horvath shouts to his men, "Five men is a juicy opportunity. One man is a waste of ammo." Walking with his squad in the countryside, Brooklyn native Reiben questions, "You wanna explain the math of this to me? I mean, where's the sense in risking the lives of eight of us to save one guy?" Jackson likewise argues that the rescue mission is a misallocation of precious resources and human capital (above all, his abilities as a sniper). Utilitarianism would reject the idea of sending a rescue mission to save Ryan, since there is little reason to think that one private is worth more than a captain, a sergeant, a medic, four experienced ranger privates, and an interpreter. Even Ryan defends what utilitarianism suggests. Upon learning that he is to be rescued, Ryan protests that his life is not worth more than the lives of the other paratroopers in the 101st Airborne: "It doesn't make any sense, Sir. Why do I deserve to go? Why not any of these guys? They all fought just as hard as me." Ryan does not see himself as being special or unique.[17]

Many of the comments made by Captain John H. Miller (Tom Hanks) are representative of the nonutilitarian position. He is motivated by the idea of returning home to his wife: "Sometimes I wonder if I've changed so much that my wife is not even going to recognize me whenever it is I get back to her. And how will I ever be able to tell her about days like today? Ryan. I don't know anything about Ryan, and I don't care. The man means nothing to me. It's just a name. But if going to Ramelle and finding him so he can go home—if that earns me the right to get back to my wife—well then, that's my mission." Notice that Miller says he does not *care* to know anything about Ryan. This seems to be because Ryan is not part of Miller's group, his squad. In the church, Miller explains to Sergeant Horvath how he justifies choices that result in the deaths of his men:

> Vecchio. Yeah. Caparzo. You see, when you end up killing one of your men, you tell yourself it happened so that you can save the lives of two or three or ten others. Maybe a hundred others. Do you know how many men I've lost under my command? . . . Ninety-four. But that means I've saved the lives of ten times that many, doesn't it? Maybe even twenty, right? Twenty times as many? And that's how simple it is. That's how you . . . that's how you rationalize making the choice between the mission and the men. . . . This Ryan better be worth it. He'd better go home and cure some disease or invent a longer-lasting lightbulb or something. 'Cause the truth is, I wouldn't trade ten Ryans for one Vecchio or one Caparzo.

Although Miller's reference to the numbers of human lives lost or saved and his allusion to Ryan's contribution to society might seem to have a utilitarian ring, these remarks actually fit better with the ethics of the family. Miller focuses on the fact that the men in question are *his* men. They are not just any human lives. Since Ryan is not part of the squad, Ryan must demonstrate his worth and earn being rescued. Miller prefers Caparzo (Vin Diesel) to Ryan, but not because Caparzo is a better soldier. In fact, Caparzo is reckless, exhibiting the vice that corresponds to an excess of courage: he eats apples as bullets fly; he disobeys Miller's orders and is killed, whereas Ryan survives. Miller prefers Caparzo because he belongs to Miller's group. Miller seems to recognize a special obligation to his men. He makes a moral distinction between members and nonmembers of his group.

Likewise, Army Chief of Staff General George C. Marshall (Harve Presnell), who issues the order to save Ryan, defends the nonutilitarian and ethics of the family position. He argues that Ryan is worth saving because all of Ryan's brothers (Sean, Peter, and Daniel) were killed in action. He reads aloud a letter (however implausibly) from Abraham Lincoln to Mrs. Bixby, who was thought to have had five sons who died while fighting in the American Civil War.[18] When Marshall reads the letter, John Williams's music ascends to the lofty, noble, and sublime. The audience is clearly supposed to follow the general into the ethics of the family camp and to root for Ryan's successful rescue. Similarly, since he has two brothers himself, Captain Fred Hamill (Ted Danson) sympathizes with the rescue mission and adopts an ethics of the family perspective ("I understand what you're doing. . . . Find him [Ryan]. Get him home").[19]

It is worthwhile to be more precise about the notion of the family that is operative in *Saving Private Ryan*. The most obvious instance of the family, of course, is the Ryan family. After all, the basic plot of the film turns on reuniting the last surviving Ryan brother with his mother and family in Iowa. But one could say that a family is constituted by Miller's squad, too, with Miller as the father figure.[20] Miller remains distant so as to be a disciplinary figure. He does not tell the squad his origin or occupation. Reminiscent of a father tucking in his children, he tells his men, "We only got a couple of hours. . . . Go to sleep." At the same time, he is open enough for the squad to trust, revere, and perhaps even love (Mellish: "He's good." Caparzo: "I love 'im"). Miller realizes when it is the right moment to confide in his squad: after the gruesome death of medic Irwin Wade (Giovanni Ribisi), he finally tells the squad where he is from and what he does. Thus, Miller is stern and demanding, but also sympathetic and kind. He is also resourceful, as he demonstrates by using chewing gum and a mirror at one point during the Normandy invasion and improvised "sticky bombs" in the defense of Ramelle.[21]

Accordingly, it seems that, in deciding to attack the German radar post, Miller acts like a bad father. He risks the safety of his men unnecessarily in order to reestablish his place with them (they have noticed his hand shaking, which he realizes could be taken as a sign of weakness). Indeed, the effects of his actions are undesirable, since Wade dies a grisly death and Reiben and Horvath fight with one another, nearly sparking a mutiny. Spielberg has Miller break down and cry after Wade's death, revealing that Miller recognizes he acted unwisely and in a nonfatherly, noncaring way. When Miller acts from bravado in rushing the radar post unnecessarily, his squad (or "family") suffers.

The concept of the family also includes the notion of *motherhood*. If *Saving Private Ryan* lends itself to interpretation in terms of an ethics of the family, then it should not surprise us to find representations of motherhood throughout the film. In the Omaha Beach scene, for instance, a suffering and dying soldier cries out for his mother. The film shows us Ryan's mother when she is told of her sons' deaths. Caparzo, bleeding to death, asks the medic Wade to write to his mother at home.[22] In the church, Wade tells the squad about his relationship with his mother. Wade's last words bring together motherhood and the home: "Mama. Mama. I wanna go home. I wanna go home. Mama. Mama. Mama." Of course, there are also mother jokes.[23]

Other familial relationships are also evident. Caparzo rescues the French girl because she reminds him of a family member, his niece.[24] *Saving Private Ryan* shows us the *brotherhood* shared by the soldiers, whether the privates in the ranger rescue squad or those in Ryan's paratrooper outfit. The bookish Corporal Timothy E. Upham (Jeremy Davies) desperately wishes to experience the "bonds of brotherhood" shared by soldiers fighting side by side.[25] He attempts to look up the meaning of FUBAR ("Fouled" Up Beyond All Recognition) to fit in; eventually he learns how to use the word and becomes a member of the group, joking with Mellish, Reiben, and Horvath before the battle of Ramelle. Moments before the fighting begins in Ramelle, Ryan tells Miller about the last time he was with his brothers. Being a Ryan brother makes Private Ryan special, worthy of rescue, Spielberg suggests. If he was not a Ryan brother and all of his brothers had not been killed, there would have been no rescue mission. To commanding officers such as General Marshall, Ryan would have been like most other soldiers. It is membership in the Ryan family (brotherhood) that sets him apart and makes him unique. In short, *Saving Private Ryan* seems to stress the importance of familial relations. This is noteworthy because advocates of an ethics of care charge that there is a tendency in Kantian and utilitarian ethical theories to overlook social and familial relations and the construction of personal identities within a social web. *Saving Private Ryan* brings out the importance of such relations.

However, the irony of the mission to rescue Ryan is that Ryan is not part of Miller's squad. Miller's squad does not owe Ryan anything in terms of either an ethics of care or an ethics of the family, because Miller and Ryan have no existing relationship at all, much less one of family or close friends. Miller sets out on the mission because he was ordered to do so. That Ryan is not a member of Miller's squad or company may, as I have mentioned, be one reason that Miller says "Ryan" is just a name to him, that he would rather have one Caparzo then ten Ryans, and that Ryan must earn his rescue. Even *after* Miller has met Ryan and the latter has chosen to stay and defend the bridge, Miller tells Ryan that he must earn his rescue. Ryan is still not part of the group. When Ryan tries to get Miller to talk about his wife, Miller keeps that to himself, drawing a line between Ryan and his family in Addley, Pennsylvania (Ryan: "Tell me about your wife and those rosebushes." Miller: "No, that one I save just for me"). According to an ethics of the family, if Ryan were part of Miller's circle of family and friends he would not have to earn his rescue; we owe certain things to our friends and family, the ethics holds, simply *because* they are friends and family.

Ryan is no Indiana Jones or Oskar Schindler. We have no reason to think that he goes on to accomplish extraordinary things, to become a noble, meritorious agent who carries out great feats or saves the lives of many individuals. He does not invent a longer-lasting lightbulb. However, he still may have earned his rescue after the war. We see Ryan, decades later, as an ordinary man wearing nondescript clothing. But Ryan is an ordinary man *surrounded by his family*, and Spielberg seems to be implying something here. Spielberg offers this grandfather as a model of the virtuous, caring person.[26] Personal identity, membership in a group, and familial relationships thus play important roles in *Saving Private Ryan*. Since James Frederick Ryan of Minnesota (Nathan Fillion) is not the sought-after James *Francis* Ryan of Iowa, the search for Ryan continues. Not just any Private Ryan will do. The correct Ryan is found on June 13, 1944, defending a strategically important bridge over the Merderet River in Ramelle, exactly a week after the Normandy invasion. Private James Francis Ryan deserves to be rescued on account of his personal identity, because of who he is—namely, a Ryan brother and a member of the Ryan family—and Ryan's full name reveals this identity. Likewise, Ryan asks about the names of the rangers who died rescuing him (Irwin Wade and Adrian Caparzo) so that he can remember them. Even the title of the film, *Saving Private Ryan*, highlights the name of the person being rescued. The film can therefore be viewed as suggesting that personal identity is morally significant or important. Indeed, this focus on personal identity as a function of one's familial relationships is one way in which the Spielbergian ethics of the family counts as an ethics of care.

Private Ryan earns his rescue because he goes on to lead a good life, develop a good character, and be a good man, not because he discharges duties or maximizes the good. This is the language of virtue ethics. Accordingly, the film portrays Ryan as a man who has lived virtuously in that he has had a family and has cared for his relatives. By being a good man—above all, a good husband, father, and grandfather—Ryan earns his rescue and affirms the sacrifice made by the rangers. Miller's last words, spoken to Ryan, are "James, earn this. Earn it." At the end of the film, the elderly Ryan, surrounded by his family, says by Miller's headstone, "I've tried to live my life the best I could. I hope that was enough. I hope that, at least in your eyes, I've earned what all of you have done for me." He asks for confirmation from his wife (Kathleen Byron): "Tell me I've led a good life. Tell me I'm a good man." His wife responds, "You are." Ryan, the film suggests, has lived up to the conditions of his rescue by being a good father and grandfather.[27] One commentator asked, "Does 'earning it' mean performing extraordinary feats, or does the valor of living a good and ordinary life with dignity suffice?"[28] The film's answer is that living a good, even if ordinary, life with dignity indeed suffices, and that Ryan is a model of virtue because he nurtures caring relationships with his family members.

Thus, we find an ethics of care and of the family in what may strike some as an unlikely place. In a film that—to judge by its DVD cover—one might have thought celebrates only male bravado and heroic acts in a time of war, we find attention to the special obligations that members of a squad (modeled on the family) place on each other, an awareness of the importance of who one is, and a positive characterization of being surrounded by a caring family.

The Color Purple

In *The Color Purple* we find similar attention to the importance of promoting caring relationships among family members and friends. Here the focus is not so much on brotherhood as on sisterhood, motherhood, and fatherhood. We are introduced to Celie (who is fourteen years old) and Nettie while they are living with their stepfather (whom they take to be their biological father) in rural Georgia in 1909. The man Celie calls Pa rapes her repeatedly and has made her pregnant twice. She bears two children who, we later learn, are Adam and Olivia.

The Color Purple, Warner Bros. Pictures/Amblin Entertainment, 1985. Sisters Celie (Desreta Jackson, *right*) and Nettie (Akosua Busia) form a lifelong bond that arguably grounds unique moral obligations between the two, including the raising of the other's children. (MovieGoods, Inc.)

The relationships among the family members in *The Color Purple* are complex, to say the least, and they develop over the course of the film, which spans several decades. Celie's stepfather gives Celie (Whoopi Goldberg) over to Mr. Albert (Danny Glover) in marriage; Mr. Albert abuses Celie physically, psychologically, and sexually. In the end, however, he helps bring Celie's children to Georgia to be with her. Albert's lover, Shug Avery (Margaret Avery), is coldly rejected by her father, a minister; but by the film's end they are reconciled. Celie advises Albert's son Harpo (Willard E. Pugh) to beat his wife Sofia (Oprah Winfrey), but she later regrets this and aids Sofia in the store; the two then become friends.

Amidst all the harshness with which these characters treat each other, Nettie (Akosua Busia) and Celie exhibit a relationship of care throughout the film.[29] Although Celie and Nettie are together only at the beginning and end of the film, they feel inseparable from each other. This feeling remains even when they are physically separated. Nettie watches over Celie's children: she takes care of and cares for Olivia and Adam. Nettie relates that Olivia and Adam, taken away from Celie after birth, are "all growin' up together, a family." She writes in one of her letters from Africa, "But Celie, my dear sweet sister, we'll all be coming home soon." At the end of the film, Nettie, Olivia, and Adam return to be with Celie in Georgia. Spielberg thus incorporates some of his favorite themes: the search, the return home, and the reunion of family members.

According to an ethics of the family, Nettie is under a special obligation to raise Celie's children because Nettie is Celie's sister and the children's aunt. This ethical theory would place an obligation on a close friend as well. If a close friend of Celie's met Adam and Olivia in Africa, then this friend would be under a moral obligation to raise the children. A person who was not a friend of Celie's, however, according to the ethics of the family, would not have a moral obligation to raise the children. A stranger may very well choose to raise Celie's children, but this would count as a noble, supererogatory act, going above and beyond the call of duty. According to an ethics of the family, in other words, sisterhood (like other familial relations) and friendship enjoin moral obligations that we do not owe to strangers.

Although sisterhood is the most apparent familial relationship in *The Color Purple*, fatherhood is also evident in ways that are relevant to an ethics of the family. For instance, Albert tells his son Harpo to beat Sofia. This is clearly a violation of the notion of a caring relationship between family members. According to an ethics of the family, family members should not only have moral respect for each other as human beings, but should demonstrate love and care toward one another. Albert's counsel turns out to be bad advice, not just because it implies that spousal abuse is morally permissible, but because Sofia defends herself well and gives Harpo a puffy eye.

Second, the relationship between Albert and his own father demonstrates the importance of rearing children well. Albert seems to give Harpo this advice because he was brought up to do so by Old Mister (Adolph Caesar). Indeed, Celie blames Old Mister for teaching Albert that it is ethically permissible to abuse one's spouse. In other words, Albert's father did not help Albert adopt the virtue of care as part of his character. Similarly, when in the fall 1937 sequence Old Mister chastises Albert for letting the house fall into disrepair ("This house is a wreck"), he does so in a sexist way that does not value care for one's spouse. But when Old Mister tries to cheer him up with his usual counsel ("I know just what you need—you need a woman"), Albert seems to reveal that he has undergone a change. Albert makes his father leave. He appears to recognize that one reason he is lonely is that he has been following his father's bad advice. This recognition may be the beginning of a moral transformation (more on this later).

Third, Shug tells Celie of her father, the local minister, "My Pa loved me. My Pa still love me, 'cept he don't know it." The film can be interpreted as a version of the biblical story of the prodigal son who comes to his senses after living unvirtuously (Luke 15:11–32). Shug is a sort of prodigal daughter who, after living freely, is eventually accepted by her father. At the end of the film (but not the book) there is a musical battle between the church choir and singers from Harpo's juke joint, led by Shug, a blues singer. Although the battle starts out as an opposition between the two groups, they end up singing together, and the father and daughter are reconciled. Hugging her father, Shug calls herself a sinner and repents: "See Daddy, sinners have a soul, too." An ethics of the family implies that Shug and her father should be reconciled and should not remain alienated from one another. It suggests that Shug's father is under a special obligation to forgive her, precisely because he is her father. Although throughout most of the film Shug's father rejects Shug (and is thus unlike the biblical father who accepts the son even before he can repent), Spielberg has him accept her in the end. The father eventually does what the ethics of the family says he should do.

The Color Purple suggests, as the ethics of the family maintains, that unique moral obligations obtain among family members and close friends. For example, Sofia fulfills the duty to protect her children by demanding that her children be taken away before she is unjustly thrown in jail. Nettie fulfills obligations to her sister Celie by writing her periodically and by looking after Olivia and Adam until they return to Georgia.[30] Shug and Celie eventually develop a loving, caring relationship. When Shug says, "I think it pisses God off when you walk past the color purple and you don't notice it," Celie responds by asking whether it just wants to be loved.[31] The implication is that by getting noticed, one puts oneself in a position to be loved and, by extension, to be nurtured or cared for. This makes good sense in light of the ethics of the family (and of care).

As in *Saving Private Ryan,* motherhood and the home are significant in *The Color Purple.* Sofia, for instance, demonstrates the virtues associated with motherhood: care, loyalty, love, and devotion. When Sofia finally sees her children after eight years in jail, she says that she does not know them anymore, and she cries. Sofia explains to Miss Millie (Dana Ivey) that she would like to spend more time with her children, but Millie forces Sofia to drive her from Sofia's home back into town. Sofia is nearly destroyed by Millie. However, at the dinner scene in which Celie stands up for herself, Sofia also regains her dignified manner. Sofia thanks Celie by using the language of the home: "I want to thank you, Miss Celie, for everythang you done for me. I 'members that day I's in the store with Miss Millie. . . . I's feelin' real down, I's feelin' mighty bad . . . and when I seed you, I know'd there is a God. I know'd there is a God, and one day I was gonna get to come home." The Celie-Sofia relationship is significant for the ethics of the family, since it illustrates that care can extend or apply to friends as well. Since Sofia is Celie's friend, Sofia and Celie owe each other special moral obligations. Moreover, when Celie's children come home, exclaiming "Mama," they return not to just any old house but to Celie's new home. It is the home in which she played with Nettie—new because she inherited it yet familiar because it is the home she shared with her sister.

Toward the end of *The Color Purple*, Spielberg juxtaposes a shot of a knife and one of a musical instrument, implying that the family bonds between Celie and her relatives reach beyond the Atlantic. The montage, in my view, does not so much suggest that the Africans are the brothers and sisters of the Georgians—this would be the idea of *fraternité*, an extension of a family-based concept to nonfamily members and nonfriends—as it connects individuals who are family members *tout court*: Celie, Olivia, Adam, and Nettie.

Thus, we find an ethics of the family (and therefore of care) in *The Color Purple*. The film reveals some of the special obligations that family and close friends place on each other, pays attention to personal identity and to family relations such as motherhood, fatherhood, and sisterhood, and offers a poignant reminder of what happens when family members do not care for one another in healthy and ethical ways.

Assessing Spielbergian Ethics

It seems appropriate to conclude with a brief evaluation of the claims made by a Spielbergian ethics of the family. One advantage of the ethics of the family is that it can account for the natural and widespread impulse to care for family members more than for strangers. (Indeed, human beings may have inborn instincts to do this.) This has the advantage of making it easier to be moral (even if one does not like every member of one's family). Feasibility is a good thing in ethics, for we want an ethical theory that we can actually live up to. Ethical principles should be practicable. However, it would be wrong to claim that this easy naturalness is the *justification* for the principle, since this would commit the mistake of deriving an ethical theory from a fact about the world (a deduction of "ought" from "is," to use David Hume's phrase[32]). A better justification is instead something like the common sense notion that one should take care of oneself or one's own before others. While this may be a good justification, there is a danger here (which is not necessarily a reason for rejecting the justification, but something to be wary of): one might always end up thinking that one should help oneself or one's family before helping others, and thus never get around to fulfilling one's obligations to nonfamily members and strangers. Instead of giving money to the United Nations Children's Fund (UNICEF), I might always think that I should contribute to my own savings account or to my child's college fund, or even splurge on my brother's birthday gift.

Second, although *Saving Private Ryan* and *The Color Purple* imply that one should develop a good character that incorporates the virtues, including care for family and friends, the films do not indicate how an individual can undergo a moral transformation. Such a transformation is not always necessary for developing a good character (as Ryan's case reveals), but *sometimes* it is (as in Albert's case). Albert's moral transformation seems rather abrupt and inexplicable. The psychological or social cause of his change is not adequately revealed.[33] Is it Celie's rebuke? His loneliness? The repudiation of his father's mistaken views? Divine grace? As one commentator notes, it is not clear *why* Albert would change, considering the social conditions under which he lives, or *how* he could change, if his moral sense is so utterly and inexplicably debased.[34] Perhaps Albert's change could be explained by a combination of the aforementioned factors. In conjunction with one another, some or all of them might be part of a broader explanation of Albert's transformation. But showing how this happens would require much work.

In any case, even if someone like Albert changes, this raises difficult questions about whether evil of any kind can be fully atoned for, or whether instead an agent should be held accountable to some standard of retributive justice. In not allowing Albert to reconcile with Celie, Spielberg implies that some sins are simply unforgivable and that it would be morally unjust for Albert and Celie to reconcile (or, to take an example from *Saving Private Ryan*, for Upham to let Steamboat Willie go free rather than killing him).[35] It is not immediately obvious that Spielberg's position regarding redemption and forgiveness is the correct one, however.

Third, the only thing that comes close to revealing the conditions of the good, ethical life is incomplete, even if headed in the right direction. Correctly, Spielberg's films do not suggest that the moral developments people undergo are exclusively individualistic and inner-directed. Ryan appears to have led a good, ethical life with the help of his family. Shug helps Celie develop, grow, and live independently. Celie helps a battered, tired Sofia remember who she is, and Sofia in turn serves as a model of strength for Celie. Spielberg's films rightly suggest that the aid of relatives and loved ones is a necessary condition of living a good and ethical life. Although assistance from family and friends is necessary for the ethical life, however, it is not *sufficient*. To flourish, human beings require more moral influences and aids than just those provided by friends and the nuclear family. Any satisfactory representation of how one can lead an ethical, flourishing life should account for other factors, such as the influence of the social milieu, the effects of the arts and aesthetic activities, the role of economic institutions, and assistance or hindrance by the political state. Although *The Color Purple* and *Saving Private Ryan* have ample opportunity to do so, they do not adequately acknowledge or gesture toward these influences on human behavior.

These criticisms notwithstanding, the ethics of the family merits serious philosophical attention, and *Saving Private Ryan* and *The Color Purple* enable us to better understand and evaluate it.

Notes

The epigraph is from William Shakespeare, *Complete Works*, ed. Stanley Wells and Gary Taylor (Oxford: Oxford University Press, 1988), 588.

This essay is for John and Martin.

1. Readers might wish to compare the Spielbergian position with that defended by Plato (*Republic*), John Locke (*Some Thoughts Concerning Education*), Jean-Jacques Rousseau (*Émile*), and Immanuel Kant (*Groundwork for the Metaphysics of Morals*). Familial relations have been discussed from the end of the nineteenth century to today; the discussion includes contemporary debates about civil unions, filial obligations, welfare, reproduction, and parental rights. See, for example, Borden P. Bowne, "The Ethics of the Family," in *The Principles of Ethics* (New York: Harper and Brothers, 1892), ch. 9, 231–46, and James Hayden Tufts, "The Ethics of the Family," *International Journal of Ethics* 26:2 (January 1916): 223–40. Part I of Jeffrey Blustein's *Parents and Children: The Ethics of the Family* (New York: Oxford University Press, 1982) summarizes the history of the philosophy of familial relations.

2. I say "Spielbergian" not "Spielberg's" since the director need not (but may) subscribe to every feature of the theory discussed, while others besides Spielberg can do so.

3. In a number of interviews Spielberg has stressed that he sees *Saving Private Ryan* as a morality play; see Lester D. Friedman, *Citizen Spielberg* (Urbana: University of Illinois Press, 2006), 233.

4. Although deontological and utilitarian positions are asserted by some of the characters in both *Saving Private Ryan* and *The Color Purple*, the films as a whole, insofar as they are viewed *philosophically*, assert and illustrate an ethics of the family, a virtue theory with care as the central virtue. I interpret both films as asserting and illustrating an ethical theory (composed of a set of philosophical claims, which I list in this essay) that I call a Spielbergian ethics of the family. For a compelling defense of the position

that a film can be philosophical by asserting and illustrating philosophical claims, see Thomas Wartenberg, *Thinking on Screen: Film as Philosophy* (New York: Routledge, 2007). Moreover, it seems to me that if a film asserts a philosophical claim, it must somehow also *illustrate* that claim, although this is not the place to defend this thesis.

5. Alasdair MacIntyre, *After Virtue* (Notre Dame, IN: University of Notre Dame Press, 1981), 146–47.

6. Ethical relativism, by contrast, maintains that what is morally right or wrong is determined and *justified* by the standards established by a particular community or group; moral standards, it holds, are nonobjective and nonuniversal. One problem with this view is that it leaves little conceptual room for moral progress and reform since it is claimed that there are no nonrelative standards to guide reform and progress. Second, it is not clear how disagreements and disputes between conflicting standards could be settled reasonably in the absence of a nonrelative standard. On the surface at least, the Spielbergian ethics of the family does not seem to be a type of ethical relativism.

7. See Hilde Lindemann, *An Invitation to Feminist Ethics* (New York: McGraw-Hill, 2006), 4.

8. Two important early sources are Carol Gilligan, *In a Different Voice: Psychological Theory and Women's Development* (Cambridge, MA: Harvard University Press, 1982), and Nel Noddings, *Caring: A Feminine Approach to Ethics and Moral Education* (Berkeley: University of California Press, 1984).

9. See, for example, Annette C. Baier, *Moral Prejudices: Essays on Ethics* (Cambridge, MA: Harvard University Press, 1994), esp. ch. 1; Peta Bowden, *Caring: Gender-Sensitive Ethics* (London: Routledge, 1997); and Margaret Urban Walker, "Feminism, Ethics, and the Question of Theory," *Hypatia: A Journal of Feminist Philosophy* 7 (1992): 23–38.

10. For a defense of the view that an ethics of care should be conceived as a distinct ethical theory, see Virginia Held, *An Ethics of Care* (Oxford: Oxford University Press, 2006), 4, 10–13.

11. Held, *Ethics of Care,* 10–12.

12. Held, *Ethics of Care,* 12.

13. Lisa Tessman, Margaret McLaren, Barbara Andrew, and Nancy Potter share this view; see their contributions in *Feminists Doing Ethics,* ed. Peggy DesAutels and Joanne Waugh (Lanham, MD: Rowman and Littlefield, 2001). Michael Slote likewise argues that caring is the primary virtue and that morality should be based on the motive of caring; see Michael Slote, *Morals from Motives* (Oxford: Oxford University Press, 2001). Although Held's point that the ethics of care focuses on relationships rather than on the dispositions and states of character of individuals (pp. 4, 19) has some plausibility, this does not necessarily entail that the ethics of care must be seen as a distinct ethical theory: perhaps virtue ethics can accommodate a focus on relationships. Even Held admits that her view is controversial and that there are similarities between the ethics of care and virtue ethics (p. 4).

14. However, I do not wish to suggest that this is the only valid or fruitful way to interpret *Saving Private Ryan* or *The Color Purple.*

15. A noteworthy feature of both *Saving Private Ryan* and *The Color Purple* is that care is directed primarily to sons and daughters rather than to parents. But some ethicists criticize a filial focus. For example, Christina Hoff Sommers and Chenyang Li both discuss the obligations that grown children have to their parents; see Christina Hoff Sommers, "Filial Morality," *Journal of Philosophy* 83:8 (August 1986): 439–56, and Chenyang Li, "Shifting Perspectives: Filial Morality Revisited," *Philosophy East and West* 47:2 (April 1997): 211–32. Jeffrey Blustein's *Parents and Children* has influenced much of the contemporary debate.

16. The search is an important theme in many of Spielberg's films. The *Indiana Jones* films (1981, 1984, 1989) concern the search for meaning or life (embodied in a precious object or relic), *E.T.* (1982) the attempt to go home, *Jaws* (1975) the hunt for a monstrous creature, and *Amistad* (1997) the quest for freedom. See Lane Roth, "Raiders of the Lost Archetype: The Quest and the Shadow," in *The Films of Steven Spielberg: Critical Essays*, ed. Charles L. P. Silet (Lanham, MD: Scarecrow, 2002), 59–67 (originally published in *Studies in the Humanities* 10:1 [June 1983]: 13–21).

17. Ryan also, however, expresses his desire to stay "with the only brothers" he has left—the paratroopers in his company. This is characteristic of the ethics of the family position, which is *not* utilitarian. The line between utilitarian and nonutilitarian views may not always be clear, and sometimes the same individual might express both types of views at different times. As another example, Private Reiben questions the mission of saving one man at the risk of eight (which is utilitarian), but he might not question a similar mission that aimed to save a private in his *own* squad (which is not utilitarian). He refers to a utilitarian calculation ("You wanna explain the math of this to me?"), yet argues in nonutilitarian and ethics of the family terms that the members of the squad all have mothers. The plurality of such arguments within one film should not surprise us, if Spielberg's intent is indeed to give us a morality play (see note 3).

18. In fact, only two brothers died in battle: Charles and Oliver Bixby; see "Letter to Mrs. Bixby," *Abraham Lincoln Online,* http://showcase.netins.net/web/creative/lincoln/speeches/bixby.htm (accessed September 28, 2007). Spielberg fudges the historical facts in interpreting the story of the Bixby sons in order to heighten the emotional sympathy for Mrs. Bixby, which is then extended by analogy to Mrs. Ryan. It makes saving Ryan that much more important: we want to avoid a Bixby-like case. This is morally significant for the ethics of the family because it is only through Private Ryan that the Ryan family can live on.

19. Since both Hamill and Miller adopt an ethics of the family perspective, it might be puzzling that Hamill supports the mission but Miller does not, seeing it as a public relations mission. But we should recall that Hamill is not the one carrying out the mission; Miller is. If Hamill were part of the rescue squad, he might very well oppose the actual mission. If Miller were *not* part of the squad, he might very well support the idea of the mission. Their behavior is consistent with their ethics of the family principles. In other words, if the mission goes against the interests of your group/family, you should oppose it; if it does not harm your group and supports your (ethics of the family) principles, you should support it. This seems to be what the ethics of the family entails. Miller shows that

he is capable of imagining having another allegiance (family). He tries to convince Ryan to go home safely: "Is that what they're supposed to tell your mother when they send you home in an American flag?" He speaks from the perspective of Ryan's mother.

20. I am indebted to Dean Kowalski for sharing this interpretation with me.

21. One might also argue (as Dean Kowalski pointed out to me) that the army itself is the operative family unit. On this interpretation, General Marshall would be the father figure (or even grandfather figure): he acts like a father in ordering Ryan to go home to his mother, who needs him. One advantage of this view is that it *justifies* the mission from an ethics of the family perspective. Justifying the mission is a good thing. There are some problems with this reading, however. First, the army seems to be too large to count as a family in any ordinary sense; it stretches the concept of the family very thin. Second, it has trouble explaining why Corporal Timothy Upham is not part of the group or band of brothers; if being in the army were sufficient for membership in the group, he would be a member, but he is not. Third, this reading does not square as well with an ethics of family interpretation as does the squad-as-family reading. According to the army-as-family reading, Miller's men owe Ryan a special obligation because he is their brother *even though* they do not know him; however, the brothers' knowing one another is more consistent with an ethics of the family.

22. Louis Menand writes, "When they're [the U.S. soldiers] not talking about the war, they're talking about their own homes and mothers which, of course, is how they come to appreciate the deeper significance of their mission"; see Louis Menand, "Jerry Don't Surf," in *The Films of Steven Spielberg,* ed. Silet, 254 (originally published in *New York Review of Books,* September 24, 1998, 78). Menand picks up on the motherhood theme: the squad's mission is "to bring him [Ryan] home to his mother" (p. 251) and dying soldiers are "screaming for their mothers" (p. 252).

23. At Omaha Beach, Horvath says to Miller, "If your mother saw you do that, she'd be very upset," to which Miller responds, "I thought you were my mother." And walking in the field, Reiben jokes that Miller does not have a mother.

24. After Caparzo dies, Miller proclaims, fatherlike: "*That's* why we can't take children."

25. As its title (taken from Shakespeare's *Henry V*) reveals, the television miniseries *Band of Brothers,* which was coproduced by Spielberg and Hanks and based on Stephen Ambrose's novel of the same name, picks up on the solidarity and brotherhood between soldiers.

26. Admittedly, the patriarchal squad and Ryan's nuclear and extended family (based on a two-parent, heterosexual model) might strike some readers or viewers as being overly traditional; they might point out, for instance, that when we meet Ryan's mother, she is doing the dishes.

27. But is Ryan a good *son?* Confronted with a choice between his two "families"— that is, either going home to comfort his mother or fighting alongside the "only brothers" he has left (the paratroopers)—he chooses the latter. This may point out problems within the ethics of the family, namely, how to prioritize *conflicting* obligations to different family members (do I help Aunt Susan or Uncle Joe?), as well as how to decide between

obligations to friends and to family when one cannot discharge both types of obligations (do I pick up my friend at the airport, or do I have dinner with my mother?).

28. See Friedman, *Citizen Spielberg,* 239.

29. Shug acts like a sister to Celie in Nettie's absence, singing the Celie Blues for her: "Sister, you been on my mind. . . . Sister, remember your name." (The lyrics are in the film but not in the novel.) When Shug kisses Celie, bells that were used to mark *Nettie's* presence begin to jingle. Shug tells Celie, "I love you"; Celie is clearly in love with Shug as well. It is somewhat puzzling that Celie sees Shug as a sister figure, since Celie has a sexual encounter with her. In Walker's book, too, both the erotic and the sisterly elements are present. Celie describes sleeping next to Shug as a "little like sleeping with Nettie, only sleeping with Nettie never feel this good" (p. 98); "Dear God, Us sleep like sisters, me and Shug" (p. 124). Alice Walker, *The Color Purple* (New York: Harcourt Brace Jovanovich, 1982).

30. Walker's Albert has nothing to do with Nettie's return to the United States; nonetheless, Albert and Celie reconcile and are friends by the end of the novel. In the book, Nettie and the children come home of their own doing; in the film, Albert plays an important role in helping Celie reunite with her family. To attempt to atone for abusing Celie, Albert (in Spielberg's version) corresponds with the U.S. immigration authorities and pays for Olivia and Adam's return home. By altering Walker's novel in this way, Spielberg emphasizes the fact that Albert has a moral obligation to Celie because he has wronged her deeply. Spielberg gives Albert the *desire* to reconcile with Celie, but Spielberg (unlike Walker) does not allow them to reconcile. See Walker, *The Color Purple,* 240. For an unsympathetic comparison of the "very bad" (p. 94) film to the eschatological, "utopian" novel (p. 104), see Gerald Early, *"The Color Purple* as Everybody's Protest Art,"* in *The Films of Steven Spielberg,* ed. Silet, 93–106 (originally published in *Antioch Review* 44:3 [1986]: 261–75).

31. Walker uses "notice" as well (p. 167).

32. David Hume, *A Treatise of Human Nature,* ed. David Fate Norton and Mary J. Norton (Oxford: Clarendon, 2000), book 3, part 1, section 1, paragraph 27.

33. Wonder is an important part of Mr. Albert's moral transformation in Walker's novel but not in Spielberg's film. Toward the end of the book, Mr. Albert begins to wonder. He connects wonder with love (or care): "The more I wonder, he [Mr. Albert] say, the more I love" (p. 239). On the concept of wonder, see Robert R. Clewis, "Heideggerian Wonder in Terrence Malick's *The Thin Red Line,"* *Film and Philosophy* 7 (2003): 22–36.

34. Gerald Early, *"The Color Purple* as Everybody's Protest Art,"* 98. Similarly, why does Shug change her habits and way of life? Celie's friendship? Divine grace? Longing to reconcile with her father? Marriage to Grady? Just plain getting older? (Of course, Shug always has a better character than Albert, and her change of habits might not necessarily count as a *moral* transformation; indeed, even when she was still drinking and living freely, she was caring for Celie and trying to reconcile with her father—i.e., she may have had an at least *partly* good character.)

By contrast, it is easy to understand Upham's and Reiben's changes in *Saving Private Ryan*. Upham's decision to kill Steamboat Willie is easily explained as a reaction to seeing the latter shoot and kill Miller; Upham wants to enforce retributive justice and defend the group to which he now belongs. Reiben's change in how he views Ryan can be understood as his assessment that Ryan is a good man and a hard-fighting soldier (although the latter turns out to be at least partly *false*, since Ryan cowers at the end of the battle of Ramelle). Upham might undergo a moral transformation of some sort, but it is easily explained in terms of retribution and group membership. Reiben does not undergo a *moral* transformation at all.

35. In having Albert *attempt* to reconcile with Celie, however, Spielberg implies that Albert has an obligation to try to do so even though he should not be forgiven.

Human Rights, Human Nature, and *Amistad*

David Baggett and Mark W. Foreman

It would take an eternity to break us,
And the chains of Amistad couldn't hold us.

Readers might recognize the sentimental refrain in the epigraph from Whitney Houston's "My Love Is Your Love." To celebrate the permanence of love, the song borrows an image from a grim but ultimately hopeful chapter of American history, a chapter that Steven Spielberg captured cinematically in his film *Amistad* (1997).

Peter Pan All Grown Up

After making films about aliens, sharks, and close encounters that stretched both the creative potential of special effects experts and the imaginative limits of moviegoers, Spielberg, in the first film he directed for DreamWorks, depicted an actual historical case brought before the U.S. Supreme Court in 1841. *Amistad* is the tale, told with a healthy dose of artistic license, of a case that figured centrally in the abolitionist cause.

In 1839, in the same decade as the death of famed English abolitionist William Wilberforce, a group of abducted Africans from Sierra Leone, led by Cinque (whose real name was Singbe Pieh, played in the film by Djimon Hounsou), revolted on the Spanish schooner *Amistad,* killing most of the crew and demanding their return to Africa. Sailing up the coast of the United States, they were taken into custody by U.S. officials off Montauk, New York, and then transferred to New Haven, Connecticut, for trial on charges of murder and piracy. The mutineers were about to be delivered back to Spain, but fortunately had by then garnered strong support from antislavery groups, for whom the case represented a watershed in the fight for human and civil rights.

The ensuing legal battle culminated in the Supreme Court, where former president John Quincy Adams (played by Anthony Hopkins), a passionate antislavery advocate in the U.S. House of Representatives, argued on behalf of the Africans. The case preceded by a few decades the start of the Civil War, a conflict ostensibly fought over the extension of slavery to new territories, and one that would exact a toll so bloody it almost defies comprehension. Sixty-three years before the *Amistad* case, America had declared her independence, insisting, in language borrowed from the English philosopher John Locke, that all men are created equal and endowed by their Creator with unalienable rights, among them life, liberty, and the pursuit of happiness. Yet despite such lofty rhetoric, equality had not been extended to all men (and certainly not to women). Slavery remained legal, and American slavery had devolved into a particularly brutal institution—yet an institution that many insisted the American economy desperately needed for its survival, particularly in the South.

In 1984, producer Debbie Allen came across two volumes of essays and articles, entitled *Amistad I* and *Amistad II,* written by African American writers, historians, and philosophers. For more than a decade she researched and developed the volumes as a film project but met with little success in generating interest among the filmmaking community. After seeing Spielberg's *Schindler's List,* she realized that "here was a filmmaker who could understand and embrace this project and help me get it done."[1] Spielberg did a great service by giving Allen this chance and drawing our attention to this important but easily neglected episode. It is a story that needed to be told, and it gives us the chance to learn some of its lessons and some philosophy along the way.

Legal or political freedom is the central theme of *Amistad.* The discussion of rights represents one of the most important and vexed ethical questions dominating the political landscape over the past several centuries. It raises issues of moral normativity, political expediency, cultural identity, and metaphysical reality. It has occupied the talents and energies of the acutest philosophical minds, from John Stuart Mill to Immanuel Kant, John Locke to Thomas Hobbes, Jean-Jacques Rousseau to John Rawls.

In this essay, using Spielberg's remarkable movie as a springboard, we hope to offer a plausible reading of Locke's account of natural or human rights and to identify some of its insights and vulnerabilities. We confine much of our attention to the historical context of *Amistad* to make the discussion manageable in scope. We are particularly interested in the right not to be

(*Left to right*) Spielberg converses with Anthony Hopkins and Morgan Freeman in preparation for a scene from *Amistad,* the director's controversial historical drama about Africans captured and sold into slavery. (MovieGoods, Inc.)

enslaved or subjugated. By focusing on a snapshot of this debate situated in its historical setting, we can broach some of the enduring questions of this ongoing dialectic without biting off more than we can chew.

What Is the Deal with Rights?

Political philosophy has for one of its salient concerns the issue of rights, which is tied closely with the notion of justice. We live in a culture exploding with rights language. Before discussing what *Amistad* says about rights, we should ask two questions: What exactly is a right and how do we know when a right is really legitimate? A right can be defined as a justified claim that individuals or groups can make on others or on society as a whole. This needs unpacking. First, a right is a claim. It is like something I own or possess. Suppose I have a DVD of the movie *Amistad*. Because it is my possession I can determine what I want to do with it, and you are limited in being able to do with it only what I allow you to do. Rights are like that.

Second, rights are "justified" claims, meaning that rights need to be grounded in something that justifies our being able to claim them. What kind of grounding this could be depends on what kind of right we are talking about. There are "legal" (or "civil") rights such as the right to bear arms or the right to an attorney when you are in court. These rights are grounded in legal documents (like the Constitution) and legal decisions and precedents established by the legislative and judicial branches of the government as representative of the will of the people. In *Amistad* the lawyer Roger Baldwin (Matthew McConaughey), as we will see, argues on the basis of the legality of property rights as established in property law.

There are also "moral" or "basic human" rights, which are not established in any documents or by the will of the people. It is interesting to note that whereas Baldwin argues on the basis of legal property rights, Quincy Adams, in his argument before the Supreme Court, elevates the issue to the question of moral rights. Such rights are grounded elsewhere: perhaps as divine gift; as a function of rationality or rational autonomy; as something intrinsic to and morally important in human beings themselves; as a way to maximize the greatest happiness for the greatest number; as a dictate of reason; by game-theoretic considerations and various thought experiments or presumed implicit social contracts; or by appeal to the common good. In fact, *Amistad* at various turns hints at several of these approaches.[2]

So some rights can be moral and not legal (religious freedom in communist lands), some can be legal and not moral (many might argue that prostitution in parts of Nevada is an example), some can be neither legal nor moral (the right of the team that won the toss to pass or receive), and some can be both moral and legal (free speech or freedom from slavery, such as we see in *Amistad*). Because legal rights derive from political constitutions and legislative enactments whereas moral rights exist independently of these derivations, moral rights can form a basis for justifying or criticizing legal rights. Legal rights can also be eliminated and changed by the will of the people, whereas moral rights, grounded in something above our will, cannot be eliminated in this way. Finally, although there is often a correlation and overlap between legal and moral rights, they do not require each other nor do they require reference to each other; they can exist independently of one another.[3]

Political philosophy, with its concerns about justice and rights, is part of value theory in philosophy. It is intimately related to, and perhaps even a subset of, standard ethics with its traditional concerns about virtue, goodness, and moral obligation and permissibility. Despite the overlap between moral and political values, though, in many ways political philosophy constitutes its own distinct field of inquiry.

To see why, remember that rights are justified claims we have toward others. Rights involve others, and the nature of this involvement pertains to the relationship between rights and obligations. There is a principle in rights talk called the "correlativity thesis," which basically says that all rights have correlative obligations. If I have a right, someone else has an obligation. If slaves have a right to freedom, others have an obligation to grant them that freedom. Because of the correlativity thesis, moral and legal issues can often be analyzed equally well by referencing either the obligations or the rights, since the correlativity thesis implies that one can go from one to the other and vice versa. Both the obligation and the right are grounded in and justified by the same overarching moral or legal principle—which is not, however, to deny that rights language has something distinctive to offer political discourse.

Although this thesis applies to all rights, it does not apply to all obligations. Whereas all rights have correlative obligations, not all obligations have correlative rights. John Stuart Mill, an English philosopher who happened to be at the height of his career during the *Amistad* events, drew on an important distinction between two types of obligations or duties. There are duties of "perfect obligation" and duties of "imperfect obligation." Duties of perfect obligation are duties for which there is a correlative right. An example would be Baldwin's relationship with his clients. He has an obligation to defend them competently and they have a correlative right to be represented adequately. Shirking such a duty violates a right. Duties of imperfect obligation, in contrast, are duties with no correlative rights. These are usually general obligations involving a range of choice of how to fulfill them. An example might be that abolitionists in *Amistad*'s time may have had an obligation to fight against slavery, but not necessarily to wage battle in every abolitionist cause. They could choose when and how to fulfill this obligation. No particular person would have a claim against them even though they have this obligation. Political philosophy and justice are more concerned with perfect duties and their correlative rights than with issues of moral obligation in general, and this is Mill's way to demarcate the specific terrain of political philosophy within the broader purview of ethics in general.[4]

So what might *Amistad* teach us about political philosophy, justice, and rights? More than you might imagine.

Locke and the Pursuit of Property

The opening scenes of *Amistad* depict in vivid detail how slaves in eighteenth-century America were treated with egregious inhumanity. Mercilessly packed into slave ships and taken against their will to a foreign land, a horrendous percentage of them would perish in the brutally harsh and unsanitary journey. If rations ran short or there was a perceived risk of getting caught, the abductors would routinely drown some or all of the "cargo," the Africans. This happens on the slave ship in *Amistad* before the transfer to the schooner —during the infamous transatlantic "middle passage." If the captives survived the voyage, a lifetime of slavery and subjugation likely awaited them. Such treatment was thought justified because the captives' humanity was denied; they were cast as subhuman, brutes, "beasts of burden," animals, and savages, rather than as human persons deserving of respect and equal treatment and imbued with rights both legal and moral.

The dehumanization of these people led to their exploitation as property and commodity. As it happens, the *Amistad* mutineers gained eventual freedom because the claim that they were the property of the Spaniards was shown to be false. In the movie, the young real estate attorney Baldwin is the one to proffer this legal strategy. Baldwin's suggestion initially offends the sensibilities of an overtly religious abolitionist who wishes the court battle to be conducted in the exalted terms of morality and justice, the "battlefield of righteousness," rather than turned into a logic-chopping wrangle over legal minutia. Interestingly, however, an important aspect of the historical and philosophical context of the case connects property and rights more strongly than many realize. To see this, we have to delve into a little intellectual history to understand some of the philosophical context of the period.

The English thinker John Locke was perhaps the foremost political philosopher of the seventeenth century.[5] The influence of Locke's political philosophy on America's Founding Fathers is generally taken for granted, although the extent of this influence has become a vexed question among Locke scholars, a question that need not detain us here. The Founders freely incorporated many of his political ideas, like a separation of powers, the need for a system of checks and balances, and a formal institutional separation of church and state. Indeed, some of his very words found their way into their bold declarations and occasionally polemical political analysis. Among what the Founders, especially Thomas Jefferson while quilling the Declaration of Independence, appropriated from Locke's work was the right of a people to revolt against a government that fails to discharge its fundamental duties. Those duties discharged by a legitimate government include upholding certain unalienable rights, among them life, liberty, and the pursuit of happiness.

Locke, much as Bentham would later write, explicitly said that things are good or evil only in reference to pleasure or pain. We call "good," he affirmed, that which causes pleasure or reduces pain, and we call "bad" what causes pain or reduces pleasure. Such hedonism represented only one aspect of Locke's complex moral theory, which has disparate parts, not all of which easily cohere; however, the similarity to Bentham in this respect is interesting. But despite such similarity, Locke's account does not belong in the same category of rights theories as Bentham's; rather it belongs in that family of theories that grounds rights in a deontic way. These theories, sometimes called "choice theories," ground rights in some morally important characteristic of the bearer, from our rationality, to our status as God's creations, to our autonomy.

The language of unalienable rights of life and liberty expressed in the Declaration borrows heavily from Locke. He had written a century earlier in his *Second Treatise of Government* that government's responsibility is to safeguard certain basic human rights, especially life, liberty, and, interestingly enough, *property*: "Man being born, as has been proved, with a title to perfect freedom, and uncontrolled enjoyment of all the rights and privileges of the law of nature, equally with any other man, or number of men in the world, hath by nature a power, not only to preserve his property, that is, his life, liberty, and estate, against the injuries and attempts of other men; but to judge of and punish the breaches of that law in others."[6]

Jefferson altered Locke's words for the Declaration, capturing perhaps the gist of Locke's meaning of "property" by replacing it with the phrase "the pursuit of happiness." Life and liberty remained as fundamental rights of human beings, although, as Mr. Joadson (Morgan Freeman) puts it in the film, the Founding Fathers left it to their sons to finish the job of uniting the states by crushing slavery.

Endowed by Our Creator

An ineliminable aspect of the historical context of the *Amistad* case, an aspect that comes through in the movie in numerous respects, is the traditional view of rights as having been conferred on us by God. There is another strong connection with Locke here as well. Locke was a firm believer that our most fundamental rights come, ultimately, from God, and also that all of us, as God's creations, are morally equal. How Locke attributed both of these important and related principles of equality and liberty to God is interesting to see.

Locke argued that our essential equality and most basic freedoms are the gifts of God. One reason for this belief was the authority Locke thought God has by virtue of creating us. Since we are here because of the work God expended in making it happen, *we* are *his* workmanship, therefore we are his property. As such, he has the authority, because he made us, and the desire, because he loves us, to endow each of us with the right to be free. Freedom from slavery is an important implication, because, since God owns us, we cannot be owned by anyone else, including by parents (a vital point of Locke's *First Treatise*); nor are wives the property of their husbands (an egalitarian point that in Locke's day and age was often needed). Among the implications of our being God's property, Locke thought, would be that we do not have the moral freedom to commit suicide, or to give ourselves over to slavery, or to enslave another.

Because we were all created by God, we are protected from being owned by one another, which is one important way Locke's account of natural law and God's workmanship leads to the moral equality of persons. Human beings are also invested with the capacity for autonomy and reason, another argument for human equality. Created in God's image, we have the capacity to work and exercise creative power, and through these to exercise dominion in the world, analogous to God's dominion over us. As part of God's dominion over us, he has also exercised his volition in making us all equal. He gave us the world over which to exercise dominion, provided that we not use more than we need. God's decision to make us share the world, not selfishly wasting resources though allowing for some inequalities in the distribution of resources, fundamentally demonstrates Locke's conviction that God's will played a role in our natural equality.

Religious motivation was an important part of the *Amistad* story. We catch a sense of this sort of reasoning early in the film when vocal abolitionists are shouting or holding signs that read, "You cannot own another human being" and "Emancipation: It's God's way." We know that, historically, not everyone channeled their religious convictions against the cause of slavery; sometimes, sadly, quite to the contrary. We see an example of this in the sentiment of a southern defender of slavery that not just the economic survival of the South depended on slavery, but that slavery, since biblical times, has been accepted as normative.[7]

Locke's understanding of natural law distinguishes his commitment to it from the version we find in one like Aquinas, according to whom, because we have been created with certain features, there is a naturalness to our behaving in certain ways. There is a natural or even eternal law, set by nature (most ultimately God's nature, and secondarily ours), which amounts to or at least approximates God's law. By seeking what gives us real fulfillment and true happiness, we can apprehend this natural law, which exists before any manmade legislation or rules for harmonious living.

We return to this version of natural law in the next section, but for now it bears emphasis that Locke's version of natural law, plausibly read, is a little different. Locke, like many theistic ethicists, struggled with the question of whether or not God himself might be subject to an eternal law if he is not directly and volitionally responsible for its contents. One way to get around this difficulty is perhaps by suggesting that, although the moral law depends on God, thereby safeguarding his sovereignty, God is not able to completely alter its contents, making good evil or vice versa. A natural law theorist in the tradition of Aquinas has this option, cashing out divine sovereignty more in terms of dependence than control.

In departing from Thomism, however, Locke seemed to embrace a more "voluntaristic" account, privileging God's *will* over his *nature*. Whereas Aquinas rooted the authority of natural law in God's mind and character, Hugo Grotius, Samuel von Pufendorf, and Locke were more inclined to root it in God's will. Natural law, as Locke conceived it, was founded in God's freedom, *his* rights, which come from his having made us—a principle we have already seen is very important in Locke. It is through acts of autonomous making that ownership is created, which demonstrates the way Locke privileged will. As Ian Shapiro puts it, "In [Locke's] moral and political writings he came down decisively in the voluntarist, or will-centered, camp. He could not relinquish the proposition that for something to have the status of a law, it must be the product of a will."[8]

Amistad itself features ambivalence in its depiction of the religious; note, for example, the unhappiness of the protesting abolitionists that, in a humorous scene, even the Africans notice. When prospects for victory for the *Amistad* Africans look bleak after concerted efforts against them by President Van Buren (in obsequious deference to Spain and the southern states), Mr. Tappan (Stellan Skarsgård), an outspoken Christian abolitionist, says, "This news, well of course it's bad news, but the truth is they may be more valuable to our struggle in death than in life. Martyrdom, Mr. Joadson. From the dawn of Christianity, we have seen no stronger power for change." To which Mr. Joadson, a former slave, replies, "What is true, Mr. Tappan, and believe me when I tell you I've seen this, is that there are some men whose hatred of slavery is stronger than anything except for the slave himself."

This powerful scene brings to mind the words of contemporary political analyst Richard John Neuhaus: "Even more perverse [than those who seek martyrdom] are those who would volunteer countless others for martyrdom. In truth, those who think 'a little totalitarianism might not be a bad thing for the church' reflect an aspect of the superficiality of American culture that they deplore. The romanticizing of persecution is only possible for those

Amistad, DreamWorks SKG, 1997. (*Center left to right*) Theodore Joadson (Morgan Free-man), Ensign Covey (Chiwetel Ejiofor), and Roger Baldwin (Matthew McConaughey) collaborate on how best to defend the basic human rights of the *Amistad* Africans. (MovieGoods, Inc.)

who have not taken the measure of history's horror, who have not read their church history nor their Solzhenitsyn."[9] In other words, willingness to be a martyr oneself is one thing; volunteering others for the task and glorifying it the way Tappan does is quite another.

This negative depiction of Tappan brings to mind a critique of *Amistad* offered by Gary Rosen in a fascinating and provocative essay in which he issues a harsh indictment of Spielberg's characterization of religion. Rosen ac-cuses Spielberg of denigrating white, Protestant Christianity by intentionally misrepresenting the racial relations of the events in question. For example, Tappan, in historical fact, was the prime defender of the Africans from start to finish. And "far from being indifferent to their fate as individuals, [Tap-pan] refused to prolong their suffering by pressing for more litigation. Far from being a closet racist, this cofounder . . . of the American Antislavery Society was extraordinary in his day for publicly condoning marriage be-tween blacks and whites." Moreover, whereas the heroic Joadson is a purely fictional character, Tappan was "the engine behind" the "*Amistad* Commit-tee," a group of "militantly evangelical abolitionists . . . who raised money for the case, publicized it, and carried it through to its successful conclusion," although this committee makes no appearance in the movie.[10]

Locke so firmly rooted basic human rights in a theistic worldview that he has been criticized by some as having promoted a theory that, in a secular and pluralistic culture, needs reinterpretation. It has been suggested—by John Dunn, for example—that the biggest ideological shift that has taken place between the context of Locke's writing and the present has been the replacement of this theistic vision of the world with more secular counterparts. For example, rather than saying that people cannot be owned by other human beings because they are owned by God, contemporary rights theories are more likely to affirm simply that human beings cannot be owned by anyone at all. We later discuss ways in which aspects of Locke's theory can be applied without assuming that rights are a function of divine whim, but perhaps dependent on God after all.

Broaching religion in public discourse is often thought of as opening a can of worms, so Spielberg deserves credit for including the religious dimension of this chapter in history so prominently; it was certainly an important aspect of the context and intellectual milieu. Moreover, since Locke was pointing to the importance of recognizing moral rights that exist prior to governmental recognition and that in fact require such legal recognition, his theory of rights, as any workable theory of rights does, requires a strong sense of underlying moral realism to retain its normative force. Historically, religion was often thought best to function in that role. Even Thomas Jefferson, whose words against slavery were excised from the Declaration by the First Continental Congress, who was a firm proponent of an institutional separation of church and state, and who was by no means a conventionally religious individual, offered the following reflections on the importance of religious belief to the issue of slavery: "And can the liberties of a nation be thought secure when we have removed their only firm basis, a conviction in the minds of the people that these liberties are the gift of God? That they are not to be violated but with his wrath?"[11] Jefferson's point here pertains more to confidence in the existence of rights rather than their true philosophical explanation.

Jefferson's mention of divine wrath resonates with Locke in another way and also points up a potential limitation in Locke's analysis. Locke closely connected God's authority to invest us with basic freedoms with his ability to mete out rewards and punishments for obedience and disobedience, respectively, to God's law. Recall again the importance of pain and pleasure as guideposts in the construction of ethics, on Locke's view. It has been speculated that this effort to understand God's authority as establishing moral foundations was due to Locke's empiricism (the view that all of our knowledge originates in our senses). Whereas later empiricists like Hume would argue that such an epistemology undermines confidence in many treasured convictions, like belief in God, Locke believed that God's existence remained, on empiricist grounds, as sure as anything; and likewise, he argued, the principles of morality, which he suggested remained as secure as those we discover in mathematics. However, an empirical grounding for moral convictions meant that he needed to resort to pain and pleasure and the power of God to dole them out; this required Locke to appeal to traditional notions of rewards and punishments rather than less empirically accessible notions of genuine divine moral authority.[12]

To sum up this section, one important reason, Locke argued, that God has the power to make us equal and give us our basic rights is that he created us. Work, for Locke, entitled the craftsman to his workmanship. Both by his creation of us and by his sovereign choice he made us equal, investing us with the right not to be enslaved by any man. We are God's alone. Our shared ability to think and reason also underscores our equality, as does our creative ability (fashioned after God's) to engage in meaningful work and craftsmanship, thereby entitling us to the labor of our hands so long as we do not forget that the world is to be shared with equals. But because of the importance of Locke's workmanship model, and the primacy it accords to will, his version of natural law likely suggests, in his mind, an important voluntaristic component, which raises arbitrariness objections. And Locke's empiricism led to an inadequate account of divine authority, rooted less in morality than in prudence.

Amistad captures both the potential and pitfalls of rooting rights in religion through its range of depictions, from the sanctimonious Tappan, to the secular Baldwin, to the pragmatic Adams, to the earnest abolitionists.

"Give Us, Us Free!"

Locke believed that, metaphysically speaking, our freedom and equality come from God; but how is it that we come to *know* this? This is a question of epistemology. For Locke, natural law helps here. On his view, we have been invested with reason, by which we can apprehend certain truths about ourselves. Locke was of the view, as a natural law theorist and strict empiricist, that we can know, normatively, how humans are to be treated by an empirical investigation into their behavior, and not just through special revelation. A universal and relentless desire for freedom, for example, would provide evidence for Locke that such a state is not just normal, but natural, and a deviation from it unnatural and bad.[13]

Spielberg vividly depicts the desperate human desire for freedom by capturing Cinque's experience of something approaching a panic attack in the midst of a court procedure. The escalating internal tensions within him finally manifest by his standing to his feet and repeating, with increasing urgency, "Give us, us free!" It is a powerful scene, and one of the many ways in which the theme of freedom reverberates throughout the film. In the climactic Supreme Court scene, Adams claims that, despite its appearance as a garden-variety property case, this case is far more, concerning nothing less than who and what human beings really are. The natural state of human beings, he claims, is freedom. The philosophical significance of the scene requires that we quote his words at length:

> Yes, this is no mere property case, gentlemen. I put it to you thus: this is the most important case ever to come before this court. Because what it, in fact, concerns is the very nature of man. . . . This is a publication of the Office of the President. It's called the *Executive Review,* [and it] asserts that "there has never existed a civilized society in which one segment did not thrive upon the labor of another. As far back as one chooses to look . . . history bears this out. . . . Slavery has always been with us and is neither sinful nor immoral. Rather, as war and antagonism are the natural states of man, so, too, slavery, as natural as it is inevitable."

Readers might recognize in these words an echo of the philosopher Thomas Hobbes, who, in his magnum opus *Leviathan,* characterized the state of nature for human beings as a "war of all against all," a pessimistic picture of the human condition indeed. Continuing, Adams reveals that, on this score, his view is much closer to that of Locke's greater optimism: "Now, gentlemen, I must say I differ with the keen mind of the South, and with our president, who apparently shares their views, offering that the natural state of mankind is instead, and I know this is a controversial idea, . . . freedom. And the proof is the length to which a man, woman, or child will go to regain it, once taken. He will break loose his chains. He will decimate his enemies. He will try and try and try against all odds, against all prejudices, to get home."

This powerful scene nicely connects with a Lockean understanding of natural law. The humor, intelligence, rationality, and desire for freedom of the Africans are accentuated throughout the film—from humorous comments by the captives about the dour abolitionists to Cinque's intelligent questions to Adams about legal jurisdiction—to highlight their humanness and their equality and rights as human beings. But a critic might insist, rightly, that just because we by nature exhibit certain characteristics, like the craving for freedom the slaves manifest, it does not necessarily follow that such a natural desire carries with it normative or moral force.

Locke himself realized the need for something else to invest such intuitions about freedom and such language of rights with determinate normative force. Earlier we mentioned his workmanship argument that, he thought, invested God with the requisite authority to give us such rights, but we suggested that such an account is, at best, incomplete. Likewise, as an empiricist Locke was limited in his resources for constructing an argument for God's authority to what could be perceived by the senses.[14] The divine workmanship theory, even joined with the divine retribution theory, does not seem quite enough.

We have hinted at a Lockean-inspired account that may avoid some of these difficulties, so now we will try to deliver. If we take some of what Locke suggests and reduce or eliminate the voluntarism, we can end up with an account of natural law closer to that of Aquinas, and perhaps in the process find a more defensible view. Locke himself emphasized that we were created by God and created in God's image, so perhaps on such a view we have been invested essentially by God with a nature that, in its healthiest, happiest state, is free. Locke's theory of morality and of rights incorporated a number of different parts, and although he attempted to synthesize them, perhaps the most defensible theory we can glean from his writings will try to separate the wheat from the chaff. Maybe, if we understand human rights as a gift from God in the sense that we were created in his (metaphysical) image of personhood, we might be able to offer a hybrid account of what grounds our basic rights. True, this downplays Locke's property of God premise, but it still suffices for an account of unalienable rights bestowed on us by our Creator, bestowed in the sense that God created us in a form analogous to his. It also helps capture Locke's desire to avoid arbitrariness despite his hesitancy to reject voluntarism altogether.[15]

Finally, despite the challenge of accounting for the full moral reasons there are for affirming our rights to be free from slavery, most of us are firmly convinced of them. So much so, in fact, that we deem them worth fighting for if necessary.

The Last Battle of the American Revolution

Some of the last lines of the movie feature Adams following Cinque's lead, invoking his own ancestors with these words: "We desperately need your strength and wisdom to triumph over our fears, our prejudices, ourselves. Give us the courage to do what is right. And if it means civil war, then let it come. And when it does, may it be, finally, the last battle of the American Revolution." Adams could have invoked at this juncture the words of his own famous father in whose shadow he lived: "Every measure of prudence, therefore, ought to be assumed for the eventual total extirpation of slavery from the United States. . . . I have, throughout my whole life, held the practice of slavery in . . . abhorrence."[16] The elder Adams had also predicted to Thomas Jefferson that a national struggle between the states over slavery "might rend this mighty fabric in twain."[17]

Abraham Lincoln, in his classic Second Inaugural Address near the end of the Civil War, would speak these immortal words: "Fondly do we hope, fervently do we pray, that this mighty scourge of war may speedily pass away. Yet, if God wills that it continue until all the wealth piled by the bondsman's two hundred and fifty years of unrequited toil shall be sunk, and until every drop of blood drawn with the lash shall be paid by another drawn with the sword, as was said three thousand years ago, so still it must be said 'the judgments of the Lord are true and righteous altogether.'"[18]

Slavery advocates continually exploited fears over the potential cost and suffering produced by a war to keep abolitionists on the defensive. Note the words of (the fictional) Calhoun, an outspoken southerner who happens also to have been Quincy Adams's vice president: "Ask yourself, . . . what court wants to be responsible for the spark that ignites the firestorm? What president wants to be in office when it comes crashing down around him? Certainly no court before this one. Certainly no president before this one. So . . . the real determination our courts and our president must make is not whether this ragtag group of Africans raised swords against their enemy, but rather, must we?"

We earlier mentioned John Stuart Mill, for whom the elimination of suffering was of tremendous importance. Nonetheless, it is instructive that Mill, himself a passionate defender of human rights, wrote this of war, echoing the sentiment of Adams and Lincoln: "War is an ugly thing, but not the ugliest of things. The decayed and degraded state of moral and patriotic feeling which thinks that nothing is worth war is much worse. The person who has nothing for which he is willing to fight, nothing which is more important than his own personal safety, is a miserable creature and has no chance of being free unless made and kept so by the exertions of better men than himself."[19]

A few decades ago, around the time President Carter proposed reinstating the draft registration, a Princeton student could be seen prominently sporting a shirt that read, "Nothing is worth dying for." Socrates said the unexamined life is not worth living; one might wonder, if nothing is worth dying for, whether or not anything is worth living for. Adams, Lincoln, and Mill, great thinkers·all, seemed to think that some wars, terrible and tragic as they may be, are worth fighting and dying for, because freedom and the life purposes it affords make life worth living.

Notes

Many thanks to Greg Bassham, Michael S. Jones, and especially Dean Kowalski and Steve Patterson for helpful comments on an earlier draft of this essay. We attribute any remaining weaknesses to them, thereby absolving ourselves of all responsibility.

1. "Special Features," *Amistad*, DVD (Glendale, CA: DreamWorks, 1999).

2. There is a third type of right that we will just mention here called "conventional" rights. These are claims grounded by the rules and principles adopted within certain conventional relationships. Examples would be the relationship between a lawyer and his client or between a priest and his confessor. There are also employee rights and even conventional rights in organized sports. Such rights need be neither morally nor legally based.

3. We also need to make a distinction between what are referred to as "negative" rights and "positive" rights. This language is not used in an evaluative sense; negative rights are not bad and positive ones good. A negative right entails an obligation to refrain from doing something. It is a right to be free from an action taken by others. Negative rights are often called rights of noninterference. The U.S. Bill of Rights is a good example of negative rights: freedom of worship, free speech, free press. These all say that the government cannot interfere with our exercising these rights without just cause. A positive right entails a right to expect another to do something. It means that someone is obligated to provide a particular good or service. Your right to an attorney is a positive right; the government must provide one for you if you cannot do so yourself. This distinction is an important one that is often confused.

4. Mill was the protégé of Jeremy Bentham, well known for his utilitarianism. Bentham was not the first to advance this principle of ethics, by any means, but he is one of its best-known advocates. Utilitarianism says that morality is a matter of maximizing utility, of generating the greatest happiness for the greatest number of people in a society. Mill would later modify and further develop this theory. We mention Bentham at this point because he was notorious for denying the existence of natural rights. Questions of rights and duties for him were to be answered by appeal to what he called the two "sovereign masters" of pain and pleasure, governing us in all we do.

According to utilitarians, for moral guidance we must look to pleasure and pain rather than anything more abstract or metaphysical. Rights described as natural or intrinsic violate utilitarianism's consequentialism; to the extent that we have rights, according to utilitarianism, they would be ways of protecting people's interests with an eye on maximizing overall utility.

Utilitarianism and other "interest theory" accounts of rights typically ground rights in morally important interests that we believe all persons who fit into the class of rights bearers have. There are important variations here, from Richard Brandt's subtle rule utilitarian reading of moral rights to Alan Gewirth's view that the universality of a particular interest across the class of rights bearers presents a grounding for the right. Most theories of legal rights typically begin from some version of interest theory.

In fairness to utilitarianism, it should be stressed that, in a great many cases, maximizing utility and treating people *as if* they possessed basic and essential human rights lead to identical results. But in cases where doing the latter produces severe disutility, utilitarianism, with the theoretical resources at its disposal, would find it hard to justify upholding such rights. In *Amistad*, we hear Calhoun (Arliss Howard) make an essentially utilitarian appeal in favor of maintaining slavery, warning of the prohibitively high price to be paid for abolition. Although such problems riddling utilitarianism have led the majority of political philosophers to see utilitarianism as inadequate in providing an account of rights, it is a view that still has its defenders. We do not explore a utilitarian account of rights here, although we wanted to mention that not everyone is convinced natural rights exist in the same way or even at all.

5. See especially Locke's *Essay Concerning Human Understanding* (1690), *Two Treatises of Government* (1689), and *Letter Concerning Toleration* (1689).

6. John Locke, *Two Treatises of Government* and *A Letter Concerning Toleration*, ed. Ian Shapiro (New Haven: Yale University Press, 2003), section 87, 136. In Locke's context of seventeenth-century England, the protection of property was one of his biggest motivations for arguing against the unchecked powers of kings and in favor of the need for an autonomous parliament. Property in fact was said by Locke to be a prerequisite for there to be any violation of justice at all, but this cryptic saying of Locke's from his *Essay* has often been analyzed in terms of a broader understanding of property, by which it means more than just ownership of land and possessions. Most expansively, it is meant to denote something like the human quest for fulfillment and happiness, which requires more than just basic needs to be met. It also requires incentives to create and engage in meaningful work. It is by work, Locke thought, that we become entitled to the fruit of our labor. By mixing our labor with the world, we acquire the right to property.

7. For reasons of space we cannot delve into the matter of biblical exegesis to see in what, if any, sense the Bible sanctioned or allowed slavery. Suffice it to say we agree with those, from William Wilberforce to Dr. Martin Luther King Jr., who affirm that slavery, especially the American version that treated humans as chattel, is antithetical to the normative force of biblical revelation rightly understood. A distinction between kinds of slavery, incidentally, is also at play in *Amistad*, when the prosecutor asks Cinque

questions about practices of slavery in his own country, refusing to acknowledge any potential moral distinctions between kinds of slavery and indentured servitude. For insightful commentary on the Christian church's historical stance on slavery and relevant disanalogies between activities called "slavery," see Oliver O'Donovan's *The Desire of the Nations* (New York: Cambridge University Press, 1998), especially pages 184–86 and 263–66.

8. Locke, *Two Treatises*, ed. Shapiro, 311. Although in recent decades there have been some very intelligent modified versions of voluntarism articulated, such as that by Robert Adams (see *Finite and Infinite Goods* [Oxford: Oxford University Press, 1999]), voluntarism in its starkest forms, like we find in Ockham (see Janine Idziak [ed.], *Divine Command Morality: Historical and Contemporary Readings* [New York: Mellen Press, 1979]), has raised notorious arbitrariness objections. For what if God were a despot? Even if not an evil despot, but rather a benevolent one, can God do just anything with us simply because he created us? Does God, for example, have the prerogative not to give us freedom and equality? On the other hand, if God did not have such a prerogative, does that mean God is bound by a moral code that exists independently of himself? Is God, for example, bound by the principle that making entails ownership, or was such a principle a function of his will? The way Locke hinted that divine moral authority gives God very wide prerogatives leaves many readers convinced that his theistic account, as it stands, is in need of further explication and defense.

9. Richard John Neuhaus, *The Naked Public Square: Religion and Democracy in America* (Grand Rapids, MI: Eerdmans, 1984), 164.

10. See Gary Rosen, "'Amistad' and the Abuse of History," in *The Films of Steven Spielberg: Critical Essays*, ed. Charles L. P. Silet (Lanham, MD: Scarecrow, 2002), 239–48.

11. Thomas Jefferson, *Notes on the State of Virginia* (New York: Harper and Row, 1964 [1861]), Query 18.

12. A fascinating issue in political philosophy introduced by this issue of religious motivation is the relevance to public discourse of religious conviction and reasons, particularly when it comes to coercive legislation. One of the admittedly vexed questions in political philosophy pertains to the legitimacy of bringing to bear one's religious convictions in the context of political discourse. On one side of the debate are thinkers like Robert Audi, who insist that religion, because of its all-encompassing scope, ambitious metaphysics, and perceived unquestionable authority, ought not to be able to provide compelling public reasons for legislation. (On this issue we might remind readers that the excesses and abuses of the French Revolution show that when a society rejects the idea of divine authority, it tends to transcendentalize alternatives, such as secular values, that themselves can come to be seen as authorities that none are permitted to challenge.) Richard Rorty and the early John Rawls were even stronger advocates for the privatization of religion. On the other side of the debate are thinkers like Christopher Eberle and Nicholas Wolterstorff, who insist that the exclusion of religious reasons from public discourse is antithetical and ultimately detrimental to the democratic enterprise; see Christopher J. Eberle, *Religious Conviction in Liberal Politics* (New York: Cambridge

University Press, 2002), and Robert Audi and Nicholas Wolterstorff, *Religion in the Public Square* (New York: Rowman and Littlefield, 1997).

13. A defender of slavery like Calhoun in *Amistad* could try to turn the tables here and offer an argument for the naturalness of slavery based on its ubiquity in history, as we saw before. Would not a natural law theorist have good empirical grounds for claiming that slavery itself is a natural process of human behavior? If so, then is not the natural law theorist committed to the claim that slavery is obligatory? It is not clear that an appeal to natural law provides anything like an airtight case against slavery. (Then again, moral arguments are rarely airtight, so this might not be too great a concern.)

14. Again, Locke's empiricism perhaps served as too great a constraint on his theorizing, because the way he had to cash out God's authority was in terms of rewards and punishments. We violate another human's freedom at the risk of divine punishment. Although this is a powerful prudential reason for respecting rights, it strikes most of us as lacking authoritative force. Locke's empiricism may have hampered his ability to construct the deeper theistic theory really needed to make sense of divine *authority* here, rather than mere divine power alone.

15. What perhaps justifies this modest revision of Locke is that it is far less radical a revision of Locke than those interpreters who, perhaps projecting, would try expunging all religious elements from Locke's account completely. We do not deny a case can be made for engaging in such radical revisionism. In Locke's own day he was denounced as a crypto-atheist for his elevation of human reason as a proper instrument for discerning the natural law and applying its principles to evaluations of justice. Locke's contemporary critics also complained that he made God irrelevant to political morality, largely by uncoupling God's will from judgments of legitimacy. The monarchical order had long rested on a presupposition that monarchy was the preferred form of government because it mirrored on earth the divine order of one lawgiver at the pinnacle of an expanding pyramid of progressively less powerful beings, each kept in place by a divine order that she live out her place in society as given to her by God, in his infinite wisdom, and sustained by divinely imposed, caste-based obligations of each class to the others. Only kings could be sovereign—never the people, who were divinely commanded to play the role appointed to them by God in virtue of their having been born into their particular station. Rebellion against the king was therefore tantamount to rebellion against God.

When Locke in effect puts dominion over civil society into the hands of the people, and when he argues that it is not divine will but human contracting that brings a political order into being, he substantially secularizes the business of evaluating the justice of political arrangements. His saying that our rights come from God has looked to some like a feeble add-on meant to keep the ecclesiastical courts away. Add to this his staunch empiricism, and it is little wonder that even in his own day he was sometimes thought to be as "godless" as the arch-materialist Hobbes. It is easy to miss the force of this argument if one reads the *Second Treatise* outside of the light of the *First*.

We do not think this argument is without merit. Locke's work marked an important move toward secularism, and his rejection of a divine right to rule was decisive. He may well have been perceived by many in his generation as a thoroughgoing secularist in a religious disguise. Nonetheless, we would suggest that this sort of radical revision simply does too much violence to Locke's intentions and convictions. It strains credulity to think that Locke was not a sincere theist who believed that our rights were rooted somehow in God. This does not make it true, of course, but the point we are making here is merely a historical one. This is not to deny that secular counterparts of Locke's views can be identified, and perhaps many readers of Locke will suggest that, since his work moved us toward secularism, there should be no end to this process until we follow secularism all the way, eliminating all references to God as the extraneous remnants of an earlier age they are. However, this requires argument, and we remain skeptical that a thoroughly secular account of rights can prove adequate.

16. John Adams, letter to Evans, June 8, 1819, in Adrienne Kock and William Peden (eds.), *Selected Writings of John and John Quincy Adams* (New York: Knopf, 1946), 209.

17. Lester J. Cappon (ed.), *The Adams-Jefferson Letters* (Chapel Hill: University of North Carolina Press, 1959), 551.

18. Spielberg, a big admirer of Lincoln, has signed on to direct an upcoming film of Lincoln's life as depicted in Doris Kearns Goodwin's wonderful *Team of Rivals: The Political Genius of Abraham Lincoln* (New York: Simon and Schuster, 2006).

19. Attributed to John Stuart Mill; see "The Contest in America," *Dissertations and Discussions, Vol. 1* (1868), 26 (first published in *Fraser's Magazine*, February 1862).

Terrorism, Counterterrorism, and "The Story of What Happens Next" in *Munich*

Joseph J. Foy

In 1972, the Israeli government instituted Operation Wrath of God, a covert response to the Munich massacre in which eleven Israeli Olympic athletes were killed by Palestinian terrorists. In 2005, Steven Spielberg dramatized these events in his film *Munich*. Using Wrath of God as an example, the movie addresses the ethics of state-sanctioned responses to acts of terrorism. It is not surprising that the film simultaneously received commendation and condemnation. For some, the film's focus on the nature and logic of counterterrorism undermines what they felt should be the proper discourse: a moral denunciation of any and all acts of terrorism.[1] For others, the film thoughtfully conveys conundrums of individual and collective "moral insanity" that can drive counterterrorist responses beyond an acceptable realm of ethics and reason.[2]

Spielberg anticipated negative reactions to *Munich*. He attempted to deflect some criticisms by publicly stating that the film was not designed as an attack on Israel or its policies. Spielberg claimed that the film was not an argument for nonresponse on the part of governments confronted with acts of terrorism. To the contrary, the purpose of *Munich* was to show that tactical response to counterterrorism—even when it is justified—still carries with it important moral and ethical dilemmas that need to be carefully thought through.[3]

Spielberg has stressed that he was not attempting to make a documentary. So much of the Israeli response to the Munich massacre is shrouded in secrecy that a completely accurate retelling would be all but impossible to achieve. It is through the interpretation and recasting of events such as those following the Palestinian Black September killings in Munich that we would typically find a filmmaker inserting himself and framing his argument.

Spielberg claims, however, that he attempted to avoid doing this. *Munich,* he explains, is not designed to offer a single argument for or against the use of violence as a response to terrorism. Instead, he sees the purpose of this film as merely raising issues that must be openly confronted without providing solutions. Ultimately, Spielberg created *Munich* as an attempt to engage audiences in asking why a "country feels its best defense against a certain kind of violence [terrorism] is counter-violence," without providing a definitive answer.[4]

Despite the claim that he remains impartial throughout the film, I argue that careful analysis shows Spielberg does not offer a disinterested portrayal of the logic and ethics of counterterrorism. This is not to say that Spielberg is lying. He may very well have intended a film that raises moral questions without attempting to provide answers. However, Spielberg's uncanny ability to create a connection between his characters and audiences may, with this movie, have undermined his own goals. The empathy that Spielberg creates throughout the film between the audience and Avner (Eric Bana) is compelling, and the protagonist's development provides an implicit argument regarding just and unjust actions on the part of the state. Whether intentionally or accidentally, *Munich* offers a foundation for reexamining the principles of vengeance and retributive justice related to counterterrorism, and calls for alternatives to the perpetuation of cyclical violence.

"The Problem is Considering Right and Wrong as Ethical Questions"

When Avner begins his assignment to carry out Operation Wrath of God, he seeks out an old friend, Andreas (Moritz Bleibtreu), in Frankfurt. There he engages in a conversation about ethics with Andreas's girlfriend Yvonne (Meret Backer). Yvonne claims that "Marcuse says Hegel's *Philosophy of Right* does not place 'wrong' in a moral category." She advises Avner to reconsider notions like right and wrong, and to begin to look at them not as ethical questions but as "ways of talking about a terrible struggle, parts of an equation, a dialectic." She concludes that the ongoing struggle between opposing forces is the inevitable product of history, devoid of such sentimentalities as the morality of right and wrong.

Yvonne's arguments are reminiscent of the postmodern movement in philosophical ethics, which often gives rise to discussions of moral nihilism. Postmodernists such as Jean Baudrillard and Jean-François Lyotard argue that moral language is dependent on culture and the timing of history. Thus, ethics is not based on objective truth, but consists of "language games" produced by, and inseparable from, the systems that create it.[5] If there is no objective form of right or wrong upon which to evaluate action, then an action could easily be condemned as unjust by one faction and articulated as just and appropriate by another, with neither side being incorrect.

Spielberg seems to play with this relativist notion, using background newscasts at various points throughout the film to demonstrate the tit-for-tat exchange of violence between the Israelis and Palestinians. Furthermore, early in their assignment the covert Israeli Mossad agents are eating dinner together when Carl (Ciarán Hinds) remarks, "It's strange, isn't it? To think of oneself as an assassin?" In reply, Avner tells him to view himself "as something else." Hans (Hanns Zischler) agrees, and tells Carl to think of himself as a soldier in a war. It is as though, in this moment, the ethical controversy of assassination can be erased if the words used to describe it are changed. Such "language games" would definitely support the postmodern perspectives of thinkers such as Baudrillard and Lyotard. However, the rest of the film seems to challenge this notion, as seen in the emotional, psychological, and physical change of Avner over time. The killing, destruction, and unending cycle of violence take a toll on Avner's psychological well-being that no linguistic manipulation can undo. The film goes even further by implying that seemingly anyone in Avner's situation would be harmed in a number of morally significant ways by undergoing this mission (the destruction internally and physically of the members of his Mossad team stands as a testament to this). Thus, although acknowledging the existence of relativist positions regarding ethics, Spielberg dismisses such positions, and in doing so he offers a very sophisticated look into the ethical philosophy of vengeance and retribution.

Avner's emotional and psychological breakdown as the film progresses clearly demonstrates a level of suffering that is devoid of well-being. He becomes paranoid, agitated, angry, and unable to open himself to happiness or to the love he and his wife Daphna (Ayelete Zurer) once shared. Because of the empathy that is generated between viewer and protagonist throughout the film, Spielberg cannot claim to be merely highlighting dilemmas and issues that need to be discussed; Avner's perspective is the audience's perspective, his suffering is our suffering. Spielberg achieves his goal of "creating empathy," which is in part what makes him such a profoundly successful director; but in doing so he undermines his rhetorical position. By rejecting the claim that we need to rethink how we view notions of right and wrong, Spielberg dismisses the postmodern perspective of relativism, and instead implicitly asserts that justice and morality are objective principles.

"We're Supposed to Be Righteous"

The question that we come to, then, is under what conditions a state can justly employ violence in response to acts of terrorism. For those in the pacifist traditions the conduct of such hostilities by states is morally bankrupt and without ethical merit.[6] An interesting variation of this idea can be found in Plato's *Crito*. Socrates engages Crito in a debate regarding the impermissibility of retaliation for wrongdoings. Socrates argues that to harm another in retaliation is morally worse than the initial wrong because your act also harms yourself. You damage your moral character in a way that the original harm to you cannot.[7] Avner reflects Socrates' position over the course of the film. It seems clear that Avner is suffering psychological and moral setbacks as a result of the harm he caused. Furthermore, near the conclusion of the film, he and Ephraim (Geoffrey Rush) come to an impasse on the value of the assassinations in furthering the cause of Israel. He tells Ephraim, "There's no peace at the end of this. Whatever you believe, you know that's true." Arguably, Avner is referring to the lack of psychological peace that is tearing away at his well-being for the acts he committed.[8]

Although it seems easy to draw the conclusion that *Munich* stands as a testament to the ineffective and self-destructive nature of violence, thereby promulgating nonviolence, such a determination overlooks the more complex dialogue in which Spielberg is engaged. Spielberg does not categorically reject the use of violence (many of the other films discussed in this volume stand as a testament to that). Instead, he seems to be advocating a just use of violence in order to achieve a more lasting peace. In this way, Spielberg seems to reflect Aristotle's dictum that "there must be war for the sake of peace."[9] *Munich* is not a unilateral call for nonviolence. It rather offers a more intricate view about the conditions under which the state is justified in applying retaliatory violent measures in response to terrorist acts in the hope of ending the violence.

So under what conditions is it acceptable for the state to use violence in response to terrorist actions? The film implicitly offers two competing positions regarding this question. The first is the argument in favor of revenge or vengeance in which retaliatory violence serves the ends of punishing others for horrific acts they inflicted. The second is that of a more deliberative form of retribution, which carries with it defensible criteria upon which to decide whether a state is justified in using the violence associated with war. The empathy Spielberg develops between the audience and Avner throughout supports the conclusion that we must shun violence motivated by revenge or vengeance but be willing to carefully undergo it for defensible reasons of retribution.

"Every Civilization Finds It Necessary to Negotiate Compromises with Its Own Values"

The concepts of revenge and vengeance have a deep and storied association with traditional notions of justice. Sources such as the Old Testament and the Homeric epics have prompted Robert Solomon to note, "Vengeance is the original meaning of justice." These conceptions of justice are linked to notions of repayment and balance. Revenge, for instance, is an action that is taken as a form of retaliation against another for causing us to suffer in some way. When one does harm to us, we respond by visiting punishment or injury upon them to even the score. However, vengeance implies that we are seeking to avenge a wrongdoing that was carried out against one who is no longer able to seek retribution for herself.[10] Although not exactly the same, revenge and vengeance are concerned with punishing crime or inflicting injury for a wrongdoing, and *Munich* is concerned with the ethics of such punishment.

The film was based largely on George Jonas's book *Vengeance: The True Story of an Israeli Counter-Terrorist Team,* and the concept of vengeance (because the athletes are now dead) is at the core of Spielberg's reflections in *Munich.*[11] But under what conditions is *state-sanctioned* violent retaliation an appropriate response to acts of terrorism? According to philosophers concerned with principles of revenge and vengeance, among them Susan Jacoby and Robert Solomon, the dual principles of deterrence and catharsis are satisfied by vengeance. Not only does punishment for a wrongdoing work to deter future perpetrators who might otherwise seriously threaten society, it also offers public catharsis—a sense of security and closure for an injured populous when those responsible are "brought to justice." Thus, when the state pursues vengeance as a part of its counterterrorist programs, it should do so to fulfill these two ends.[12]

Solomon offers an analysis of the role of vengeance as it applies to theories of justice. He claims that vengeance is often inappropriately attacked as a result of misunderstandings over or the improper conflation of revenge and hatred, two distinct concepts, which distorts the very idea of revenge as a component of justice.[13] He links justice with the desire to even the score. Even if it is plausible to seek revenge as a way of deterring future transgressions, Solomon argues that the desire to get even comes first and the rationalization to justify that desire follows. He argues that denying a community vengeance can lead to a deep "psychological disaster." In essence, part of Solomon's defense of vengeance is that it is cathartic, serving a deep emotional need to seek (communal) payback for a wrong that has been committed. Retribution, on the other hand, does not offer such catharsis in that it does not fully satisfy the emotional desire for payback. Because there is value in the kind of catharsis vengeance brings, and this value (allegedly) cannot be met with retribution alone, there is a role to be played by vengeance in our conception of justice.

Solomon admits that only some acts of vengeance are legitimate or justified. It is just to (publicly) expel a student for burning down the library; it is not appropriate to fail a student for disagreeing with his professor's pet theory. Borrowing from Robert Axelrod's work on the "tit-for-tat" model of the evolution of cooperation, Solomon uses the notion of rational revenge to explain how "an optimum strategy for discouraging [undesirable behavior] is to respond, dependably, with retribution." He thus concludes that "sometimes vengeance is wholly called for, even obligatory, and revenge is both legitimate and justified," since vengeance carried out to punish wrongdoing ensures the preservation of social patterns of cooperation.[14]

Solomon's argument requires criteria to evaluate when vengeance is sought justly and when it is being unjustly applied. For example, he claims that hanging a poor man for stealing bread to feed his family is a "barbaric" act that not only is unacceptable, but also seems to work in direct opposition of justice. Likewise, sentencing the same person to life in prison would also be an unjustifiable act. But why? Should we, as a society, not seek to punish thievery? Would society be in the right if the same man murdered someone who was hoarding food in order to redistribute that food to his family? What if the poor man was trafficking crack-cocaine to high school kids to make money that will buy the bread that will keep his family from starving? Such questions reveal how a just response may not be as clear as merely seeking to get even for a wrong committed. Solomon is correct that vengeance must contain, or at least be cultivated to contain, "the elements of its own control, a sense of limits, a sense of balance."[15] What is not clear is how a society achieves, or is meant to achieve, such balance and how it should temper vengeance with rationality when seeking to placate the furies.

The very nature of vengeance makes this determination unclear. Vengeance and revenge are first and foremost emotional actions. They may have positive externalities (deterrence or rehabilitation) that result as by-products, but these are not a consideration within the initial calculus. Solomon, for example, cites Nietzsche: "'The urge to punish' comes first; the reasons and attempts at justification come later." He also provides insights from A. S. Neill: "I think that the deterrent argument is simply a rationalization. The motive for punishment is revenge—not deterrence.... Punishment is hate." But these borrowed insights ironically provide the foundation for the ultimate criticism of Solomon's view. Emotional reactions to (real or perceived) wrongdoings are subjective. What is an unforgivable sin to one may not be so bad to someone else. Likewise, the degree and depth of the injury relates entirely to the perception of the person who is injured. Some people may seek a divorce to punish a spouse for infidelities, while others may be so filled with rage and hurt over a partner's rendezvous that they feel violence is the only way to subdue their anger. As Solomon points out on more than one occasion, although vengeance is not necessarily contrary to rationality, the "emotion of 'getting even'" need not necessarily be rational either.[16] Thus, we are left with the curious predicament of concluding that vengeance is justice—except when it is not.

Furthermore, Solomon's position that vengeance does not necessarily lead to an ongoing loop of retaliatory violence seems dubious. Such a cycle likely results from the issue of the subjective calculus described above. As Solomon explains, there is a tendency to confuse vengeance with a hostile feud in which actions move from retaliation for a specific event (or series of events) and transform into cyclical violence without regard to origin or purpose. In such cases, hate, not a desire to set things right, is the primary factor motivating action. This hatred causes one side to overestimate the other side's attempt at getting even by seeing it as an "overpayment." Each side then escalates beyond what the tenets of a just response would call for, prompting the other side to escalate its response as well. Interestingly, Solomon highlights the Middle East as an example of when such violence takes on a life of its own. Such violence has no "natural end," and therefore cannot be said to further a rational interest that serves the goal of either the state or those involved. Consequently, as *Munich* seems to suggest, revenge within the context of the tensions in the Middle East seems impermissible even to those who are otherwise sympathetic to it.

That vengeance does not always lead to ongoing tit-for-tat punishment may be true, but when one becomes deeply mired in such activities, such actions become easier and easier to justify. This seems to be the case with the Mossad agents in *Munich*. When Carl is murdered by the Dutch assassin Jeanette (Marie-Josée Croze), the remaining members of the team (minus Robert) hunt her down to avenge his death. This was not part of their mission, and they are later criticized for it by the Israeli government.[17]

Likewise, the way in which the assassination takes place seems to emphasize Spielberg's own reflections on this murder. The assassination is both intimate and clumsy. There seem to be moments of hesitation and inner struggle tearing at Avner and his crew. Jeanette pleads for her life as calmly as she can, exposing her naked breasts to Avner and Steve (Daniel Craig) as if to magnify the rawness and brutality of the act. They fire. Hans enters and shoots her once more in the head. Her naked body is exposed as she falls into a chair with her robe lying open. The Mossad agents stare for a moment into her dead eyes and at the holes in her body before Avner steps forward to close her robe. Hans instructs him to leave it. Rather than merely killing her quietly to get even for her silent assassination of their friend, she is to be made an example. The group here is not acting for Israel or the security of its people, and the scene clearly demonstrates the type of escalation that corresponds with acts of vengeance.

Perhaps this is why Solomon admits he is not attempting to defend vengeance categorically. Instead, he argues that the role vengeance plays in fulfilling the emotional desire to get even for a wrong committed means that it should be considered in legitimate conversations about justice. Although Solomon wishes to include vengeance in an understanding of what motivates different theories of justice, he concludes that emphasizing it can be dangerous and ultimately self-destructive. Borrowing from an older Chinese maxim, Solomon states, "If you seek vengeance, dig two graves."[18] Here he acknowledges that vengeance can devolve into self-destructive activity that does not further either individual or collective interests.

If one is concerned about the results and consequences of one's actions, vengeance must be carefully considered and applied in a just sense to ensure it produces the desired outcomes. However, that vengeance is an emotional, not necessarily a rational, response undermines its potentially just application. Vengeance is essentially arational, an emotional response to being wronged. On the other hand, justice is essentially rational, a nonemotional response to wrongdoing. If justice implies rationality, and vengeance is essentially arational, these two concepts are not identical. Thus, justice and vengeance are not the same. If vengeance is tempered with reason and carefully exacted to bring balance and avoid escalation, then it is just. However, the addition of these conditions transforms the nature of the act from vengeance to a different form of retaliatory act—retribution. In fact, tempering vengeance with rationality undermines the emotional catharsis that Solomon earlier ascribed to acts of revenge. Therefore, although vengeance might fill a primal desire to strike back at someone who hurts us, it is clear that vengeance and justice are not synonymous.

Spielberg seems to share Solomon's concerns about the direction in which vengeance can take its perpetrator. If the state is to move us beyond our primitive self, as Francis Bacon argues, it must develop the types of institutions that can replace and suppress the desire for such a primal urge as revenge. This conclusion is supported by psychologist Sandra Bloom, who argues that "acts of 'wild vengeance' . . . can be seen not only as the failure of the violent individual, but also the failure of the social group. Revenge is justice gone awry and takes over when society's institutions fail." Bloom goes on to argue that "if, as a society, we are to eliminate violent perpetration, then we must socially evolve systems of justice that effectively contain and manage the human desire for revenge." Thus, it is possible for the state to help us move beyond our primal urges for seeking personal vengeance, even in the most extreme cases. The state can be used as a tool to move us past the rubric of revenge and into the realm of retributive justice.[19]

"Some People Say We Can't Afford to Be Civilized—I've Always Resisted Such People"

In dealing with the principles of justice involved in an evaluation of counter-terrorist actions by the state, it is important to distinguish between vengeance and retribution. Unfortunately, it remains easy to confuse the two, even for philosophers. Some, such as Jacoby for example, see the term "retribution" as a euphemism for revenge, a sterilized version that is meaningless beyond its ability to offer a greater sense of civility when speaking of the base desire for retaliation. Likewise, Solomon argues that the distinction between revenge and retribution is a false dichotomy that creates misunderstandings about the very nature of revenge as a form of retributive justice. However, many other intellectuals disagree with such conflation. Immanuel Kant, for example, sees retribution as an act that is impersonal and rational, whereas revenge is a form of irrational rage that is unjustifiable as a pursuit.[20] Retributive justice relies fundamentally on the principle of desert: the belief that people ought to receive what they are due. What people have coming to them, of course, varies along the lines of reward and punishment depending on the behavior and character of the individual in question, and retributive justice demands that retribution be sought only in cases where collective or individual responsibility can be assigned. Identifying and properly addressing the issue of culpability is therefore essential to the principles of just action when seeking retribution.[21]

Robert Nozick offers a series of procedural arguments to illustrate the important differences between retribution and revenge. According to Nozick, retribution differs from revenge in five fundamental ways. First, retribution is carried out in response to an actual "wrong," as opposed to revenge, which may be sought for some personal harm or slight that may not be an actual wrong. Second, retribution carries with it limits on the level of punishment that is sought in response to the wrong committed. Such a measure of proportionality need not necessarily be a part of revenge. Third, revenge is personal. This personal attachment to revenge leads thinkers such as Kant to support the rational pursuit of retribution while rejecting the emotionally irrational act of revenge. Fourth, whereas retribution is a detached act, revenge carries with it a perverse form of schadenfreude—a delight and pleasure born from witnessing the suffering of another. Such perversity of pleasure from witnessing suffering outweighs any positive value or virtue associated with the communal catharsis of revenge. Finally, because of the personal nature of revenge, there is no way to extract from the specific case to the general when proceeding with an ethical code of behavior. Whereas retribution is committed in accordance with principles (often legalistically codified) of what level of punishment is acceptable in response to a specific act, no such established principles exist for an act of revenge. What is acceptable in terms of what constitutes a wrong and an appropriate response in a revenge scenario would be entirely dependent on the feelings of the individual.[22] These important distinctions demonstrate why it is important not to conflate vengeance and retribution, contrary to Solomon.

Distinguishing between retribution and revenge is critical to understanding the philosophy contained in *Munich*, because Spielberg does not explicitly discount the use of violence on the part of the state in response to acts of terror. He does, however, develop a theme throughout *Munich* about the need for thoughtful reflection and careful decisionmaking when responding to terrorism with violence. Like Nozick, Spielberg seems to imply that there is a distinction between justified acts of rationally applied retribution and unjustified acts of irrational revenge. In much of the film, Spielberg seems highly critical of the headlong rush into violence as a response to terrorism. This begins when Avner is first offered his assignment and General Zamir (Ami Weinberg) tells him, "If you can't decide in one day, you can't decide."

This headlong rush into action is revisited as Avner's covert Mossad team works quickly to install a telephone bomb in the home of Dr. Mahmoud Hamshari (Yigal Naor). Hamshari, whom the Israelis believed to be the head of Black September in France, provides a unique look into the theme of cyclical violence. In setting him up for assassination, Robert (Mathieu Kassovitz) pretends to be interviewing him for an article about the Middle East.

He asks Hamshari whether the attack in Munich was justified. Hamshari, while publicly proclaiming that the "PLO [Palestine Liberation Organization] condemns attacks on civilians," begins to try to justify the murder of the Israeli athletes. He argues that "for twenty-four years our civilians have been attacked by the Israelis. Israel just bombed two refugee camps in Syria and Lebanon, two hundred people killed, right after Munich they did this." His wife joins in the verbal assault on Israel's actions, illustrating the deep-seated hatred felt from their perspective about the ongoing conflicts in the Middle East. Thus, even though Hamshari offers an official condemnation of attacks on civilians, he and his wife demonstrate that they feel the murders in Munich were somehow justified acts of vengeance. Robert pretends to make a call and installs a bomb in Hamshari's phone. The Mossad agents then call his house, and when he finally is alone and answers, they detonate the bomb.

After this assassination, Carl begins to question Avner as to the role Hamshari played and whether the Israeli government was using them to carry out unethical or unnecessary acts against high-profile Arabs. Avner rejects the need for evidence that what they are doing is right because he, at this point, believes completely what the Israeli government has told him about the necessity of his actions. He tells Carl that in a "war, a crisis, you don't always have to . . . think." This conversation is interrupted by the completion of the bomb installation, but is echoed later when Carl tells Avner, "I knew guys like you in the army. You'll do any terrifying thing you're asked to do, but you have to do it running. . . . The only thing that really scares you guys is silence." His critique is that the silence would provide Avner and people like him with the opportunity to think about and confront their actions, which is what truly scares them. Carl's skepticism is revealed at the end of the film as being warranted, as Avner asks his Israeli contact Ephraim to provide evidence that all those Avner was sent to kill had a hand in Munich. Ephraim scolds him by saying that Hamshari "was implicated in a failed assassination attempt on [David] Ben Gurion, he was recruiting for Fatah France, enlisting sympathetic non-Arab fanatics eager to destroy the international Zionist conspiracy. You stopped him." What is obviously missing from his repudiation of Avner's concerns, however, is evidence linking Hamshari to the Munich massacres.

The call for thoughtful and careful reflection in responding to terrorism is where we first see Spielberg distinguishing between acts of retributive justice and acts of blind vengeance. Spielberg seems to be unwavering in his call for careful deliberation before engagement in a program of violence as a part of state counterterrorist efforts, and in many ways seems to be playing the role of armchair philosopher, using his film as argument. As a director, Spielberg is not a pacifist. Films like *Saving Private Ryan* and *Empire of the Sun,* for example, are not antiwar or antiviolence; nor should one assume that his perspective changed in filming *Munich.* However, with *Munich,* Spielberg seems to establish that deliberative, careful reflection may be what separates just and unjust violence. For example, in commenting on *Munich,* Spielberg says, "When we respond to terror today, what's relevant is the need to go through a careful process; not to paralyze ourselves, not to prevent us from acting, but to try and assure that the results we produce are the ones we really intend." He goes on to speculate that it is the "unintended results that are probably some of the worst."[23] An example of Spielberg's reflections on unintended consequences working against state interests occurs in one of Avner's many conversations with Louis (Mathieu Amalric). After assassinating Hussein al-Chir (Mostefa Djadjam), Black September's KGB contact, Avner assumes the job is done and the name can be crossed off his list. Louis, however, gives him another name, Zaid Muchassi (Djemel Barek). Avner tells him that name is not on the list, but Louis explains, "You put a bomb under Monsieur al-Chir's bed in Cyprus, and now he's defunct. Muchassi is his replacement. I hear he's much tougher than his predecessor." Not only does the assassination of al-Chir not accomplish the goal of eliminating Black September's connections with the KGB, but it also leads to the replacement of al-Chir with an agent who is even worse.

Here, Spielberg is clearly concerned with evaluating the consequences, or final causes, of state action when responding to terrorism. He does not argue that the state should do nothing, nor does he seem to regard all violence as necessarily unjust. Instead, the appropriateness of violence is, by some measure, gauged by its ability to produce the intended outcomes and avoid unwelcome results. Without clarity of purpose and thoughtful design, the consequences of violent action may not produce desired ends. Therefore, for the very reason of furthering state interests, Spielberg clearly advocates the deliberation of retributive justice over the quick strikes of vengeance.

But did Israel achieve its desired results with Wrath of God? Did the killing of the Black September operatives responsible for Munich serve to prevent future acts of violence against Israel while satisfying the demands for retaliation from the people of Israel by holding those culpable accountable? Throughout the film, as I have said, Spielberg reminds us of the unending cycle of violence in the Middle East through actual newscasts highlighting the retributive acts on the part of both the Israelis and the Palestinians. Likewise, Ephraim admits to Avner that his one small group was not the only force working for the state of Israel in this capacity. Finally, history itself stands as a testament to the ineffectiveness of such retaliatory violence in the Middle East. More than three decades after the violent attacks at Munich, violence continues in the Middle East, and the violence between Israel and Palestine is showing no natural end.

A second way in which Spielberg engages the philosophy of retribution as distinct from revenge is in his consideration of the notions of discrimination and proportionality when executing retaliatory actions. Traditionally associated with the classical principles of "jus in bello" (just conduct in war), discrimination refers to the fundamental notion that anyone falling outside the bounds of the "combatant class" must be immune from attack. All reasonable efforts must be taken to protect against collateral damage, as well as to ensure against the targeting of civilians and noncombatants. In terms of proportionality, the actions of the state must not exceed what is reasonable to the attainment of stated objectives. There should be a reasonable association between the type and amount of force applied and the goals set forth by the state in declaring war.

The Mossad agents portrayed in *Munich* clearly make all attempts to abide by the principles of discrimination and proportionality, as demonstrated in the most dramatically intense scenes in the film. When the team attempts the assassination of Hamshari with a bomb planted in his telephone receiver, they wait until his wife and daughter have left the apartment before putting the final pieces of the assassination in motion. However, unseen by the team, Hamshari's daughter Amina (Mouna Soualen) returns to retrieve the glasses her mother left behind. The phone rings, Amina answers, and Carl rushes to call off the detonation. The intensity of the scene serves to highlight the care the agents put into making sure that no innocent lives are taken in their quest to seek retribution against those responsible for the Munich massacre. Likewise, Spielberg seems to use this scene to make a claim about carefully considering our involvement in political violence. Hamshari's daughter is nearly killed in an attempt on his life, just as Avner's involvement puts his own family at risk (forcing them to seek refuge in New York). Modern terrorism does not distinguish between solider and civilian, or in the case of *Munich,* guilty and innocent. Thus, a terrorist response to antiterrorist measures might threaten the very innocents we are trying to protect. The pronounced involvement of family throughout the film seems to draw attention to this point.

Additionally, when setting off the bomb in the top floor of the Olympic Hotel, Avner rushes to the aid of a newlywed couple who were accidentally injured in the explosion and helps them find their way to safety before fleeing himself. That the couple was injured, and that Avner realizes his obligation to them, highlights Spielberg's basic position that we must exercise extreme caution in engaging in such retaliatory actions. With each operation, great care is taken by the Mossad agents to try to protect against collateral damage. Such deliberate purpose is reflective of the principles of retribution and not of the blind rage that is often associated with the violence of revenge. Therefore, Spielberg, as both filmmaker and philosopher, conveys a message reminiscent of the fifth book of the Torah, Deuteronomy 19:10, "that innocent blood be not shed in the midst of thy land, which the LORD thy God giveth thee for an inheritance, and so blood be upon thee." Throughout the film there is a clear statement about the obligation that a state has to protect against the harming of innocents, which is strongly correlated with Spielberg's message about careful deliberation guiding retaliation.

It is important to note that Spielberg recognizes that states have an obligation to protect their citizens, and that governments should not become frozen into nonaction by ceaseless deliberation. He does not even entirely dismiss violent retaliation as a justified response to terrorism. However, his implicit call for more careful deliberation by the state in response to terrorism has left him open to criticism. Given the ability for terrorist organizations to rapidly strike and disappear, quickly adapting with flexibility unavailable to state actors, the deliberative process might be seen as paralytic, leaving the state vulnerable to future attacks. What is traditionally made as an argument of using force only as a last resort before engaging in violence may not apply between state and nonstate combatants in the same way that it does between two states. Spielberg acknowledges these types of arguments when he has General Yariv (Amos Lavi) explain while recruiting Avner that "this is something new. What happened in Munich changes everything. The rules, everything."

In response to the notion that traditional approaches to warfare need to be abandoned in the face of modern terror, some ethical philosophers, such as those belonging to the Pontifical Council for Justice and Peace, have argued that, although the state has the right and obligation to defend itself from acts of terror, which are of the worst and most depraved form of human action, "this right cannot be exercised in the absence of moral and legal norms, because the struggle against terrorists must be carried out with respect for human rights and for the principles of a State ruled by law."[24] Within the bounds of international law, the only principle that has been recognized by the international community and codified in international law as establishing "just cause" is that of "self-defense." Furthermore, as St. Thomas Aquinas persuasively notes, the actions of the state must be carried out with "just intentions."[25] This means that war should be waged with an eye toward creating the conditions for peace, and that the state must be willing to engage in peaceful negotiations when conditions are met. Motivating factors such as vengeance, retribution, and retaliation do not form an internationally recognized foundation for using violence, nor do they form the basis of just intention on the part of the state.

Such principles also entail a contractual obligation between the soldier and the state regarding counterterrorist tactics. Governments have a moral obligation to act in an ethical manner when engaging in or carrying out the act of war. They also have a contractual obligation to their soldiers not to place them in harm's way without just warrant. Finally, because states must employ violence only as a means of restoring conditions for peace, the state is obligated to its soldiers to provide a clear strategy for ending the conflict as quickly as possible and with as little harm as situations allow. In *Munich,* Spielberg shows his affinities for such a relationship between state and soldier. Soldiers like Avner and his Mossad team are willing to risk everything, including their lives, in defense of the state. All they ask in return is that the state does not send them forth without just purpose. It is the responsibility of political officials to be certain that what they are doing is rational, just, and necessary, and possesses a reasonable chance for success. Without that, the state is not living up to its obligations to its civilians or its soldiers. That such a contract is not upheld between Israel and Avner's agents may explain in the end why Avner chooses not to return to his homeland.

The notion that the state is responsible for avoiding the base, emotional act of revenge when seeking retributive justice is articulated in the philosophy of Pietro Marongiu and Graeme Newman, who argue that vengeance is a personal action built into private social organizations and is separate from government action.[26] Such a position supports that of Nozick, who sees the rationally impersonal aspects of retribution as built into the state through a system of legalism. The state is bound by the impersonal, rational codes that form the basis of the rule of law. When it begins to act in a manner befitting a label of blind rage, as opposed to the more deliberative act of retribution, the state expends its soldiers in an irrational and unjust manner. In *Munich,* this is revealed when, after Avner has given his everything for the state of Israel—having killed and witnessed the killing of his friends—he asks Ephraim for proof that what he did was not performed under false pretenses. Like Carl before, Avner begins to question whether the men he killed actually had a hand in committing the Munich massacre, or whether he was being used for other violent purposes by the state. Ephraim does not answer his charges. In the end, the soldier and the state turn from one another, and walk away.

"Go Ahead—Tell Me What You Learned"

Munich is not a film that categorically rejects violence. It is a film that artistically portrays how the use of violence, regardless of the reason, always carries with it significant moral considerations and dilemmas. In reconsidering the morality and ethics of state-sanctioned violence in response to terrorism, it is clear that the use of violence purely for the sake of fulfilling the desire for vengeance is not a justifiable position for the state to take. However, the state may justly seek retribution as an appropriate response to acts of terrorism. By engaging in actions that remain within the rubric of retributive justice without slipping into the realm of blind rage, the state improves its chances of achieving desired political results. It thereby upholds its moral responsibilities to the soldiers who carry out orders on behalf of the state.

In the film, Golda Meir (Lynn Cohen) remarks, "Every civilization finds it necessary to negotiate compromises with its own values." However, *Munich* stands as a testament to not abandoning ethics and morality for the sake of security or vengeance. As Robert tells Avner before seeking revenge on Jeanette, "We're Jews, Avner. Jews don't do wrong because our enemies do wrong. . . . We're supposed to be righteous." Through the empathetic connections he develops between Avner and his audience, Steven Spielberg masterfully reminds all of us living with the bitterly dark and complex realities of terrorism what it means to be righteous.

Notes

1. This included the Zionist Organization of America, who called for a boycott of *Munich* because of Spielberg's artistic choices that call into question the same moral dilemmas for acts of counterterrorism as for terrorism itself. Morton A. Klein, "ZOA: Don't See Spielberg's 'Munich' Unless You Like Humanizing Terrorists & Dehumanizing Israelis," *Zionist Organization of America*, December 27, 2005, http://www.zoa .org/2005/12/zoa_dont_see_sp.htm (accessed July 11, 2007); Leon Wieseltier, "The Case against Munich," *Jewish World Review*, December 12, 2005, http://www.jewishworldre view.com/1205/munich.php3 (accessed April 24, 2008).

2. Eleanor Ringel Gillespie, "Murder Takes Its Toll in Munich," *Atlanta Journal-Constitution*, December 23, 2005, http://www.accessatlanta.com/movies/content/ shared/movies/reviews/M/munich/ajc.html (accessed April 24, 2008); Manohla Dargis, "An Action Film about the Need to Talk," *New York Times*, December 23, 2005, http:// movies2.nytimes.com/2005/12/23/movies/23muni.html?ex=1180670400&en=0adcc1f 7d1656418&ei=5070 (accessed April 24, 2008).

3. "Introduction by Steven Spielberg," *Munich*, special ed. DVD (Hollywood, CA: Universal Studios, 2006).

4. "Introduction by Steven Spielberg," *Munich,* DVD (2006).

5. Jean-François Lyotard, *The Postmodern Explained* (Minneapolis: University of Minnesota Press, 1992).

6. In various Asian traditions, but most notably Jainism, the primary emphasis that is placed on having compassion for all living things gives rise to the principle of *ahimsa,* the complete avoidance of violence. Violence in any form is inherently destructive, and one must reject all violence out of concern and compassion for all that is living.

7. Plato, *Crito,* in *Five Dialogues: Euthyphro, Apology, Crito, Meno, Phaedo,* trans. G. M. A. Grube (Indianapolis: Hackett, 1981).

8. Admittedly, this scene can also plausibly be conveying the broader context of revenge killings and retaliation in the Middle East. More subtly, Spielberg uses this moment to invite connections with the United States' global war on terror in response to the terrorist attacks on September 11, 2001: it is certainly no coincidence that the film ends with a shot of the World Trade Center towers dominating the New York City skyline. Regardless of the specific reference, Avner on some level seems to be rejecting the use of such violence in order to bring about peace on either an individual or a social level, since he expresses his concern as to whether his actions might have done nothing more than create new and more dangerous terrorists.

9. Aristotle, *Politics,* book 7, section 14.

10. Robert C. Solomon, "Justice and the Passion for Vengeance," in *A Passion for Justice* (Reading, MA: Addison Wesley, 1989), reprinted in *What is Justice? Classic and Contemporary Readings,* ed. Robert C. Solomon and Mark C. Murphy (New York: Oxford University Press, 1990), 292; Ted Honderich (ed.), *The Oxford Companion to Philosophy* (Oxford: Oxford University Press, 1995).

11. Jonas's book was originally published by Simon and Schuster in May 1984.

12. Solomon, "Justice and the Passion for Vengeance"; Susan Jacoby, *Wild Justice: The Evolution of Revenge* (New York: Harper and Row, 1983).

13. For example, Solomon writes:

Vengeance is not [merely] punishment, no matter how harsh. It is a matter of emotion, and like punishment, it is always *for* some offense, not just hurting for its own sake (even if, in some other sense, it is deserved). Vengeance, then, always has its reasons (though, to be sure, these can be mistaken, irrelevant, out of proportion or otherwise bad reasons). Vengeance is no longer a matter of obligation . . . or rationality. . . . Vengeance is the emotion of "getting even," putting the world back in balance, and this simple phrase already embodies a whole philosophy of justice, even if (as yet) unarticulated and unjustified. (Solomon, "Justice and the Passion for Vengeance," 293)

14. Solomon, "Justice and the Passion for Vengeance," 292–93, 297.

15. Solomon, "Justice and the Passion for Vengeance," 293.

16. Solomon, "Justice and the Passion for Vengeance," 292–93, 298.

17. Interestingly, the movie suggests that the Israeli government is engaged in vigi-

lantism, using Avner's covert Mossad team to assassinate people not directly responsible for the Munich massacre.

18. Solomon, "Justice and the Passion for Vengeance," 301.

19. Sandra L. Bloom, "Commentary: Reflections on the Desire for Revenge," *Journal of Emotional Abuse* 2 (4): 61–94.

20. Jacoby, *Wild Justice*; Solomon, "Justice and the Passion for Vengeance"; Immanuel Kant, *The Metaphysical Elements of Justice,* trans. John Ladd (Indianapolis: Hackett, 1999).

21. Honderich, *The Oxford Companion to Philosophy.*

22. Robert Nozick, *Philosophical Explanations* (Cambridge, MA: Belknap Press of Harvard University Press, 1981).

23. "Introduction by Steven Spielberg," *Munich,* DVD (2006).

24. Pontifical Council for Justice and Peace, *Compendium of the Social Doctrine of the Church,* United States Conference of Catholic Bishops (Washington, DC: Liberia Editrice Vaticana, 2005), 223.

25. Timothy McDermott (ed.), *St. Thomas Aquinas's Summa Theologica: A Concise Translation* (Notre Dame, IN: Ave Maria Press).

26. Pietro Marongiu and Graeme Newman, *Vengeance* (Toronga, NJ: Rowman and Littlefield, 1987).

Part III

Realism, Mind, and Metaphysics

Spielberg and Cinematic Realism

Keith Dromm

> There are many conceivable ways of telling a story, some of them
> known and some still to be discovered.
> —Bertolt Brecht, "A Short Organum for the Theatre"

Soon after the theatrical release of Steven Spielberg's World War II film
Saving Private Ryan (1998), there were reports of veterans suffering symptoms of post-traumatic stress disorder after watching it.[1] Referring to his
own experiences in the war, one World War II veteran said of the film, "It
brought it back like a flash. Like I was there." The film's ability to do this may
be explained by another veteran's comment: "I want to say that it's just a war
movie, but it's too close to being realistic."[2] Film scholars have echoed this
opinion of the film. One scholar writes of its opening sequence depicting
the landing at Normandy that it "set new standards for battlefield realism."[3]
But it is perhaps the reactions by veterans to the film that are the better
endorsement of its realism.

Saving Private Ryan is not the only film by Spielberg that can be recognized for its realism. His portrayal of the Holocaust in *Schindler's List* (1993)
matches *Saving Private Ryan* in the richness and detail of its depiction of
the same period of history. *Amistad* (1997), about a revolt aboard a slave
ship in 1839, is another historical film that aims to provide a convincing
portrayal of a certain time and part of the world. All three films are equally
unflinching in their depiction of acts of brutality and their consequences.[4]
Many of Spielberg's films, including those not based on historical events,
are commendable for their realism, even his science fiction films. The film
scholar Lester Friedman says of *Jurassic Park* (1993), referring in particular
to its depiction of dinosaurs, that it "raised the bar for acceptable renditions

of 'reality' that audiences would ultimately require for their disbelief to be suspended."[5] The future imagined in *Minority Report* (2002) is similarly convincing. For example, it is not hard to imagine the technology it envisions for our future actually being a part of our world someday. It seems that no matter the subject matter, Spielberg aims for realistic portrayals of his films' stories. He uses the screen canvas to present us worlds that we can easily imagine ourselves occupying, some reluctantly, in either our past, our present, or the future.

Whereas art forms such as painting and sculpture have perhaps peaked in their abilities to represent reality *realistically* and have subsequently moved away from realism as an ideal, film directors such as Spielberg are still striving for greater levels of realism in their films. But what does it mean to call a film realistic? The topic of cinematic realism can profitably be explored through an examination of Spielberg's films. Because so many of his films aspire to be realistic, and for the most part succeed, they offer a valuable resource for testing theories of cinematic realism.

Although cinematic realism is a topic in the philosophy of art, it also has connections with the rest of philosophy. For example, it is different in interesting and illuminating ways from "truth," a subject that has always intrigued philosophers. We can evaluate a historical fiction like *Saving Private Ryan* on its truthfulness or accuracy in representing the Allies' landing at Normandy. Its realism, however, is a separate matter. Those who have no experience of war or knowledge of the Normandy landing can still be struck by and commend the film's realism. As it has been applied to other artworks, such as painting, the label "realistic" is not restricted to truthful portrayals or those that take their subjects from history. So even a film like *Minority Report,* whose story line is entirely imagined, can be realistic. Fictitious portrayals still owe their realism to their relationship with reality, but it is a relationship importantly different from that between truth and reality. For example, realism comes in degrees, whereas a representation is simply either true or false. *Saving Private Ryan* can be more realistic than *The Longest Day* (1962), but they can both be described as realistic films about the Normandy landing (as opposed to some other cinematic portrayals of World War II, such as Spielberg's comedy *1941* [1979]). Also, a portrayal is true simply if the depicted events occurred. Assessing realism, however, is not so straightforward, since there can be realistic portrayals of events that never occurred.

In this essay I propose three interrelated criteria for cinematic realism that work for both entirely fictional films and those that take their stories from history. I derive and defend these criteria through consideration of a variety of Spielberg films. The criteria should help us determine whether a film by any director is realistic, and to what degree. However, although most of this essay is devoted to answering the question, what is cinematic realism? it concludes with the question, *why* cinematic realism? That is, should other directors strive as much as Spielberg to make their cinematic portrayals realistic? There might be good reasons against doing so. The example of veterans suffering from symptoms of post-traumatic stress disorder after watching *Saving Private Ryan* might suggest one such reason. In addition, many people refused to watch the film solely because they were averse to seeing its realistic battle sequences. However, it might be that the subject matter of a film somehow warrants—even requires—a realistic portrayal. Films that do not take their topics from history have been criticized for their realistic—in other words, graphic—portrayals of sex and violence. Such depictions are sometimes described as gratuitous.

In the final section of this essay I consider an objection to realism ever being an ideal in filmmaking. I draw on the proposed three criteria for cinematic realism in defending realism as a legitimate goal for filmmakers, while acknowledging that it need not be the goal of every film. There might be stories that should not be filmed realistically. I do not attempt to say which sorts of stories these are, but I suggest that whether a story should be filmed realistically should be determined, at least in part, by the reasons for telling the story.

"It's Life Itself!"

There seems to be something about films that makes them intrinsically more realistic than any other sort of artwork. The film scholar André Bazin writes that "photography and the cinema . . . are discoveries that satisfy, once and for all and in its very essence, our obsession with realism." He points out that whereas a filmmaker, like any sort of artist, will select what she wants to represent in her artwork, the photographic images that constitute the film are produced mechanically or "automatically, without the creative intervention of man." For Bazin, this gives film a "credibility" that other artworks lack and that "force[s] us to accept as real the existence" of whatever is represented by the image.[6] This view was perhaps being attested to by the audience member at one of the first public showings of a film (made by the Lumière brothers), who reportedly yelled at the screen, "It's life itself!"[7] The film contained no special effects and the direction was rudimentary. It was simply the nature of the medium that elicited this response.

Given their photographic basis, all films automatically enjoy a high degree of realism. All properly exposed photographs are realistic with respect to what we can call their pictorial properties. But since all photographic images are equally realistic in this respect, we must consider more than pictorial realism in order to distinguish realistic from nonrealistic films. Bazin and the audience member at the Lumière film are commenting only on the pictorial aspects of film. *Cinematic* realism involves much more. In addition to what films and photographs share with painting (pictorial realism), there is the realism of the aural aspects of the film—for example, the sound effects and other diegetic sounds on the film's soundtrack.[8] Also, there are what films share with theater—for example, costume, set design and construction, acting, dialogue—and what both share with literature, the realism of the story.[9] The quality of these components determines how realistic a film is; in the next three sections we will see how.

Disguised Representation

One thing that consistently detracts from an audience's judgments about a film's realism is their being reminded that the events they are watching are unreal. The philosopher William Earle puts it this way: "In a purely realist film, every effort is devoted to making the audience unaware of the camera, unaware that they are seeing only a reflected reality."[10] The more that a film calls our attention to its status as a representation, as a mere "reflected reality," the less realistic it will be. We will in a moment review the various ways, both intentional and unintentional, that a film can make us aware of its representational status. But we should first note that a film is not necessarily unrealistic if it fails to make us "unaware of the camera." In fact, this awareness can sometimes contribute to the realism of the film.

In *Saving Private Ryan,* Spielberg and his cinematographer wanted the shots of battle sequences, such as the landing at Normandy, to resemble color newsreel footage from the time. All the cameras used for these sequences were handheld. They and their lenses were manipulated to photograph like those used to make newsreels in the 1940s. In postproduction the images were desaturated (drained of color) and made to appear grainy.[11] The image is also sometimes splattered with blood and dirt. In manipulating the image in these ways, Spielberg increased our awareness of the camera. He was not disguising the fact that we are watching a film. However, he was trying to make us unaware that we are watching merely *reenactments* of battles and other events. The manipulation of the image, as well as costuming, acting, special effects, and so on, all contribute to the impression that we are not watching a "reflected reality" of the portrayed events. The crew members and equipment, sounds extraneous to the fictional action, and anything else that might indicate its representational status are hidden from the audience.

This is a typical ambition of fiction films. Some films, however, consciously try to call our attention to their status as representations. For example, *Dogville* (2003), directed by Lars von Trier, is filmed entirely on a soundstage with a minimalist set. There are a few necessary props, such as pieces of furniture; however, instead of roofs, walls, floors, and so on, buildings and streets are indicated by painted outlines and labels on the soundstage floor (as if it were an enormous blueprint for a set). Films often contain more subtle revelations of their representational status—for example, the use of captions to indicate time or place, such as "Isla Nubar, 120 miles west of Costa Rica." Expressionistic lighting, such as the backlighting of characters, which Spielberg often uses in his films, can also reveal the filmmaker's hand in creating the image.

Filmmakers can also *un*intentionally reveal the film's status as representation. For example, films often contain continuity mistakes in which one shot does not match another shot of the same person or action. The scene from *Jurassic Park* in which Drs. Grant and Sattler first meet John Hammond contains such a mistake. In two shots we see Hammond drying a glass for the champagne he has opened; the first a long shot, the next a medium shot. But the color of the towel he is using to dry the glasses is different in the two shots. Some time likely passed between the filming of the two shots, and the crew failed to keep track of the towel used.[12] Other things that can unintentionally reveal the film's status as representation include bad acting, poorly constructed sets (including obviously fabricated backdrops), and the poor use of special effects.

In attempting to disguise a film's status as representation, filmmakers are engaged in the construction of an illusion of sorts. The film scholar V. F. Perkins writes that "the most 'realistic' films are the ones which convey the most complete illusion."[13] The more a film reveals its construction, the less effective the illusion. Some have objected to using illusion as a criterion for realism. Dominic Lopes, for example, has argued that pictorial realism "does not depend on realism as illusionistic experience" that "dupes" the viewer into taking what they are viewing to be real.[14] Nelson Goodman similarly rejects the idea that "a picture is realistic just to the extent that it is a successful illusion, leading the viewer to suppose that it is, or has the characteristics of, what it represents. The proposed measure of realism, in other words, is the probability of confusing the representation with the represented."[15]

However, these philosophers are tending to conflate illusion and deception. The two are different. Although illusions can cause deceptions, one does not need to be deceived in order to be subject to an illusion. Consider an optical illusion like the famous Müller-Lyer illusion.

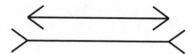

This consists of two parallel lines of equal length; one line has outward-pointing arrows at its ends, the other inward-pointing arrows. The latter will invariably appear longer to us. Until we measure the lengths of the lines and discover that they are equal, we might be deceived by the illusion into believing that they are of different lengths. But even after we learn that the two are equal in length, they will still appear to us to be different. To be deceived is to believe wrongly.[16] To be subject to an illusion is only to see things as they are not, not necessarily to believe they are so. Realistic films present audiences with an illusion. Goodman and Lopes are still correct, however, in believing that deception cannot be a criterion for realism.

Deceiving, or "duping," audiences into believing that what they are seeing is real is not an ambition of filmmakers, nor is it even a capability of film, at least given current technology. A film would have to be capable somehow of causing the audience to forget that they are sitting in a movie theater or at home, as well as such things as that World War II ended several decades ago, that the future has not yet arrived, or that dinosaurs are not at present walking the earth. The quality of its images and other typical aspects of films are alone incapable of causing this sort of deception. Films can certainly be used to deceive in other ways. Propaganda films sometimes use fabricated images to deceive audiences into believing that certain events have occurred. Typically, however, filmmakers do not attempt to deceive audiences, but rather to present them with an illusion.

What kind of illusion do filmmakers try to create? In the first place, all films, including documentaries, evince an illusion of motion.[17] A film consists of still photographs. When these photographs are run through a projector at a rapid speed the photographed objects appear to be moving. Fiction films attempt to create a further illusion that is often dependent on this first one. We have seen that films are incapable of deceiving us into believing that we are watching actual events as they transpire. Films are also incapable of simulating human perception to the extent that they can give us the illusion of watching actual events (as the technology used in the Cyberparlor in *Minority Report* is able to do). But films typically do not even make an effort to do this. As we have seen, the images in one of the most realistic films ever made, *Saving Private Ryan*, were manipulated so that they would not resemble direct perception of the represented events. Similarly, *Schindler's List* was filmed in black and white, which arguably added to rather than detracted from the film's realism.

Although not all filmmakers manipulate the image in these ways, they typically do other things that are in tension with creating the illusion that we are watching actual events as they occur. Camera angles often give us perspectives on events that humans ordinarily do not occupy (e.g., extremely low-angle or high-angle shots). Films also may present us perspectives from a viewpoint that a camera could not occupy, precluding even the illusion that we are watching a filmic record of the events (e.g., within the dreams or memories of characters). Such techniques, in addition to the scale of the images we are watching, make it impossible for us to imagine that we are seeing the portrayed events as ordinary observers. As F. E. Sparshott explains, we observe these events "from a vantage point that contrives to be at once definite and equivocal or impossible."[18]

That a film does not duplicate the ordinary perception of events might seem to detract from its realism. Faux-documentaries such as *The Blair Witch Project* (1999) present, along with their fictional events, an explanation for the dissimilarities between ordinary perception and our perception of the cinematic images. We are supposed to be watching documentary footage of events that occurred in the past; that is the illusion created by such films. The contrasts with ordinary perception play an important part in the construction of this illusion. But for other sorts of films, Sparshott recommends that we do not analogize our watching them with ordinary perception. Instead, we should compare them to our perception of dreams, both the nocturnal and the daytime variety. In dreams, Sparshott explains, "I see from where I am not, move helplessly in a space whose very nature is inconstant, and may see beside me the being whose perceptions I share."[19] In our dreams, we are free to imagine events in an unlimited number of ways. The illusion of our dreams in this respect resembles the illusion of films.

Sparshott is not suggesting that filmmakers consciously, or even un-consciously, model their works after dreams. Rather, the analogy is meant to explain the illusion that films create, and in a way that is not in tension with the ambitions of realism. Although in our dreams we can, and typically do, imagine the most fantastic *un*realistic events, our dreams also contain recollections and other imagined events that are capable of a kind of realism. Sparshott also intends this analogy to explain the facility with which we are able to understand what we see happening on the screen, even though we are watching events in a way we never do in ordinary perception; we are familiar with this form of perception from our dreams. We will return to this analogy later to explain how these photographic techniques actually add to the realism of a film.

So the illusion of films is the illusion that we are perceiving certain events and persons, although not as we would perceive them in the actual world. It is not an illusion of the ordinary perception of those events. It achieves this illusion by disguising the fact that what we perceive are mere representations. However, this is an ambition of many sorts of films. Even the most unrealistic of films—a slapstick comedy, for example—will try to evince this illusion. Therefore, the criterion of disguised representation is not enough to distinguish realistic films from most other varieties of film.[20] We need additional criteria for cinematic realism.

Fidelity

We have noted that a realistic film does not need to be true. Its source can be the filmmaker's imagination and not actual events. But a realistic film cannot be entirely the product of the filmmaker's imagination. It still owes something to the real world. What could that be? A film like *Hook* (1991), while disguising its status as representation, revels in its status as a product of imagination. It presents us, unapologetically, with images and events that we would never encounter in the real world. Yet it still borrows from the real world. In order for a film to be an effective drama, we must be able to see something of ourselves and our world in it. Most importantly, the characters must behave as we do. They should be fearful of danger, happy at fortune, sad at loss, and so on. The inanimate objects of the imagined world must also behave like those of the real world, at least some of the time. If they did not, we would have difficulty recognizing them and we could not establish the expectations that are necessary for suspense. For example, if the swords in the imagined world of *Hook* did not behave like those in our world, the fight scenes would fail to be suspenseful. But a realistic film borrows much more from the real world. Although it has the freedom of a fantasy like *Hook* to present events that have never occurred, the illusion it presents must still be of the real world and not an imagined one. That is, audience members must be able to accept what they see and hear as something that could very well be, or has been, found in *our* world.

We can call this quality of realistic films their "fidelity" to the real world. Rather than being truthful, a realistic film will attempt to be faithful to the world in other respects. The events, objects, and persons it portrays will be like their counterparts in the actual world. Not only must they look like their counterparts in the real world (though not, as I have argued, be perceived as we perceive their counterparts), they must behave like them as well. We might say that a realistic film, in contrast to a fantasy or comedy, must obey the *logic* of the real world. For example, humans talk, animals do not, nor do trees and candlesticks; few things are capable of flying; nothing is capable of disappearing or performing other magical feats; moral perfection is rare, as are happy endings; aesthetic perfection is also rare, some sights are ugly and unpleasant to look at.

The design of sets and props is important in the making of a film that meets the criterion of fidelity. For example, the realism of *Jurassic Park* is due to more than its dinosaurs. The use of a recurring motif, the T-rex head, helps make the island setting *look* like a theme or amusement park, as do the designs for the rides, gift shop, and visitors' center. In designing *Minority Report,* Spielberg and his crew consulted scientists who shared their visions of the future, and the film therefore contains technology that we can easily imagine existing. The widespread use of retinal scanners for not only surveillance but also marketing purposes is a real possibility, as are newspapers that are continuously updated and cereal boxes with moving images. The way users interact with computers in the film is modeled on technology that is currently being developed.[21] Even though it is set in the future, then, the props of *Minority Report* are indebted to the present, real world.[22]

Several of Spielberg's other films portray the past, and their realism depends upon fidelity to that period. *Munich* (2005) is faithful in a variety of ways to the past it depicts—it incorporates the clothes and technology of the 1970s, for example. But the most interesting example of its fidelity is its use of existing archival footage of its story's subject, the hostage-taking of Israeli athletes at the Munich Olympics, which it deftly incorporates with footage made for the film. The best example of this is its use of the famous video of one of the hostage-takers standing on the balcony of the athletes' dormitory. Spielberg created a shot of this figure from the rear, which we see while the archival footage of the hostage-taker is playing on a television in the foreground.

Another way that a film can be faithful, or not, to the real world is in its informativeness, or detail. A realistic representation will be as rich and varied as the real world. Both the aural and visual images in Spielberg's films achieve a density that is comparable to what we perceive in the actual world. We see this, for example, in the rich textures of the soiled and battered uniforms and bodies of the soldiers in *Saving Private Ryan.* But the most obvious example of this film's fidelity to the real world is its graphic portrayals of injury and death. Although death is an inescapable element of any war film, *Saving Private Ryan* shows us more than do most of its predecessors the *way* in which soldiers and others die in war. This amount of detail and information is found in many of Spielberg's films. Something comparable is achieved in *Schindler's List, Amistad,* and *The Color Purple* (1985). Various crafts are responsible for this aspect of a film's fidelity, including costuming, makeup, set design, and special effects.

Acting is another important component of a film's realism, and the realism acting brings is due to a kind of fidelity to the real world. The characters should sound and behave as people do in the real world. In order to elicit convincing portrayals from the actors in *Saving Private Ryan,* Spielberg subjected them to a mini boot camp. This preparation was meant to familiarize the actors with life as a soldier, in the expectation that this knowledge would transfer to their performances. However, such preparation must be paired with dialogue and a story that are in their own ways faithful to reality.

A story is realistic to the extent that the events it comprises are typical of the real world. Happy endings, for example, typically form the conclusions to Spielberg's films and most other so-called Hollywood productions, but occur much less often in the real world. *Saving Private Ryan* is an exception to this: almost all of its heroes die by its end (although Ryan himself lives). The realism of the story is also enhanced by the behavior of these characters. Their actions are not always morally commendable. Similarly, *Munich* presents us with morally conflicted characters, who are more faithful to reality than the confident, self-assured heroes that populate many films. Even when a story's events are ones that have never occurred in the real world, as in science fiction, the story can still be realistic. For example, *Jurassic Park* strives to convince us of the possibility of bringing dinosaurs back to life by taking us, along with its characters, through a lengthy introduction to the science and technology that is responsible for their creation. By contrast, the idea of the precogs in *Minority Report,* no matter how realistically they and their visions might be portrayed, may strike many as unrealistic. For some (including myself), the very notion is metaphysically suspect, and therefore fantasy on the order of that in *Hook*.

The fidelity criterion is related to the criterion of disguised representation. The less realistic the acting, the less plausible the future or past imagined, the more apparent is the film's status as representation. The illusion of a real world suffers the more we see or hear things that we cannot believe to be likely constituents of that world. Both criteria are connected to the final and perhaps most important criterion, which we will examine in the next section.

Emotional Response

The third and final aspect of cinematic realism that I want to identify is not only a criterion for realism; it is also a consequence of the first two criteria, and what typically motivates their inclusion in a film. It is the tendency of a film to evoke emotional reactions in the audience to the events being portrayed on the screen.[23] A strong emotional response is indicative of a film's realism. The more faithful a film is to reality, the more it disguises its status as a representation, the more likely we are to respond emotionally to the events being portrayed. Although emotional response is not restricted to realistic films, the more powerful and lingering emotions can be evoked by realistic films, especially those that draw their stories from history.

Some have found our liability to respond emotionally to fictional events to be paradoxical. This is because when we respond emotionally to events being portrayed by the film, we at the same time know that those events are fictional. We feel anxious when watching the progression of E.T.'s illness; we feel relief when the shark in *Jaws* (1975) is finally killed (or so it seems); and we anguish over the indignities suffered by Celie in *The Color Purple*. The emotions we feel in response to historical films might be more understandable, since they depict actual events, but some of these emotions are felt in response to what happens to the fictional characters of these dramas. Although the Normandy landing was a historical occurrence, the central characters of *Saving Private Ryan* are imagined. We nevertheless share some of their fear, sadness, and occasional hope. No one could ease our emotions by telling us that these characters are not real. We know this, yet we still feel these emotions.

I do not want to explore this apparent paradox in any depth here, except to note two things that I hope will make the phenomenon of responding emotionally to fictions seem less paradoxical.[24] First, other visual arts and literature are also capable of eliciting emotional responses to the fictional events they portray. We can, for example, worry over the plight of characters depicted in a painting or a novel. Second, this phenomenon occurs most often, and perhaps most forcefully, in response to what we imagine on our own. Our nocturnal dreams, and even our daydreams, can elicit strong emotions from us. A thought or a mental image can delight or disgust us, so that we either revel in it or try to banish it from our minds. Our techniques for controlling the emotional power of our imaginations can help explain some of the techniques used by filmmakers to elicit our emotions.

There are various ways of tempering or increasing the emotional power of a perception, whether of something imagined or something actual. The

Saving Private Ryan, DreamWorks SKG/Amblin Entertainment, 1998. The sense of realism that Spielberg often achieves in his films uniquely raises our feelings of empathy, which in turn lead to important ethical and aesthetic insights. (Movie-Goods, Inc.)

fearful can appear innocuous when put directly before us and shown in bright light. The benign can appear sinister if seen from an oblique angle or in the shadows. Looking at something up-close—for example, a human face—can foster epistemic and emotional connection with it. Distance tends to decrease understanding or sympathy. Looming figures convey menace or authority. We can feel as if we possess these qualities when we look down onto something. These are the means by which our dreams scare or delight us, and they are the techniques we use to control our emotional responses to what we perceive. They are also the very techniques that filmmakers use to elicit emotional responses from us. Such things as extreme camera angles, close-ups, and expressionistic lighting can all be used for this purpose. We have discussed how the use of these techniques results in images that do not correspond to ordinary perception. We drew an analogy with dreams in order to explain the kind of illusion they manufacture. And although we mentioned that our dreams, even our nocturnal dreams, can be realistic, we have yet to show how these techniques can add to the realism of a film.

When these techniques are used effectively in a film, they can commit us more forcefully than anything else to the reality of what is portrayed. They do this by eliciting from us emotional responses to the portrayed characters and events. While we *know* that what is portrayed is unreal, while it might not even look real, we *feel* as if it is real. What can be a better test of a film's realism than our responding emotionally to what it portrays? Rather than detracting from the illusion that we are watching actual events, the techniques for eliciting these emotional responses are the most effective tool for constructing a realistic illusion.

The black-and-white images of *Schindler's List* and the desaturated images of *Saving Private Ryan* can elicit emotions that will commit us to the reality of what is portrayed more powerfully than seemingly more realistic photography. Such techniques of cinematography lend the images a "documentary" quality, which tends to add to their credibility. More importantly, however, colorless or washed-out images convey a mood more appropriate to their stories than would color or highly saturated images. We are more likely to feel dark and somber emotions when watching images that are equally lacking in color and vibrancy. Although we do not ordinarily perceive events from extremely high or low angles, or at extreme distances, these ways of viewing characters or events will have the same effect in film as they do in our dreams. They enhance the emotional power of the images we perceive, and they determine which emotional responses we will have. Without these techniques, the realistic illusion would be difficult to achieve. Therefore, our emotional reactions to the portrayed events are an important part of the realistic illusion.

This third criterion for cinematic realism is dependent on the first two. An undisguised representation or a film that lacks fidelity to the real world will be less capable of eliciting emotional responses to the events it portrays. This criterion probably does not constitute a necessary condition for realism. It is possible for a film to be realistic yet evoke no emotional responses in the audience.[25] However, evoking these responses is likely the most popular motive for making a film realistic. Nevertheless, as I discuss in the next section, this motive has not gone without criticism.

A Criticism of Realism

Challenges to realism in film and art in general have been made on a variety of fronts. One challenge in particular is critical of realism as an aspiration in dramatic arts because of its tendency to produce emotional responses in audiences. The German playwright Bertolt Brecht believed that emotions preclude an audience's cognitive understanding of the events portrayed by a drama. He did not reject pleasurable entertainment as a legitimate function of drama. Entertainment can be pedagogically useful; for example, it engages the audience's attention. But the evoking of emotions, although having the same tendency to engross us in the drama, will not facilitate our understanding of the events it portrays. Brecht created a new style of performance employing what he called "alienation effects" that were meant to forestall certain emotional responses in the audience, particularly empathy.

Brecht adopted the name "epic" for his new form of theater. His purpose was to provoke the active and intellectual capacities of the audience, rather than their passive emotions: "The theatre leaves its spectators productively disposed even after the spectacle is over."[26] Brecht was a committed Marxist, therefore a revolutionary, and believed that theater could be an instrument for social transformation. However, he thought that, instead of inspiring the audience member to participate in such transformations, traditional theater merely "provides him sensations" or an "experience"; epic theater, in contrast, "arouses his capacity for action."[27] It does this by provoking his thoughts, rather than his emotions: "The essential point of epic theatre is perhaps that it appeals less to the feelings than to the spectator's reason."[28] For traditional theater, the custom has been that the "audience hangs its brains up in the cloakroom along with its coats."[29] Epic theater demands the intellectual engagement of the audience.

Brecht believed that empathy, in particular, tends to dull the intellectual capacities of the audience. It induces in the audience a kind of "hypnosis" or "intoxication."[30] Most importantly, it inclines them to take for granted the events that are portrayed by the drama rather than questioning them and their causes. He says of a portrayal of a character's suffering in a drama, "I must know why he's suffering." To do so, it does not help to *feel* that suffering ourselves; as he rhetorically asks, "Why should I suffer too?"[31] Merely inducing empathy in me will not enable me to understand the cause of his suffering and it will dull my capacity to engage in such reflection. I should not merely feel the character's suffering; I should also attempt to figure out a remedy for it.

We saw in the previous section how the more realistic a portrayal, the greater its tendency to induce emotional responses in the audience. Brecht sought to eschew from his dramas any of the techniques used to provoke such responses. His so-called alienation effects were meant to desiccate the drama of all sense of familiarity. It should seem alien to us, not an imitation of the actual world. The acting, for example, should "be as bad as possible"; the set designer should not attempt "to give the illusion of a room or a locality when he is building his sets."[32] Brecht also encouraged the use of such "unrealistic" elements as projections, placards, music, and anything else that would prevent the "engendering of illusion."[33] All these devices are meant to be a "barrier to empathy."[34] The effect of these techniques should be that the audience is no longer content with just feeling things about the drama; they will make an effort to understand what it portrays and then be disposed to act on that understanding. A drama that successfully employs alienation effects, according to Brecht, will be "for philosophers, but only for such philosophers as wished not just to explain the world but also to change it."[35]

Although Brecht was writing principally about the theater, he said that "for the film the principles of non-aristotelian drama (a type of drama not depending on empathy, mimesis) are immediately acceptable."[36] We have seen that Spielberg aims for the opposite in most of his films: a kind of imitation (mimesis) of reality that is capable of eliciting empathy for the film's characters. But is it the case that our understanding of the events portrayed in his films is hindered by the emotions they elicit? His most realistic films draw their stories from history. Is the empathy we feel for the characters of these stories a barrier to our understanding them and their situations?

I believe the situation is rather as Lester Friedman puts it: "feeling does not necessarily eliminate thinking."[37] But also, understanding is not confined to knowing just a list of facts about persons or events. Consider John Quincy Adams's advice to the lawyers for the Africans in *Amistad*. They understand, as he puts it, *what* their clients are, namely Africans. However, he tells them, "what you don't know—and as far as I can tell haven't bothered in the least to discover—is *who* they are." There are different, more thorough ways of understanding others. We can understand the emotions of others, and doing so involves more than just knowing that they are in an emotional state (which is still just to know a fact about them). Consider the familiar refrain, "You don't understand how I feel." When someone says that to us, he typically does not mean that we do not understand *that* he is sad or angry. He means that we are not feeling, or have never felt, what he is currently feeling. We place a great deal of importance on such understanding, but it is difficult to acquire.

The empathy that films are capable of provoking can equip us with this sort of understanding. Not only does such understanding *not* disable us from acting, but it is the strongest possible motive for acting. It is our strong emotions that compel us to perform the most ambitious or self-sacrificing actions. It is not simply their knowledge that, for example, there are Germans over that hill and that defeating them will help win the war that compels Spielberg's characters in *Saving Private Ryan* to risk their lives. It is their emotions that motivate them to act: both their patriotism and, perhaps more urgently, their fear of dying. We understand something important when we empathize with the characters in a film, even entirely fictional characters. Our empathy is capable of increasing our understanding of others, as well as ourselves. Such understanding has the potential to influence our behavior, since these emotions have a tendency to linger outside of the theater or after the DVD ends.

As Brecht implies in the quote I chose as the epigraph for this essay, realism is just one among many ways of telling a story. Brecht's epic theater has its own purposes, as does realism. We should use these purposes to decide on the best method for telling the story. But a legitimate purpose of stories is to elicit emotions in its spectators. Such emotions can have revolutionary potential, and—although this might sound trite—they can also make revolutions less necessary by giving us the understanding that will compel us, more than anything else, to treat others humanely.

Notes

1. Pat Nason, "Some Vets Having Tough Time with Movie," *United Press International,* July 30, 1998; Steven Komarow, "'Ryan' Triggering Memories of Combat," *USA Today,* July 28, 1998, D1 (this article also reports that the Department of Veterans Affairs had anticipated these reactions and kept a telephone hotline open over the weekend of the film's release).

2. Quoted in Amanda Riddle, "Those Who Lived War Moved by 'Saving Private Ryan,'" *Associated Press,* July 29, 1998.

3. Lester D. Friedman, *Citizen Spielberg* (Urbana: University of Illinois Press, 2006), 229.

4. This is in contrast, for example, to Michael Bay's *Pearl Harbor* (2001), which shied away from the graphic portrayal of wartime violence characteristic of *Saving Private*

Ryan. Some have suggested that the film did so in order to avoid a less economically valuable R rating. This was a choice (along with other things, such as poor acting and dialogue) that detracted from its realism.

5. Friedman, *Citizen Spielberg,* 133.

6. André Bazin, "Cinematic Realism," in *The Philosophy of Film: Introductory Texts and Readings,* ed. Thomas E. Wartenberg and Angela Curran (Oxford: Blackwell, 2005), 59, 60.

7. Jack C. Ellis and Betsy A. McLane, *A New History of Documentary Film* (London: Continuum, 2006), 6.

8. "Diegetic" sounds are those that come from within the imagined world of the film. "Nondiegetic" sounds, such as a musical score, come from outside that world and are added by filmmakers to do such things as influence our emotional response to the events taking place in the imagined world.

9. For example, films can be criticized for the implausibility of their plot twists or resolutions, the unbelievability of their story lines, and so on. We will consider other examples later.

10. William Earle, "Revolt against Realism in the Films," *Journal of Aesthetics and Art Criticism* 27:2 (Winter 1968): 145–51.

11. "Special Features," *Saving Private Ryan,* D-Day 60th Anniversary Edition DVD (Glendale, CA: DreamWorks, 2004); see also Friedman, *Citizen Spielberg,* 251–52.

12. There is another example in *Hook.* In the scene in which Robin Williams's character meets a trio of mermaids underwater, a member of the crew in a wetsuit is briefly visible behind one of the mermaids.

13. V. F. Perkins, "Film as Film," in *Film Theory and Criticism,* ed. Gerald Mast and Marshall Cohen (Oxford: Oxford University Press, 1985), 45.

14. Dominic Lopes, "Pictorial Realism," *Journal of Aesthetics and Art Criticism* 53:3 (Summer 1995): 277–85, at 277 and 278.

15. Nelson Goodman, *Languages of Art* (Indianapolis: Hackett, 1976), 34. We do not have space in this essay to examine it, but Goodman makes an objection in his book to the very project of this essay. He argues that judgments about realism vary across cultures and over time, concluding that "realism is relative, determined by the system of representation standard for a given culture or person at a given time" (p. 37); thus, it is not an inherent relation between the artwork and what it represents that makes the former realistic. If this is the case, then this essay can at most succeed in specifying criteria for realism specific to our culture. However, even if Goodman is correct that there is cultural variation among judgments about artistic realism, that does not show that the *concept* of realism is relative. Disagreements about artistic realism might only reveal differences in the application of the concept (analogously, different cultures and time periods might differ in the moral judgments they make, but not in their understanding of the concept of morality). In fact, this is all that the relativism claim could amount to, because if different cultures truly have different understandings of the concept of realism, then they lack a shared concept about which they could disagree. Therefore,

this essay can succeed in specifying the criteria for the concept "realism," but there will inevitably still be disagreements between, and within, cultures and time periods about how those criteria are correctly employed.

16. That is, to believe on wrong or inappropriate grounds. To be deceived is not necessarily to hold a false belief, because it is possible to be deceived into holding a true belief. For example, someone who has no other evidence available might fabricate evidence (e.g., a photograph) to convince me of the truth of a claim of hers (e.g., that she once met Steven Spielberg). If I come to believe the claim based on that evidence, I have been deceived. Nevertheless, what I believe may still be true (she actually did once meet Spielberg).

17. A classic example of an exception to this is the science fiction short *La Jetée* (1962), which consists almost entirely of still photographs that do not try to evince an illusion of motion.

18. F. E. Sparshott, "Vision and Dream in the Cinema," in *Philosophy of Film and Motion Pictures,* ed. Noël Carroll and Jinhee Choi (Oxford: Blackwell, 2006), 85.

19. Sparshott, "Vision and Dream in the Cinema," 85.

20. Even documentaries often try to disguise their status as representation. For example, they typically conceal the crew and equipment from the audience.

21. So-called gesture-based interfaces are being developed by several companies, including Microsoft and Apple; see "The Trouble with Computers," *Economist,* September 8, 2007, Technology Quarterly, 21–22.

22. Even some of the more fantastic elements of the film reveal a commitment to realism. In designing the precog visions, Spielberg's crew consulted with cognitive scientists who have studied witness testimony. "Deconstructing *Minority Report*: Precog Visions," *Minority Report,* DVD, disc 2 (Glendale, CA: DreamWorks, 2002).

23. A film can provoke emotional responses in other ways. An offensive or irreverent film, even a poorly made film, might cause audience members to feel a variety of emotions (e.g., disgust, nausea, amusement). But these are responses to the film, and not the fictional events portrayed by the film.

24. For literature on this topic, a good place to start is Christopher R. Trogan and Dean A. Kowalski's "The Paradox of Fictional Belief and Its Moral Implications in *Jaws,*" in this volume. More advanced examinations include Kendall Walton, "Fearing Fictions," *Journal of Philosophy* 75:1 (January 1978): 5–27 (a seminal work on this topic); Noël Carroll, *The Philosophy of Horror or Paradoxes of the Heart* (London: Routledge, 1990), especially pages 59–96; and Malcolm Turvey, "Seeing Theory: On Perception and Emotional Response in Current Film Theory," in *Film Theory and Philosophy,* ed. Richard Allen and Murray Smith (Oxford: Clarendon Press, 1997), 431–57.

25. An example of such a film might be one that resembles security camera footage from, say, a parking garage. What we watch looks like such footage, but it is only a representation (the parking garage is a studio set, the drivers are actors, some of the cars are plastic mock-ups, and so on). Not only is it filmed in a way that would not elicit emotional responses (except, perhaps, boredom), nothing eventful happens to any of

the film's characters, or their cars. This would not be a very interesting film to watch, but it would be highly realistic.

26. Bertolt Brecht, "A Short Organum for the Theatre," in *Brecht on Theatre*, ed. and trans. John Willett (New York: Hill and Wang, 1992), 205 (hereafter *BT*).

27. Brecht, "The Modern Theatre Is the Epic Theatre," in *BT*, 37.

28. Brecht, "The Epic Theatre and Its Difficulties," in *BT*, 23.

29. Brecht, "A Dialogue about Acting," in *BT*, 27.

30. Brecht, "The Modern Theatre Is the Epic Theatre," 38.

31. Brecht, "Conversation about Being Forced into Empathy," in *BT*, 271.

32. Brecht, "A Short Organum for the Theatre," 187, 203.

33. Brecht, "The Street Scene," in *BT*, 122.

34. Brecht, "A Short Organum for the Theatre," 192.

35. Brecht, "Theatre for Pleasure or Theatre for Instruction," in *BT*, 72. This is a variation of the philosopher Karl Marx's famous lament, "The philosophers have only *interpreted* the world, in various ways; the point, however, is to *change* it"; Marx, "Theses on Feuerbach," in *The Marx-Engels Reader*, ed. Robert C. Tucker (New York: W. W. Norton, 1978), 145. As Brecht was not content with merely presenting realistic portrayals of the world, Marx was not content to merely interpret or explain the world. Both believed that there was something wrong with the social and economic organization of people in this world and that their respective disciplines were capable of bringing about change in these areas.

36. Brecht, "The Film, the Novel, and the Epic Theatre," in *BT*, 50.

37. Friedman, *Citizen Spielberg*, 241.

A.I.: *Artificial Intelligence*

Artistic Indulgence or Advanced Inquiry?

V. Alan White

Film critics tend to be clumpy in their craft. It is the rare film indeed that divides them as sharply as did *A.I.: Artificial Intelligence* (2001), which puts it ironically in the same category as another film with a two-part title—Stanley Kubrick's *2001: A Space Odyssey*. When *2001* first debuted in 1968 reviews were a morass of giddy delight with the "psychedelic" visuals, bitter disappointment with an unintelligible script, and "what-the-hell-was-that?" head-scratching.[1] *A.I.* produced much the same reaction, with critics generally pleased with its sensory cinematic elements but otherwise at war about plot, point, and philosophy.[2] The irony of this comparison arises from the well-known fact that *A.I.* was itself the constructed child—many would say the bastard child—of both Kubrick and Spielberg, since Kubrick first obtained the rights to the story and began scripting before his death, with Spielberg taking the project to completion.[3] However, although the two films shared rough-going at their premiers, *2001* has evolved in critical regard to become one of the most respected films of all time.

One may wonder whether *A.I.* might also someday age into something of a surprise vintage. This essay will argue that it will, and for similar reasons that its companion did. The cosmic themes of *2001* were too much for its 1968 audiences to absorb all at once, and required time to be understood in all their complexity and subtlety. Similarly, I will argue that *A.I.* has not yet been adequately appreciated for its own thematic overtures about humanity and intelligence, and that future reassessments might well launch the film into the starry firmament of *2001*. Its fate in this respect is probably tied to future developments in the field of artificial intelligence. Thus, in part I will claim there is good reason to believe that the portrayal of AI in *A.I.* augurs—if I may be forgiven a mildly abusive film reference—things to come.

Plot and Major Themes

The film is set in a future where climate change has transformed the earth, drowning the coasts in the oceans and forcing the government in what was the United States to enforce strict childbearing laws. Society is a mixture of carefully controlled civility and Wild West lawlessness, depending, it seems, on economic class and location. Humans and androidlike robots, distinguished respectively as "orga" and "mecha," freely intermingle, although it is clear that mecha are viewed as merely subservient instruments of orga, have no status politically or morally, and are "legal" only if properly licensed.

Enter the Swintons, Henry (Sam Robards) and Monica (Frances O'Connor), whose only child has been cryogenically stored to await a cure for a serious illness. Henry, it turns out, works for Cybertronics, one of many mecha manufacturers and headed by Professor Allen Hobby (William Hurt), who wishes to create a mecha who can love rather than merely simulate human activity. The mecha prototype (Haley Joel Osment), named David and designed after Hobby's own demised son, is offered to the Swintons for a trial, which they accept. After initial awkwardness the couple accepts David, and Monica activates in him an imprinting program that produces unconditional love for Monica, thereafter "Mommy" in David's eyes. But soon the frozen son is revived and rejoins the family, and friction develops between him and David as they both seek favor with Monica.

The son, Martin (Jake Thomas), feels displaced by a mere thing, and resents Monica's overtures to David in his absence, such as her giving David his favored supertoy, Teddy (voiced by Jack Angel), a robotic teddy bear with considerable AI properties himself. In an act of thinly disguised cruelty, Martin has Monica read *Pinocchio* to them to force the issue of who is a boy and who is a toy, like Teddy. At another time, Martin deceives David into sneaking into his parents' room to snip off a bit of Monica's hair, which causes Monica and Henry to awake and find their mecha son next to their bed with scissors frighteningly in hand, as Martin intended. Later, at a pool party, other children try to test David's "pain response," causing David to clutch Martin in seeking protection from them and to fall with him into the pool, nearly drowning Martin. Henry insists on returning David to Cybertronics for destruction, but Monica flees with David, Teddy in hand, to a forest; here she releases him to fend for himself, warning him to avoid "Flesh Fairs," where feral robots are variously destroyed in a macabre carnival atmosphere for the enjoyment of paying orga.

David is soon captured and slated for destruction in such a fair, but he manages to escape with Teddy after being aided by Gigolo Joe (Jude Law), a

A.I.: Artificial Intelligence, Warner Bros Pictures/Amblin Entertainment, 2001. A proper appreciation of Spielberg's portrayal of the three "mecha"—Gigolo Joe (Jude Law, *right*), Teddy (voiced by Jack Angel), and especially David (Haley Joel Osment, *left*)—can lead to surprising conclusions about the nature of consciousness and personhood. (MovieGoods, Inc.)

mecha sex surrogate who is himself an escaped illegal, having been framed for murder. The three go on a quest to find what David only knows as the Blue Fairy, which he comes to see as both associated with the circumstances of his origin and, following the scenario of *Pinocchio*, the only hope of making him into a real boy that Monica could love. Eventually, they make their way to a partly submerged New York and find Hobby, David's creator, where David discovers he is in fact nothing but a replicated mecha with special programming. In despair, David throws himself into the ocean surrounding Manhattan; he is rescued by Joe and Teddy in a submersible helicopter, but not before—as luck would have it—David actually glimpses the Blue Fairy as part of a deluged Coney Island *Pinocchio* display. Joe is immediately captured (shouting "I am, I was!"), but he just manages to submerge the craft with David and Teddy aboard. David takes the controls and makes his way awkwardly to the Blue Fairy statue, accidentally pulling a teetering Ferris wheel on top of the submersible and trapping it before the smiling Fairy. Pleading repeatedly to make him "into a real, live boy," David, with Teddy, fades into the darkness of time.

Abruptly, the time is 2,000 years later, and we see an advanced silent aircraft making its way between the dilapidated skyscrapers of a New York now encased in a frozen ocean. Aboard are advanced mecha—confusingly resembling classic aliens from other Spielberg films—who have just discovered David in his icy tomb. Reviving him (and Teddy), the mecha "download" his experiences and find him to be the only remaining remnant of mecha originally made by humans. They reconstruct his Swinton home to provide familiar surroundings but tell David (through an animated Blue Fairy, voiced by Meryl Streep) they cannot revive Monica, whom David still pleads for, because they have no DNA sample to work from. Teddy then produces from a storage pouch the hair David was coaxed into snipping from her, and David insists on bringing her back. The future mecha comply, but with a warning: the technology will only revive orga for one single day, after which they slip into irreversible oblivion. With careful warnings given to David as safeguards to prevent her disorientation, Monica returns to David for one day of companionship and playful abandon. Going groggily off to bed, her diurnal existence near its end, Monica tells David she loves him. David, now weeping but finally fulfilled in his wish (and along with Teddy), settles beside her, lights dimming, to fall asleep in the only way mecha can—by shutting down.

The themes in this complex and at times bewildering tale are large and numerous—themes about the social nature of identity, the problem of mind and brain, the place of emotion in thought and action, the many appearances of prejudice, the relation of technology to human development, the status of thinking beings beside humans, and more. It is easy to argue that the inherent flaw of such an ambitious film is that it attempts to do too much, and I cannot say that I am unsympathetic to that complaint as lodged against *A.I.* But to focus only on overreaching aspirations of the production can miss flashes of brilliance in its details, and this film sparkles with them. For my own purposes I will limit my attention to some of those more successful elements of *A.I.* as they relate to various themes of the central problem of what minds are. It is from a consideration of these themes that I will advocate the critical rehabilitation of *A.I.* overall.

Can Machines Think?

Readers may recognize that my section heading here is borrowed from a momentous article by Alan Turing, "Computing Machinery and Intelligence."[4] Turing's answer to the question is yes, but if and only if the candidate machine can pass what has come to be called the Turing test. Roughly, that test is a purely conversational one, and not unlike what David and Joe experience in putting questions to Dr. Know (akin to a generic Einstein, voiced by Robin Williams) in search of the Fairy. We place the machine and an ordinary human being behind screens and put questions—any questions—to both. If after sufficient time we could not confidently say which screen concealed the machine, then we should declare that that machine can indeed think. Note that the machine need not communicate verbally (though neither then should the human)—the test can be validated with printed responses.

Turing's test has been both very influential in the emergence of AI technology and at the same time highly controversial for what it purports to show. Many philosophers of mind complain that such an operationalist/functionalist (externalist) definition completely misses the point of what it is to be intelligent in the ordinary self-reflective sense that human minds are. They argue that human minds are self-conscious, with a unique first-person perspective that cannot be assessed by a third-party Turing test, either for people or for machines.[5]

These latter philosophers are concerned about the mind-brain (or mind-body) problem. Since before Plato it has been noted that minds function in a way that is quite different from the way bodily organs work. Arms and bowels move (though in distinct ways), lungs heave, teeth grind, eyebrows arch, and so on, but minds perceive, reflect, remember, anticipate, plan, and recognize others and themselves without any sort of obvious physical marker. So it seems possible that minds and physical items might be very different kinds of things or occurrences. Dualists claim just that—minds and brains are distinguishable in some ultimately real (metaphysical) sense. Monists demur, claiming that metaphysically the mind and the brain are one. Both camps are packed with variations on these two themes, and there are dozens of particular views on how to map out the mind-brain relationship. Within both camps, however, there are a considerable number of philosophers who agree that, whatever minds and brains finally come to in reality, the Turing test simply misses the point of the necessity of inner subjective mental experience to account for mind.

Return to the case of David. Does David think in the subjectively qualitative sense? In part it seems that *A.I.* is dedicated to showing across the span of the film that this is at least possible. When he is introduced to the Swintons, David is portrayed as highly machinelike; he moves in hesitant ways, tests surroundings but adjusts immediately as a feedback mechanism would, mimes eating at the dinner table, and forces a bizarre laugh stimulated by Monica's messy pasta repast. He, of course, cannot eat; he is also incapable of sleeping, although he closes his eyes and lies still to mimic it. But the change in David at the time of Monica's imprinting him is poignant and startling. His face changes from his normally fixed simper of a smile to a vague distraught expression of real need—he immediately falls into Monica's arms, hugging her with a palpable hunger for affection. His overall behavior becomes much more human, too. After he is imprinted, he tries to eat in imitation of Martin (who caustically teases David with the fact that he can really do so), but damages himself in the process. His reactively stubborn but imprudent disregard for his own welfare just to spite someone is uncomfortably recognizable as a trait of our own.

Back to the Turing test for a moment, where it is the audience that must make the call on David's intelligence. This is a tougher Turing test, however (call it the "strengthened Turing test," or STT), because David is not behind a screen—he is on it. We know he is a robot; therefore believing that he not only is intelligent but also has a mind sufficiently like ours is going to be an uphill battle. In part this is because of what I must call "anthropoph-ronism"—our tendency to accept that minds exist only in human beings. The fact that David is not an orga is an intuitive basis for believing that, for all his humanlike behavior, he cannot have the inner subjective aspects of mind we experience.

The difference between Henry's and Monica's reactions to David's nearly drowning Martin gives some insight into this point. Henry, after all, is part of the mecha industry itself—he knows that David is composed of parts that imitate human behavior well enough, but still are mere constructs of human ingenuity. Monica, on the other hand, has known David from the get-go as a being—a mecha, yes, but still an entity she willingly elected to interact with. Although these interactions were awkward and hesitant at first, they worked well enough to produce in her a curiosity about whether, after imprinting, they might improve. From Monica's perspective, they thereafter certainly did—David and Mommy grew closer together. To some extent, Monica demonstrably buys in to David's elevated status as assessed by her version of the STT—she elects to defy her husband (and probably the law) and release David rather than have him dismantled, even warning him of the Flesh Fairs that could destroy him. However, her love for David, if you can call it that, is not stronger than that for her family—she never considers leaving with David, and even becomes angry when he tries to cling to her as she flees from him. Her post-imprinting STT assessment is definitely a mixed one, but still one that is certainly less anthropophronic than Henry's. Of course, David was imprinted *only* with Monica and not Henry, and there are no scenes in which David and Henry have significant social truck with one another. There is a strong clue here about how mecha like David can pass the STT not just for Monica, but for all of us. I will discuss this clue later. But first, I must return to some philosophical concerns mentioned above that would undermine any possibility of passing the STT, and put those sufficiently to rest.

Of Bats and Brains

Earlier I mentioned that mind-body theorists of all stripes frequently excoriate supporters of the Turing test for failing to account for inner subjective experience. They argue that while the test provides some empirical ground for believing that robots can successfully *imitate* human intelligence, it cannot ever approach the problem of "qualia." The latter term is one philosophers use to refer to the nature of subjective experience, which includes thought, imagination, self-awareness, feeling, emotion, and sensation. The popularity of the use of that term is traceable to the influence of an article by Thomas Nagel in 1974, famously entitled, "What Is It Like to Be a Bat?"[6] Therein Nagel posits that the sense of the title question turns crucially on the meaningfulness of our knowing in first-person fashion the sensibleness of the phrase, "What is it like?" from that inner perspective. We do know what it is like to see and smell a rose, or to feel rage and pleasure, or to imagine kissing Scarlett Johansson or Jude Law (take your pick). These inner-known items are "qualia" of experience. Do we know what it is like to be a bat? Well, that is certainly arguable, but since we know what it is like to be a human being, the question posed for bats (but not bricks) is certainly not nonsense. So qualia in some sense are part of what it is to be or to have a mind. If this is so, then David should have some qualia—what it is like to be a truly thinking, experiencing machine.

However, some philosophers have expressed severe doubts about the possibility of this. The most famous dissent in this regard is due to John Searle, who disputes the significance of the Turing test for judging intelligence, as well as the prospect for machines having a humanlike inner life. His skepticism is expressed in his famous "Chinese room" thought experiment, a version of which I will now supply.[7]

Suppose we have a room with a person inside. There are two slots in the room, one for input and one for output. Strips of paper containing Chinese writing are put into the room in the input, and strips of paper with English translations emerge later from the output. Should one not know what the internal structure of the room involves, one would in Turing terms be justified in believing that the room "understands" Chinese because it can successfully translate it. But the real force of Searle's example comes in his description of what goes on inside the room. The person inside does not understand Chinese or English; rather, the person is given intricate instructions (in another language) on how to match Chinese characters with English words so that the output paper results from the matching. Searle's ingenuity is clear: the "mechanism" of the room (the person) does not know *intelligently* how to translate even though it spits out correct translations—it just follows step-by-step instruction. So although the room externally would pass a Turing-style test for translation intelligence, it actually is *not* intelligently translating. Perforce, no machine that does anything like such pure rule-following, as pocket translators now commonly do, can be considered intelligent.

Searle's Chinese room also demonstrates something about qualia. The person inside the room definitely has qualia—he or she sees the strips of paper and word characters, correlates images, and so on—but does not possess the qualia of *understanding* Chinese or English. That is, he or she does not know or experience *what it is like* to understand Chinese or English, or to be bilingual. But now replace the person in the room with circuitry, as we do with pocket translating devices. They are programmed in a machine language for rule-following that matches symbols in one language with those of another. By analogy the machine certainly does not know what it is like to know a language or be bilingual, but presumably it also does not know what it is like *to see* symbols or *to match* them by recognition. That is, the machine has no qualia at all. So something like a real translation device can pass a limited Turing test for intelligent translation, but actually is not intelligent and does not have a mind.

Searle argues that these points generalize to dim the prospects for anything like real intelligence being realizable in computing devices. They may get more sophisticated and do more things, but they are never more than complicated rule-following devices that can have no intelligent inner qualia life. Like David, they may be constructed so as to fool the best of us who know nothing of their working internal mechanisms, and they may be able to pass the most stringent of classic Turing tests. But no machine can pass the Strengthened Turing Test in which we know that a computing machine is involved—for by Searle's reasoning, we know that there can be no mind therein.

Searle would say that Monica hoodwinks herself—she allows herself to be betrayed by her own emotional reactions to David and does not consider what he really is. David, by Searle's lights, cannot feel or experience love, although he can meticulously imitate it. Therefore, insufficient reflection on or awareness of David's nonmind status could lead to mistakes, such as that of the crowd at the Flesh Fair where David is slated to be destroyed. In that watershed scene, David and Joe are literally positioned for destruction, because the Fair's producer establishes that they are indeed mecha and deserve nothing more than a creative way to be sent to the junk pile. However, David pleads for his life, and the crowd responds by believing that David is a real boy ("Mecha don't plead for their lives!" cries one crowd member [Lily Knight]), throwing trash at the Fair's producer, and chanting for David's release. The ensuing chaos results in David and Joe's freedom. However, Searle again would insist that the crowd gives in to close-to-human imitation, mistaking it for the real thing. The crowd does not really *know* that David is a machine—if they did, this would license their erstwhile call for David's destruction. Searle would probably say that David is an interesting articulated mannequin at best, and his destruction would be of no grave moral importance.

A considerable number of philosophers and AI researchers would disagree with Searle, maintaining that there is no reason David cannot achieve real consciousness since we (real-life orga) manage to do so, and at bottom there is no real difference between us and comparably complex machines.[8]

From the mind-body perspective, "physicalist" (or "materialist") monists argue that if the human brain is able to produce conscious states, and the brain is nothing but fancy biological "wetware" much like the hardware of a computer, then the mind is somehow a product of the proper function of the brain. Just as the screensaver program running on a monitor is nothing more than software instructions firing in binary code through a microprocessor, the mind is a special, private, internal monitor produced by the brain's neurons firing. No one would seriously propose that the screensaver has a special metaphysical existence in its own right independently of the hardware; similarly, physicalists argue that neither does the mind exist in any way independently of the brain.

It has been argued that because mental phenomena have characteristics that are not describable in terms of physical properties, the physicalist project of explaining and reducing consciousness to brain states may not be in principle achievable. The classic alternative dualism of René Descartes, however, which makes mind and brain separate entities, has intractable problems of its own, since there seems to be no way to account for how mind and brain can interact to produce ordinary human behavior. How can we make headway (as it were) about David's metaphysical mental status when we cannot even explain our own?

Hard-Headed Physicalists versus Empty-Headed Zombies

In the highly influential book *The Conscious Mind,* the philosopher David Chalmers created a furor by arguing that physicalism is provably wrong and that therefore some sort of dualism is more likely correct.[9] Chalmers's argument against physicalism is most frequently referred to as "the zombie argument."

The zombie argument depends crucially on the idea of the very conceivability of the concept of zombies—humanlike beings who in every outward aspect look, act, and appear indistinguishable from people, but are devoid of consciousness or any such mental states. Since such zombies are atom-for-atom *physically* identical to us, if physicalism were correct then such zombies would not be zombies at all: they would have to have minds. So if zombies are merely *conceivable* in a clear, self-consistent way, then physicalism cannot possibly be correct.

Chalmers sets out a rather complex logic and semantics of why zombies are conceivable, and although many philosophers have hailed this account itself as a major philosophical achievement (and many contest its adequacy as well), it need not concern us here. For our purposes let it be posited that the zombie argument is sound; after all, just *intuitively* it seems we can consistently conceive of zombies. In that case, physicalism is wrong not just in accounting for *our* minds, but for AI minds such as David's as well. Then what is left?

Chalmers realized that Cartesian dualism will not do as a substitute because of the interaction problem. But what if one abandoned metaphysical dualism for a monism that included a dualism of physical and mental properties? (I should immediately add that Chalmers was not the first to propose this sort of view.) By such a monistic dual-properties view, the physical brain and conscious mind are two sides of one metaphysical coin. Physical properties of a thing are those publicly accessible to all observers; mental properties are those accompanying the physical that are inherently private and privileged to the bearer. Both sets of properties are further unified in being causally effective, so that their interaction is a built-in feature. So, for example, the proper functioning of a brain betokens the accompanying inwardness of mental consciousness, just as a properly thinking mind betokens that same functioning brain. There is a necessary connection between these two sets of properties such that one type of property entails the other, especially in terms of the sophistication and complexity of the parallel properties. Complex minds *must* have complex brains—that is all there is to it.

This view is not without commitments that many philosophers see as problematic. For one, the monistic "thing" that manifests brains and minds is a je ne sais quoi that cannot be known directly as separate, purely physical or mental things can. For another, the necessity of irreducibly tying mental with physical properties means that *all* existing things have these two sides—that something like "panpsychism" (mind is everywhere anything is) is true. Still, Chalmers's property dualism is compatible with much of what we know about ourselves. Damaged brains seem to involve equally damaged minds. Alter a brain temporarily with drugs or alcohol, and there are altered states of consciousness. But most intriguingly, it seems possible that (from one side of the equation) it is *only* the sophistication of physical property states that makes for equally sophisticated mental states. This introduces the plausibility of "multiple realizability" of consciousness; that is, as long as certain complex types of physical states are realized, the accompanying types of mental states are too. If we can build brains out of silicon and metal that produce behavioral physical states *sufficiently similar* to those produced by biological human brains, then we can automatically instantiate conscious minds in those artificial brains. AI, compatibly with

Chalmers's view, therefore becomes possible not merely as at best imitative of human beings, as Searle argued; rather, a sufficiently complex AI David is as conscious as any of us are.

David's Love: Good, Bad, and Ugly

There is a crucial weasel-word phrase in what I just said, which I empha-sized for further analysis here. What constitutes the meaning of *sufficiently similar* behavioral physical states that might signal true AI consciousness? Of course, if I could parse out the exact meaning of that phrase I would be way ahead of contemporary AI theory, and clearly I am no expert in the area. However, *A.I.* does give me fodder to speculate on how the portrayal of David fails to live up to certain current widely accepted criteria of AI, as well as how it might augur other aspects of where AI must go in the future to achieve true AI consciousness. The discussion will at least move in the direction of nailing down what such sufficient similarity must be.

Current research in AI is by no means unilateral in its methodology or interests. Some researchers concentrate on machines' perception and ad-justment to environment, others focus on linguistics and natural language communication, and still others study heuristics: learning and problem solving. No doubt real advances in AI that would approach the depiction as embodied in David would involve all of these areas and more. To appreciate how far AI must go in the future, however, I will examine only one issue in the last-mentioned area of research: belief revision in learning and problem solving—what for David might best be termed "the Blue Fairy problem."

There seems to be consensus among AI researchers in this area that true AI must involve "nonmonotonic logic" in acts of reasoning. This point is due to remarks on the issue by an esteemed founding researcher in AI, Marvin Minsky, in 1975.[10] Minsky observed that classical logic involved "monotonic" (purely deductive) reasoning. That is, if a given body of as-sumptions logically entailed a consequent or result, then further addition of assumptions would not change the entailment. So, for example, if it is assumed that the addition of 2 + 2 entails 4, then the addition of the further assumption that 2 + 4 entails 6 does not change the conclusion that 2 + 2 entails 4. Monotonic reasoning does not tolerate the alteration of proven reasoning by added assumptions or evidence.

But clearly monotonic reasoning is incompatible with the ordinary understanding of intelligent belief revision owing to added evidence, as when children find that, despite some good initial evidence from parents that Santa exists, evidence accrued over time shows that he does not. In *A.I.,*

David reasons that if Monica abandons him in the forest and thus does not love him as she does Martin because he is not "a real, live boy," and that, drawing from the *Pinocchio* story, the Blue Fairy exists and can transform him into a real boy, then to make Monica love him he must seek out the Blue Fairy. Much of the plot line from the film is dependent not only on David initially drawing this conclusion from the information he received while with the Swinton family, but also on his ultimately never swerving from his conviction that this conclusion is true. So in one way David is portrayed as a simplistic (but genuinely—and thus positively—*childish*?) non-AI monotonic reasoner—he cannot be dissuaded from his fantasy of transformation even though he observes, for example, that mecha are just grist for the bloodlust mill of the Flesh Fairs.

However, the film shows some real sensitivity for the necessity of nonmonotonic reasoning in David's behavior, too, although perhaps too briefly for full impact on the audience. When David finally finds Hobby he discovers many facts not consonant with his reasoning about the Blue Fairy. His vague recollection of the shape of the fairy, elicited by Gigolo Joe's inquiries, turns out to be the icon of Hobby's company that David presumably saw when first activated. He realizes as well at this point that he is not in fact a unique creation—there are a number of Davids like him (and female versions, Darlenes)—one of which he destroys in a fit of rage. He then despairs, having suffered disillusionment full force, sits on a precipice over the ocean swamping New York, and (seemingly deliberately) falls into it, presumably to corrode and extinguish himself. The significance at this point is that *because of added knowledge* he has lost his vision of hope for transformation. His belief in the Blue Fairy is temporarily gone. That is, until—Spielberg/Kubrick *ex machina*—David just happens to glimpse the undersea Blue Fairy Coney Island exhibit, restoring reason to believe in the Fairy's existence. And so he subsequently does believe—acting on that belief to his and Teddy's powered-down oblivion in the submersible before their ultimate resurrection by the futuristic mecha.

The film thus *weakly* demonstrates nonmonotonic reasoning; however, because of the prevalence of David's monotonic obsession with the Blue Fairy through much of it, and reinforced by David's improbable sight of her as he tries to commit suicide, this presented aspect of his AI might be lost. But it is there nonetheless. Still, as evidence of full-fledged AI, an AI commensurate with the best of human intelligence, this sequence is not up to the task of representing how machines can nonmonotonically duplicate insight, creativity, and true inventive genius.

I doubt, of course, that Kubrick or Spielberg in any way overtly wished to show that David was capable of vigorous nonmonotonic reasoning. In the attempt to characterize his angst, however, David's capacity for revised belief is at least unveiled. One should recall that although this film is about AI, it is not a documentary—it is a from-the-heart commentary on so many aforementioned themes of our own humanity, and it aggressively inquires if and where human essence might be found beyond our own skin.

That is an offshoot, I will now argue, of the most important aspect of AI displayed by *A.I.* It is a theme that runs throughout the film and is its ultimate salvation as cinematic art and philosophy. That is, individuality, identity and intelligence—ours or David's—is at least a partial function of full-blooded social interaction. David's flaws in this regard form the backbone of the pathos of the film—but they are ironically some of the best demonstrations of what AI requires to make David a "real, live boy."

In the beginning, with his placement in the Swinton family, David reflects nothing but programmed and purely reactive social skills, and this makes him alternately creepy and comical. For example, Monica places David in a closet just to be rid of him after he inappropriately interrupts her. He obediently sits where she has placed him, then when she finally lets him out he automatically asks, "Is it a game?" He is clueless about his being treated as if he were an incontinent pet. I have averred to the fact that David in another case initiates laughter in a way that betokens situational programming—he is stimulated by a slapstick instance of Monica's messy eating. These reactions merely *affect* humanity, but not in a convincing way. In effect, the narrative poses the STT for David first to show how he fails it. Of course, this is to set up the audience for David's transformation after imprinting, and thus to challenge the audience to take the STT on David's behalf again.

The narrative device of imprinting is an inspired one for the film—and may well foreshadow similar advances in AI in the future—for it embodies in black box fashion a particular instilled *need* in David. (*This* is the clue I referred to earlier.) I have already alluded to the transfiguration of David's expression at this crucial moment. It is theatrically important for the audience, for it offers the chance to regard David as "instantly emotionalized," and sends the audience on its merry way thereafter to assess him by the STT. But the imprinting is also crucial to the narrative sense of the film because it conveys the possibility of David's embodying a real mind with real mental properties. David is presented as *needing* Monica in the fashion of any truly social creature—as recognition that another being can provide fulfillment, comfort, and reciprocal caring. As reflected in some nonhuman social interactions, such as monogamous "lovebirds" caring for one another, it is not even clear that this recognition need be self-consciously held to be genuine—bird brains may be simple, but clearly something genuinely mental accompanies this phenomenon. With David, however, we have strong behavioral clues that he *knows* his craving for Monica's affection. In STT terms, he gives every indication of thinking about, feeling strongly about, and even loving Monica, and with imprinting he begins to enjoy a real social relationship.

One problem with this represented form of imprinting, however, is that it is person-specific: from the point of imprinting onward only Monica will do to fulfill David's needs, even if at the end of the film it is only a recreated Monica that finally does so. (And note—this ameliorates the nonmonotonic criticism above. With such imprinting, who else *can* David treat in the same social way?) David accepts others into his social sphere—Martin, Henry, Teddy, Gigolo Joe—but he never betrays anything like a need for them in the same way he does for Monica. And some, like the doppelganger David he *viciously kills* in a jealous rage, and Teddy, whom he thoughtlessly and unapologetically entraps with him in his obsessive pursuit of the Blue Fairy, are not seen as worthy of regard in achieving his eventual goal. However—remember the minimal case of "lovebirds"—this focus is the device by which the story line of *A.I.* narrows and enforces the audience STT assessment. Does David *really* love Monica or not?

One complaint among critics with at least an intuitive sense of the issues here is that the ending of the film illegitimately sledgehammers home the message that David indeed passes the STT test; he *must* turn out to be a real, live boy after all. The complaint is defensible to an extent. Tears are jerked from the audience in part because they flow freely from David's eyes, presumably because this capacity was built into his original mecha-nism. As audience emotions are tugged, something like the STT affirmative supposedly comes in tow. However, the audience knows that Monica at the end of the film is not his imprinted mother. She is at best a recreated Monica, though apparently with enough intact personality and selective memory of David and their circumstances that she seems genuinely to enjoy their fleeting time together, thus finally allowing David to find contentment and peace with his yearning for her. Nevertheless, the presented conceit works—the viewer is drawn into believing David's tears *are* ones of real happiness, the kind of happiness that cooing lovebirds, avian and otherwise, know as the emotional height of experience. David may love *only* Monica—or what adequately stands in for Monica—but love her he does. The STT is passed, because by audience acclamation David is a minimally acceptable truly social being.

A.I. Reassessed?

It may seem like quite a stretch to conclude that *A.I.* presents anything special or new in bringing AI to the screen, and thus that, while it is an inspiring and even bold depiction of the possibility of artificial intelligence, it advances anything of substance beyond, say, *Blade Runner* (1982) or *Bicentennial Man* (1999). These latter films—and others—pose the same questions as *A.I.*, and even advance the possibility that the social ability to love and to be loved is sine qua non for recognition as something equal to ourselves. The trial to attain membership in the tribe is an ancient rite of passage for many cultures, after all, and all of these films press that issue for admission into the human world at large in a similar manner.

But no film that I am aware of places this issue of admission to the human tribe squarely on one capacity among many: the triggered need within even an artificial being for at least one other person to complete *itself.* The narrative black box device of imprinting, as I have argued, is the one poignant and episodic turning point of this whole film, and the plausibility of David's passing the STT is thrust entirely upon the plot track of David being first embraced by his one object of need, Monica, only to be rejected by her, leading to his hopeless adventure in pursuit of transformation for gaining her acceptance. In the end, however, *it is just his original and unchanged imprinted need,* ironically focused on a *transformed* Monica, that gains him entry to the tribe of humanity—certainly by his own lights in the context of the film, but finally from the audience perspective as well. His hope of becoming a real, live boy ultimately depends on nothing but himself as he has been all along post-imprinting—needing only acceptance in his single-minded need for another to achieve final personal fulfillment.

Ray Kurzweil, an inventor, futurist author, and advisor to Bill Gates, has predicted (and bet $10,000) that the Turing test will be passed by a machine by 2029.[11] That may be so—but the STT? I predict passing *that* stringent test will require a machine much like David, one who is constructed to yearn deeply for at least one other indisputably conscious being who completes it in the minimal sense of true social existence. When that will happen—if it ever does—I cannot predict. But if the threshold of the STT *is* crossed, I predict that *A.I.* will be seen to have been a monumentally prescient and accurate prediction of how that was finally achieved, and the film's elevation to classic status will thereby be assured.

Notes

1. An illustrative example is Roger Ebert's original review, which was positive but not exactly glowing; see "A Review of *2001* (1968)," *The Kubrick Site*, http://www.visual memory.co.uk/amk/doc/0046.html (accessed September 23, 2007).

2. A representative sample of decidedly and strongly mixed reviews can be found at http://www.rottentomatoes.com/m/ai_artificial_intelligence (accessed September 23, 2007).

3. The original story was Brian Aldiss's "Supertoys Last All Summer Long," *Harper's Bazaar*, December 1969.

4. Alan M. Turing, "Computing Machinery and Intelligence," *Mind* 59 (1950): 433–60.

5. The views of many such philosophers, including Ned Block and John Searle, may be found in David Chalmers's definitive bibliography for papers about the philosophy of mind, *MindPapers*, http://consc.net/mindpapers (accessed May 1, 2008). For papers about artificial intelligence, see http://consc.net/mindpapers#.6; for the Turing test, see http://consc.net/mindpapers/6.1a.

6. Thomas Nagel, "What Is It Like to Be a Bat?" *Philosophical Review* 83 (1974): 435–50.

7. John R. Searle, "Minds, Brains, and Programs," *Behavioral and Brain Sciences* 3:3 (1980): 417–24. Note that I have strengthened the example by having the individual in the room know neither English nor Chinese—in keeping with how the mechanisms of contemporary translation devices "know" nothing of the input/output languages.

8. See, for example, Paul M. Churchland, *Matter and Consciousness* (Cambridge, MA: MIT Press, 1984).

9. David J. Chalmers, *The Conscious Mind: In Search of a Fundamental Theory* (Oxford: Oxford University Press, 1996).

10. Marvin Minsky, "A Framework for Representing Knowledge," in *The Psychology of Computer Vision*, ed. P. H. Winston (New York: McGraw-Hill, 1975), 211–77.

11. The bet is officially listed at http://www.longbets.org/bets (accessed September 23, 2007).

Minority Report, Molinism, and the Viability of Precrime

Dean A. Kowalski

Spielberg is famous—or notorious—for inserting endangered children into his screenplays even when the original novel or short story depicts only adults. Two glaring examples of this are *War of the Worlds* (2005) and *Minority Report* (2002).[1] Spielberg's approach to adapting these two stories, however, is far from uniform. His adaptation of *War of the Worlds* keeps H. G. Wells's original ending, even at the risk of implausibility. The alien tripod-wielders are advanced enough to bury their weapons of mass destruction far enough into the ground so as not to be discovered for thousands of years. They carefully study Earth for all that time, but inexplicably do not discover that they would lack immunity to the deathly microbes that inhabit it.[2] Spielberg's adaptation of *Minority Report* eschews Philip K. Dick's original ending. Dick's protagonist goes to great lengths to keep the Precrime unit viable. Spielberg chooses to close it down.

This essay explores three reasons one might have for dismantling Precrime. First, it is tempting to argue that Precrime police science is inherently unjust and thus conceptually unworkable. The alleged problem is philosophical. Many believe that if someone has knowledge of our future choices then those choices are not freely done. But because we are (personally) responsible only for what we freely do, we are unjustly punished for acts the precogs have foreseen.[3] However, I argue that this kind of reasoning invariably misconstrues how statements about the future are true.

A second reason is that the precogs (in both the film and the novella) allegedly possess foreknowledge of events that never happen. Some philosophers across history have embraced the kind of knowledge attributed to the precogs, but many others argue that such knowledge is impossible (even if freedom and foreknowledge are compatible). Unless such arguments can be met, Precrime's conceptual viability remains unclear. A third reason—one that Spielberg has publicly endorsed—is motivated by the broader, social ramifications of Precrime. Spielberg seemingly believes that, even if the precogs' "previsions" do not rob of us of our metaphysical freedom to act otherwise than we do, Precrime is dubious because of the potential threat it poses to our political rights and freedoms. Because the values associated with our political rights and freedoms outweigh those garnered via Precrime, it ought to be jettisoned.[4] The essay concludes with an analysis of Spielberg's position, presenting reasons for the claim that Spielberg's conclusion is based on a fallacious "slippery slope" argument.

The Freedom and Foreknowledge "Problem"

The opening scenes of *Minority Report* are eerily striking. Hazy sepia images pass in and out of focus, revealing an apparent love triangle—one that ends violently. A new image quickly comes into bright focus. A blue-eyed, pallid woman hoarsely whispers "murder" as she slowly submerges into milky water. The woman is a precognitive. She and her two associates have just had a prevision of Howard Marks (Ayre Gross) committing a "future murder."[5] Twenty minutes from now, he will repeatedly plunge a pair of scissors into his wife and her lover. But through elaborate technology of which they are not aware, the three precogs have alerted the Precrime police force of Marks's future act. Their job is to prevent Marks—and anyone else in the Washington, D.C., area—from perpetrating the awful deeds the precogs foresee. Since its inception in 2049, the joint venture has been unbelievably successful. Not one murder has been committed within two hundred miles of D.C. in the past five years.

The premise of the known future is captivating. It is also unsettling. The idea that someone foreknows how a person will choose leads many to draw the same conclusion: that a person thus cannot choose otherwise. But having the ability to choose otherwise is necessary for free choice. If someone has foreknowledge of how you will choose, then you are robbed of your freedom to do otherwise. Lacking the ability to do otherwise, you cannot be held responsible for what you do. Howard Marks, then, does not murder his wife and her lover freely, and he is unjustly "haloed" as a result. If he acts freely, then the precogs cannot foreknow that he will commit the double homicide. But they do foreknow: his future deed is revealed in a prevision. This is why the Precrime police are able to barge into his house and prevent Howard's raised, scissor-clutching hand from making its murderous strike. Thus, the unsettling conclusion remains.

This philosophical worry has a long history. It began with Aristotle nearly 2,500 years ago.[6] It preoccupied medieval philosophers. Augustine, Boethius, Aquinas, and Ockham all wrestled with it. But the problem remains pressing. In his foray into the literature of popular culture, the contemporary philosopher Theodore Schick describes it this way:

> If someone knows that something is going to happen, then it's true that it is going to happen because you can't know something that is false. You can't know that 1 + 1 equals 3, for example, because 1 + 1 does not equal 3. But if it's true that something is going to happen, then it cannot possibly not happen. If it's true that the sun will rise tomorrow, for example, then the sun has to rise tomorrow, for otherwise the statement wouldn't be true. So, if someone knows that something is going to happen, it must happen. But if it must happen—if it's unavoidable—then no one is free to prevent it from happening.[7]

If someone possesses foreknowledge, then there are now truths about how the future will unfold. If there are now truths that accurately describe future events, then the future must obtain in just that way. This leads Schick—and many others—to starkly conclude that the price of having foreknowledge is our freedom.

Schick is correct that having knowledge of a statement requires that the statement be true. One cannot know that which is false (even if one can know that it is false). He is also correct in that, if someone has foreknowledge, then there are truths about the future to be known and what the foreknower believes about the future will obtain. But Schick's position becomes dubious at the next step because the fact that something will obtain is distinct from the idea that "it cannot possibly not happen." Even if it is (now) true that the sun will rise tomorrow, this does not entail that it is impossible for the sun not to rise tomorrow. And if a precog knows that Marks will commit murder, then it is true that he will, but this does not entail that it is impossible for Marks not to commit murder. Aristotle fell into this subtle logical error long ago, and many (like Schick) continue to do so.

The beginning of Schick's argument—that if a statement is true, what it describes must obtain—initially seems quite plausible. The statement 'Steven Spielberg marries Kate Capshaw' is true only if Spielberg and Capshaw are indeed wed.[8] But the force of the word "must" in this context is ambiguous. Philosophers such as Schick seemingly intend something like: If a proposition is true, then the event it describes necessarily happens. Because true propositions are those things that describe reality, this interpretation entails that each and every thing that happens does so necessarily. But there is a second interpretation that avoids this fatalistic result, thereby preserving contingency in the world. It reads: Necessarily, if a proposition is true, then the event it describes happens. This interpretation merely expresses a necessary relationship between true propositions and the events to which they accurately correspond. But this entails neither that true statements are necessarily so, nor that the relevant states of affairs obtain necessarily. Because the alternative interpretation retains all that is crucial to the correspondence between truth and reality without sacrificing contingency, it is preferable to the first.

Consider the following claim, noting the use of the term "must": 'If Tom Cruise has now (as of 2008) starred in two of Spielberg's movies, then they must have now completed an even number of films together'. It is true that Cruise has currently starred in two Spielberg-directed pictures. But what follows from this? It might be concluded that it is necessarily the case that they have now (as of 2008) completed an even number of films together. On this interpretation, it is impossible for them not to have completed an even number of films together by this time, and believing otherwise involves a contradiction. However, because believing otherwise does not involve a contradiction—it is possible that they have now completed three films, for example—we thus have reason *not* to conclude that it is necessarily the case that they have now completed an even number of films together. We thereby have reason for rejecting the first interpretation of how the term "must" works in such contexts. Therefore, the force of the word "must" regarding whether these two Hollywood moguls have currently made an odd or even number of pictures together pertains only to the necessary relationship between the exact number of films they have currently made together and whether that number is equally divisible by two. The original claim of the paragraph should thus read as follows: 'Necessarily, if Cruise has starred in two of Spielberg's movies, then they have completed an even number of films together'. This rendering leaves the number of their movie collaborations a contingent matter and not a fatalistic one.

Regarding the debate about freedom and foreknowledge, it is true that if someone foreknows a (future) event, then that event must obtain. By now it is clear that this truth is best interpreted as: Necessarily, if someone foreknows a (future) event, then that event obtains (and not as: If someone foreknows a future event, then that event obtains necessarily). So, necessarily, if the precogs foreknow that Marks will commit double homicide, then he will. But their knowing this does not lead to the conclusion that Marks necessarily or unavoidably murders his wife and her lover in a way that renders his terrible act unfree. Claiming otherwise commits the same logical error as in the Spielberg/Cruise example. The crucial difference between what *contingently* will happen and what *necessarily* will happen remains intact on the second interpretation of how true statements must match up with reality (even if not the first).

Therefore, concerns about the incompatibility of freedom and foreknowledge are invariably grounded in misconception. It is true that foreknowledge requires that there are now true statements about the future. But we fall into error if we interpret this to mean that the antecedent truth of such statements determines how events unfold. This misconstrues the dependency. Because true propositions are merely descriptions of how things are, how future events unfold thus determines why some statements about the future are true rather than others. So, if it is a contingent matter, as it seems, that the sun rises tomorrow, then the antecedent truth of the corresponding statement cannot make its so rising necessary or unavoidable. If it is a contingent matter, which this debate must initially assume, that Marks will commit double homicide in twenty minutes, then the antecedent truth of 'Howard Marks kills his wife and her lover at 8:05 A.M.' cannot make his act necessary or unavoidable in a way that renders it unfree. Thus, how events unfold determines which statements are true, and not vice versa. Once this is realized, worries about freedom and foreknowledge begin to subside.

They continue to subside once we likewise grasp that what is foreknown about the future is explained by what will happen. The obtaining of future events as they do explains why there are (or can be) now true propositions about the future, and the current truth of those propositions explains (in part) why they can be known. Therefore, assuming the purported knower is in a position to know the antecedently true statement about the future, knowing it does not impact how the corresponding events unfold. This knowledge cannot make a contingent fact necessary; knowing the facts cannot make them true or impact how they are true. Rather, how the corresponding events unfold determines what can be known about them. If Marks does not choose to kill his wife and her lover that morning, then the precogs would never have known that he does kill them. Or if he chooses to kill them with a handgun rather than scissors, then the precogs will know this and never know that he uses scissors. Thus, what the precogs know depends on what we will do, and not vice versa.[9] Once these dependency relationships are kept straight, it is easier to see how the antecedent truth of statements about the future—or having knowledge of them—poses no logical threat to human freedom.[10]

"But It's Not the Future If You Stop It"

Scene 4 ("Predetermination") of *Minority Report,* one that does not appear in the novella, is particularly informative regarding the philosophical underpinnings of Precrime. The Justice Department representative Danny Witwer (Colin Farrell) quizzes the Precrime team about the paradoxes of Precrime methodology. Witwer points out that the primary "legalistic drawback" of Precrime police science is that the team "arrests individuals who have broken no laws." Anderton's executive technical assistant Jad (Steve Harris) quickly responds, "But they will!" Anderton's second-in-command Fletcher (Neal McDonough) immediately adds, "The commission of the crime itself is absolute metaphysics. The precogs see the future, and they're never wrong." Witwer coolly replies, "But it's not the future if you stop it. Isn't that a fundamental paradox?" Chief Anderton (Tom Cruise) arrives and interjects, "You're talking about predetermination, which happens all the time." The chief picks up a wooden ball and rolls it across a curved desk. As it falls off the edge, Witwer catches it. Feigning astonishment, Anderton asks, "Why did you catch that?" Witwer retorts, "Because it was going to fall." "You're certain?" "Yeah." "But it didn't fall. You caught it." From this Anderton confidently concludes, "The fact that you prevented it from happening doesn't change the fact that it was going to happen." After a quick exchange between Anderton and Witwer about how the precogs can tell the difference between what a jealous husband merely intends to do but does not carry out, and what he will do, Anderton sums up, "The precogs don't see what you intend to do, only what you will do."

Some explanations are informative even if they ultimately fail. This is true of scene 4. Two untenable positions about Precrime are presented here. First, we cannot interpret Fletcher as claiming that what the precogs see in experiencing a "future murder" is akin to normal eyesight. Visual perception occurs almost simultaneously with what is seen. But when the precogs "see" Marks murdering his wife and her lover, Marks is standing behind a tree in his front yard. So if we interpret Fletcher's claim literally, it leads to the contradiction that Marks is and is not standing behind a tree in his front yard when the precogs perceive him murdering his wife and her lover.[11] Second, although there is a sense in which the ball is "predetermined" to hit the ground upon rolling off the desk, and it would do so if Witwer had not intervened, this example is unsatisfactory. Given what we know about the laws of physics, our belief that the ball would hit the ground if allowed to do so is well justified. We can thus know that 'If uninterfered with, the ball Anderton rolled across the desk would hit the ground', even though the ball never actually hits the ground. However, the ball does not *choose* to fall off the desk. The precogs allegedly know what a person will choose if she is left *free* in some situation. This sort of knowledge cannot be a matter of "predetermination," contrary to Anderton's suggestion. If it were predetermination, then one does not act freely; the choice would simply follow from the laws of physics, as does the ball rolling off the edge of the desk. If one does not act freely, it is inappropriate to punish that person for it. And this applies generally. Thus the conceptual viability of Precrime requires a different sort of explanation than the one Anderton provides.

However, scene 4 successfully clarifies the *kind* of knowledge the precogs allegedly have. Surprisingly, it is not best characterized as foreknowledge. Foreknowledge is prior knowledge of *actual* future events. Recall that Marks never actually murders his wife and her lover. Anderton rushes up the stairs of the Markses' home and the rest of his team crashes through the skylights of Howard's bedroom. They successfully prevent the murder of Howard's wife and her lover. If the prevision was accurate and it is true that Marks was to commit murder if left free in this situation, but foreknowledge only pertains to what *actually* happens, then only one conclusion presents itself: the precogs do not strictly speaking have foreknowledge. They rather possess a different kind of knowledge, what we might call knowledge of the *conditional* future.

The idea of the conditional future illuminates the basic paradox of Precrime police science. Witwer points out that the people arrested via previsions have actually committed no crimes. The Precrime police intercede before any blood is spilled. But the "future criminals" are arrested nonetheless because they presumably would commit murder if left free in those situations.[12] In this regard, Anderton's explanation from scene 4 is accurate—just because future murderers are prevented from acting does not change the fact that they were (freely) going to commit murder.

The viewer is initially led to believe that the precogs can see only future murders. Fletcher quotes the profound words of Precrime founder Iris Hineman (Lois Smith), "There is nothing more destructive to the metaphysical fabric that binds us together than the untimely murder of one human being by another." Presumably, the alleged metaphysical tear is disruptive enough to be recognized by those sensitive to such things even if other smaller tears are not. But this (opaque) account of the precogs' "previsions" turns out to be misleading. Some precogs, Agatha (Samantha Morton) especially, are able to recognize smaller so-called metaphysical tears. Agatha's knowledge indeed seems incredibly extensive. As the film progresses, Anderton has been identified in a prevision as committing the future murder of Leo Crow

(Mike Binder), a man the chief has never met. In the attempt to prove his innocence, Anderton kidnaps Agatha. Agatha's astounding knowledge of the conditional future is demonstrated in two scenes.

The first is in the mall, scene 17 ("The Balloon Man"). Agatha demonstrates to Anderton that her knowledge abilities persist outside of the "temple" by providing him some examples of simple foreknowledge. She informs him that a man will drop a briefcase and that a woman will recognize him. The truth of both predictions is quickly verified. This establishes the probability that Anderton can escape his old comrades if he listens to her advice. After all, she presumably knows how this will unfold. Anderton subsequently follows her advice by inexplicably standing still in the mall rotunda and dropping change for a homeless man. We soon discover that Agatha already knows the following claims: 'If Anderton and I were to stand perfectly still in the center of the mall rotunda, then Precrime's view of us would be blocked by the balloon man' and 'If Anderton were to drop some change in the hallway near the homeless man, then the pursuing Precrime officers would trip over the man'. At first, these appear to be further examples of Agatha's foreknowledge. However, they seem better categorized as examples of knowing the conditional future because her knowledge of them remains even if Anderton does not take Agatha's advice about the balloon man and homeless person. Had Anderton refused to stand still in the rotunda or drop the coins, it remains the case that Agatha knows what would have happened had he decided to trust her.

This point about Agatha's knowledge of the balloon man or the homeless person may seem unnecessarily subtle. But it is not. It sets up the move to clearer examples of knowing conditional future free choices. Recall Agatha's advice (or command) to pilfer the umbrella from the mall kiosk. What she presumably knows is: 'If Anderton were to take the umbrella, then he would freely choose to use it as camouflage' and 'If Anderton were to freely choose to use the umbrella outside the mall, then the Precrime team would chose to momentarily cease pursuing us'. Here we have better examples of Agatha knowing what individuals would do if left free in a specific situation; that is, Agatha's precognitive abilities extend to knowledge of what agents would freely choose if placed in a specific set of circumstances.

Furthermore, recall Agatha telling the young woman in the mall, "Don't go home; he knows." Agatha is seemingly conveying her knowledge of what the woman's husband would choose to do now that he knows of, presumably, her affair. Agatha knows: 'If this woman were to meet her husband today, he would choose to seek revenge for her infidelities'. Importantly, if the woman heeds Agatha's advice and does not go home today, Agatha's knowledge of what would happen if she did remains intact. This is akin to what Agatha knows about Howard Marks: 'If Howard remains home from work and surprises his wife and her lover in the bedroom, he would freely choose to kill them'. Even though the Precrime team prevent Howard from committing the double homicide, it remains the case that Agatha knows what would have happened if Anderton did not stay Howard's hand. In a way, this is akin to what Witwer knows about what would have happened if he did not catch the ball as it rolled off the table, with the crucial difference that what Agatha knows is grounded not in the laws of physics, but simply in what Marks would have done if left free in that situation.[13]

The second example of Agatha's extensive knowledge occurs near the end of the film when Anderton takes her to his ex-wife's cottage; this is scene 20 ("So Much Love in This House"). In the upstairs bedroom, with an angelic light behind her, Agatha informs the estranged Andertons what would have happened had Sean (Dominic Scott Kay) not been abducted six years ago. Agatha prefaces her knowledge of Sean's conditional future with an episode from the Andertons' past: Sean running up and down the beach with his mother, Lara (Kathryn Morris). This gets the Andertons' attention; they immediately realize that Agatha is about to tell them about their son as he would have been if he had not been abducted that day at the Baltimore public swimming pool. Agatha begins by telling them that when Sean is ten, he informs his parents that he wishes to be a veterinarian; his parents subsequently allow him to keep a rabbit, a bird, and a fox. In high school, Sean joins the track team and runs the two mile and the long relay. At twenty-three, Sean runs track at the university he attends, and Anderton watches in the stands. Agatha further informs them that after making love to his girlfriend Claire, Sean asks her to be his wife. He calls the cottage to inform Lara, and she cries at hearing the news.

But Sean in fact tragically died at the hands of his abductor six years ago. So what Agatha reports cannot be the actual future. Nevertheless, we are led to believe that Agatha knows the following claims: 'If Sean were to attend University X and meet Claire, he would freely ask her to marry him' and 'If Sean were to attend University X and become a member of the men's track team, Anderton would freely choose to attend his meets'. If Agatha knows these claims, they must be true even if Sean has actually died. Their being true is therefore neither a matter of what will actually happen, nor merely a matter of what might have happened. Rather, their truth is simply a matter of what Sean would have (freely) done had he not fallen prey to his abductor. This is why they are best described as truths about the "conditional future."

Molina and Knowledge of the Conditional Future

The idea that there can be knowledge of the conditional future reached historical prominence with the Spanish Jesuit Luis de Molina in the late 1500s. In his *Concordia* (1588), Molina argued that God, being omniscient, knows what every possible person would do if left free in any set of specific circumstances. God knows what I would freely do if I were to win the Powerball jackpot and God knows what my older sister would have done if she were accepted to both Harvard and Yale—even though I am the oldest sibling in my family (remaining sadly indigent). According to Molina, God knows

> the free choice of any creature, . . . given the hypothesis that [God] should create it in this or that order of things . . . though the creature could, if it so willed, refrain from acting or do the opposite, and even though if it was going to do so, as it is able to freely, God would have foreseen *that* very act and *not* the one that [God] *in fact* foresees would be performed by that creature. . . . That is . . . [God] knew whether or not they [i.e., which truths] were going to be, *not absolutely speaking* but rather *on the hypothesis* that [God] should decide to create this or that order of things with these or those circumstances.[14]

Armed with this sort of knowledge, God is able to exercise incredible providential control without impinging on human freedom. If God chooses not to allow a person to act as God knows that person freely would in a specific situation, God simply does not place the person in it. But if God allows a person to freely act as God (already) knows she would in that situation, God makes this a part of God's providential plan. In either case, the person in question remains free. What God knows, remember, is informed by what we would freely do; what we do is not determined by what God already knows about us.[15]

Note that the Precrime police act analogously to Providence in this way. The Precrime team is informed by the precogs what murders would happen if certain individuals were left free. Armed with this knowledge, the Precrime team can act to prevent these tragic acts by making sure that the "future murderer" is not left free in those circumstances. By not leaving the future murderer free to act, Precrime can ensure that the future murderer is not placed in just the circumstances that the precogs have foreseen.

Someone has knowledge of the conditional future only if the relevant statements are true and the alleged knower is justified in believing them.

Philosophical opponents to this kind of purported knowledge argue either that the relevant statements descriptive of how free agents would choose cannot be true or that no alleged knower could be justified in believing them. The first objection is more popular in the literature. This is probably because this debate typically assumes that the alleged knower is God. If God is omniscient, then God knows all true propositions and believes none that are false; it is simply impossible for God to not know a true proposition or to believe one that is not true. It is therefore difficult to argue that God lacks proper justification for his true beliefs.[16] However, if the purported knower is a precog—even one as talented as Agatha—the question of what justifies her beliefs becomes pressing. Interestingly, it might be argued that even if the precogs (themselves) lack proper justification, the Precrime police derivatively might be so justified. Anderton's team sees many "future murderers" about to commit their crimes just as the precogs predicted (even though they subsequently prevent the murder from actually happening). Precrime police also realize that homicides in the D.C. area are next to nil since the inception of Precrime. The precogs are not aware of either fact. Thus it indeed seems that the Precrime team is in a better position to claim that the precogs have knowledge of the conditional future than the precogs themselves. This raises some difficult issues in the area of epistemology, calling for further study.[17]

The more prevalent objection to Molina's view is that the statements descriptive of how free agents would choose lack the proper grounds for their being true.[18] Contingently true statements are so in virtue of how the facts turn out. Because the world contains horses, but no unicorns, the statement 'Horses exist' is true, but the statement 'Unicorns exist' is false. No contradiction occurs in assuming that the world could have contained unicorns and no horses, but that is not how things turned out. Philosophers opposed to Molinism argue that statements about how free agents would choose are not grounded in how things (contingently) are. After all, the relevant statements invariably describe situations that agents will never actually be in (like those pertaining to Sean Anderton). Furthermore, Molina believed that it was possible to know such truths about people who never actually exist, like my older sister. Therefore, even if there is a sense in which someone could have foreknowledge of an agent's *actual* free choice (because the relevant agent will eventually perform the act described), it is widely believed that statements merely descriptive of how agents would choose cannot be true.[19]

This objection weighs heavily on Molinists.[20] Perhaps the most elegant response is the surest. If an agent were placed in a fully determinate set of circumstances and left free with respect to the choice at hand, it seems that either she would freely make the relevant choice or she would freely refrain from it. Because no other option seemingly exists, it seems that either 'If agent S were left free in just these circumstances, then she would freely perform action A' or 'If agent S were left free in just these circumstances, then she would freely refrain from doing A' is true. If so, then perhaps it is possible to possess this kind of knowledge even if agent S is never actually in the relevant circumstances and indeed even if agent S never actually exists.[21] But this type of response remains quite controversial, inviting further exploration.

If *Minority Report* presupposes that the precogs have knowledge of the conditional future, as seems to be the case, then in order for the Precrime unit to be conceptually viable, it must be possible to have this knowledge.[22] This is why the philosophical objections to it are important. But the importance of these objections reaches beyond the movie. After all, many theistic believers—like Molina—believe that God must have knowledge of the conditional future in order to be truly provident. If it is impossible for anyone to possess this kind of knowledge—including God—then the believer must devise alternative ways to understand God as Providence without impinging on human freedom.

Spielberg as Philosopher

However professional philosophers finally (if ever) decide the debate about Molinism, Spielberg the armchair philosopher seemingly believes that freedom and foreknowledge are compatible. This claim is supported by Agatha's insistence ("You can choose! You can choose!") that Anderton can still choose to refrain from shooting Crow once they meet in the hotel room. He indeed does refrain, at least from what the precogs originally perceived. This idea is reinforced during the penultimate scene with Lamar Burgess (Max von Sydow) and Anderton on the terrace. Anderton reminds Burgess that the precogs have no doubt foreseen this, leaving Burgess (who is also the director and cofounder of Precrime in Spielberg's version) with a choice. He is free to go through with his plan to murder Anderton, thereby keeping Precrime intact but sending its director to "halo prison," or he can refrain from murdering Anderton, thereby avoiding prison but with the further result of closing down Precrime. Either way, Burgess will lose a "child" (Anderton or Precrime) dear to his heart. Burgess instead takes his own life, but Precrime is nevertheless shut down.[23] These two scenes leave us with the following perhaps paradoxical position: the more you know about your future, the freer you are to act. By being privy to the relevant prevision, we get a chance to rethink what we are about to do, thereby making us freer with respect to our choice.

Spielberg's position here deserves further study, but the remainder of this essay will delve into his motivation for changing Dick's original ending. Spielberg's version of the story is largely about governmental involvement in our private lives. Lester Friedman writes, "*Minority Report* hit movie screens while an ongoing debate was being stimulated by questions about how much personal liberty Americans were willing to sacrifice for the promise of public security. Can we trust government agencies to exercise appropriate restraints if given the power to patrol our lives? Will they monitor only those who endanger our safety and not those who hold unpopular opinions? . . . Does prevention justify the surveillance?"[24] Retinal scans are prevalent in *Minority Report*, from security checkpoints in classified buildings to consumer-specific advertising and marketing. The artificially intelligent spiders that Precrime is legally authorized to use for reconnaissance serve as an incredibly vivid example of the government's ability to intrude in people's personal lives under the guise of public safety. These tiny robotic computers literally invade an apartment building looking for Anderton and mercilessly seek retinal identification of everyone in the building. They eye scan a single mother and her two children, a couple making love, and a man using the toilet. As Friedman notes, in Spielberg's futuristic world, "even in their most private moments, none can find sanctuary from the government's intrusive, and ultimately oppressive, tactics."[25]

Spielberg thus presents Precrime as the most intrusive and oppressive of governmental surveillance tactics. It is noteworthy that the public is told the precogs are comfortably kept, receiving more mail than Santa Claus. Furthermore, the public is led to believe that the precogs can perceive only future murders. Both statements are false. The precogs are kept sedated in a milky pool, never having a choice in their service of public safety. Agatha at least appears to have unlimited knowledge of the actual and conditional future. Why might the public be told these falsehoods? The obvious answer is so that the people of futuristic Washington, D.C., can revel in the fact that they are kept safe from murderers without having to worry about too much governmental interference. If the precogs are kindly people, they would never peer into matters that they should not; and, anyway, they can see only future murders. But Agatha and presumably other precogs (if there are others) could be trained to perceive any part of the future, including the choices of those who are deemed politically unsavory by those currently in power. The knowledge of what these people would do in various situations puts the person with this knowledge at an incredible political advantage.

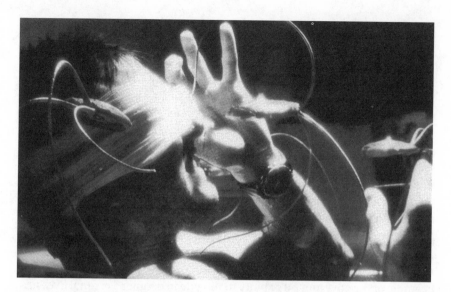

Minority Report, DreamWorks SKG, 2002. Spielberg uses vivid images of the shiny metallic recon spiders to bolster his implicit position that Precrime should be shut down. If the spiders are an infringement on our rights to privacy, what the precogs are able to see about our lives should not be under anyone's jurisdiction. (MovieGoods, Inc.)

Spielberg believes that this sort of political advantage must be prevented. He claims that Precrime gives the government too much power. If future murders can be seen and prevented so can petty theft. And if we begin preventing petty theft, what is stopping the government from preventing people from exercising unpopular political ideas or choices?[26] The hollow tapping of unstoppable metallic spider legs is one thing—although that is bad enough—but having the power to alter the future for political gain is something altogether different. To prevent this unwanted political state of affairs, Spielberg believes that Precrime should be disbanded even if freedom and foreknowledge are compatible.

What Spielberg offers us here can be classified as a slippery slope argument. Arguments of this type have the following general form: If A is allowed to happen, this will lead to B happening. B will lead to C and C to D. But D is clearly unacceptable. Therefore, we ought not to allow A to happen.[27] Not all slippery slope arguments are fallacious, but many are. An argument is fallacious if it represents some failed piece of reasoning; that is, if the premises do not logically support the conclusion. Slippery slope arguments tend to become fallacious if many intermediate steps are relied on to establish the conclusion or if the causal links between the steps (regardless of how many) are dubious. For example, it might be argued that we ought not to legalize euthanasia. If we do, then the elderly or infirm may feel pressured into (unduly) ending their lives because they are being a social or financial burden to family or society. Once the social or financial burdens of supporting the elderly are fully realized, then the government will institute a policy requiring everyone to commit suicide on their sixty-fifth birthday. Because it is morally objectionable to require healthy adults to commit suicide, we ought not to allow euthanasia (in any form). This argument is fallacious because both of its steps are suspect. It is not clear that allowing strictly regulated euthanasia programs will lead to the stipulated psychological pressures among the elderly, and it is simply fantastical to think that allowing strictly regulated euthanasia programs will lead to government-sanctioned mass suicide.

It seems true to say that some should not enjoy undue or irrepressible political advantage over others. Spielberg is also correct in that governmental involvement in our private lives requires careful assessment. It is easy to cloak the sacrificing of political liberties under the rubric of public (or national) security. However, it simply is not clear that Precrime, were it possibly instituted, would necessarily be used in the way Spielberg fears. It seems that regulations and sanctions could be put in place through a series of checks and balances that would prevent political rights infractions. True, it would forever remain possible for a cunning official like Lamar Burgess to misuse the system—any technology is subject to potential misuse for personal gain. But Burgess (and his ilk) might be deterred if there were additional oversight by a separate department—like Justice—so long as it was clear that Justice could not take over Precrime.[28] Furthermore, it could be stipulated that Precrime police may neither hold public office, nor be appointed by politicians. And we cannot forget the great benefit of Precrime: because murder is such a tragic state of affairs, preventing it amounts to a great good. Precrime can achieve that great good. Therefore, abandoning Precrime should not be taken lightly.[29] If there is a way to keep it intact and ward off potential misuses of it—political or personal—then those strategies should be explored carefully and fully.

Steven Spielberg is not a professional philosopher. It might therefore seem trite to critique his philosophical arguments. To his credit, his slippery slope argument is not as obviously fallacious as some offered by professional philosophers. As a result of studying this volume, you will no doubt realize that sometimes Spielberg's implicit philosophical positions are laudable, sometimes they are susceptible to criticism. The same can be said of professional philosophers. Perhaps I have misjudged Spielberg's argument; it might be that no system of checks and balances on Precrime can adequately guarantee our political freedoms. This is the beauty of philosophy—almost every interesting position is up for debate or revision. Nevertheless, this professional philosopher has not lost sight of the main point here: Spielberg's films are regularly of a caliber that make them proper candidates for philosophical exploration and scrutiny. This clearly cannot be said of every filmmaker. For that, I am incredibly grateful; it provides me (and the other contributing authors) a novel and invigorating platform from which to discuss philosophy.

Remaining Philosophical Issues

This essay leaves many philosophical issues associated with *Minority Report* untouched.[30] Should Precrime be allowed to function even if the precogs are not infallible? Should the precogs be given the choice to serve the public with their unique gifts? If they refuse, is that decision impermissible? Should future murderers be prevented from committing their heinous deeds, but not be punished if no harm results? Should they somehow be rehabilitated rather than "haloed"? What should be done about those who discover truths about their conditional future (as do Anderton and Burgess)? Should everyone be instructed about their conditional futures, thereby making everyone freer? These questions and the issues driving them are difficult. They are further testament to the philosophical complexity of Spielberg's corpus and further justification for this volume.

Notes

1. For more on Spielberg's textual choices in this regard, see Gary Arms and Thomas Riley's "The 'Big-Little' Film and Philosophy: Two Takes on Spielbergian Innocence," in this volume.

2. Although perhaps this familiar criticism of Spielberg's adaptation overlooks the *spirit* of the ending. Sometimes catastrophe inexplicably strikes without warning and sometimes it inexplicably ceases without warning. What is truly important is how we respond to the events in between. Something like this is certainly the point of the character arc for Ray (Tom Cruise) in *War of the Worlds*.

3. A related, potential objection to Precrime police science takes the form of a dilemma: Either the precogs have infallible knowledge of the future or they do not. If they do, then we could not have done otherwise than they have foreseen. If they do not, then it is possible that we are punished for acts that we will never do. Either way, punishments doled out by Precrime are unjust. Addressing this argument properly is no

doubt an essay in itself, but the first reason offered in the text incorporates the intuitive heart of the first half of the dilemma.

4. Spielberg's position on the viability of Precrime is surmised from two sources. The first is his commentary in "Deconstructing *Minority Report:* The Story, the Debate" (*Minority Report,* DVD, disc 2 [Glendale, CA: DreamWorks, 2002]). Here, he suggests that if Precrime were absolutely infallible and if it passed the proper national referendum, he would find it to be acceptable. However, he has his doubts about any human process being infallible. In the second source, *Spielberg on Spielberg* (Turner Classic Movies, first aired July 9, 2007), Spielberg is clearer that he believes Precrime would certainly be abused by those in political power; thus, to safeguard our political rights and freedoms, Precrime ought not to be enacted. Lester Friedman seems to concur with my reconstruction of Spielberg's position; see Lester D. Friedman, *Citizen Spielberg* (Urbana: University of Illinois Press, 2006), 51–56.

5. Spielberg hired a two-man production team to construct the precogs' previsions. After consulting cognitive psychologists, the team decided on the layered, dreamlike imagery that appears in the movie. Evidently, the eeriness of the previsions is predominantly a matter of their realism. "Deconstructing *Minority Report:* Precog Visions," *Minority Report,* DVD, disc 2 (2002). For more on cinematic realism, see Keith Dromm's "Spielberg and Cinematic Realism," in this volume.

6. For an accessible rendering of Aristotle's views on the freedom and foreknowledge problem via popular culture, see Dean A. Kowalski, "'Clyde Bruckman's Final Repose' Reprised," in *The Philosophy of* The X Files, ed. Dean A. Kowalski (Lexington: University Press of Kentucky, 2007), 195–200.

7. Theodore Schick Jr., "Fate, Freedom, and Foreknowledge," in *The Matrix and Philosophy,* ed. William Irwin (Chicago: Open Court Press, 2002), 93. Given the overall tenor of Schick's article, he clearly is not merely espousing this argument; he embraces the conclusion that freedom and foreknowledge are incompatible.

8. A statement—what philosophers tend to call a proposition—is the exact meaning of a declarative sentence. Statements are abstract objects that possess the property of "being true" or "being false" (but not both). If what they declare corresponds with how things are, then they are true. If what they declare does not correspond with how things are, then they are false. Philosophers often mark a proposition by surrounding it with single quotation marks.

9. This does not necessarily lead to the counterintuitive position of the effect (what the precogs know) existing prior to the cause (what we will do), as some have claimed; see, for example, Schick, "Fate, Freedom, and Foreknowledge," 94–95. The relationship is not causal in the straightforward sense; thus, the claim that freedom and foreknowledge are compatible does not commit one to the position that effects predate their causes. Philosophers tend to characterize the relationship as counterfactual dependence. This complex notion at least involves the idea that the knower would not believe the agent will choose to do something unless it were true.

10. The lesson here is somewhat surprising. The debate about freedom and fore-

knowledge, at its core anyway, is not about epistemology—the study of knowledge. It rather concerns how true statements are related to reality, which is more a matter of metaphysics—the study of what ultimately exists. This lesson leads to another that many find more surprising: the core debate about freedom and foreknowledge is not necessarily about God's knowledge. Many people believe that God's *infallible* knowledge creates the logical problem between freedom and foreknowledge. However, as both Augustine and Boethius seemingly saw, because knowledge requires truth, the (alleged) problem is actually generated by the antecedent truth of statement about the future. Should anyone falsely believe what happens in the future, they cannot be said to foreknow it, but should anyone truly believe future events, the alleged problem manifests.

11. This feature of foreknowledge might indeed lead us into some difficult epistemic issues. We are left asking, how could anyone then see the future? The answer initially seems to be that the future cannot be seen because you cannot see what does not (yet) exist. One kind of response to this issue invariably relies on providing the alleged foreknower an incredibly unique vantage point. Some philosophers believe that the future (or what we understand as "future") is readily "seen" by someone who exists outside of time. The precogs do not exist outside of time, but *Minority Report* (again unlike the novella) goes into some detail attempting to account for their unique powers of clairvoyance. (Even if that account is ultimately unsatisfactory, note that Schick's argument against freedom and foreknowledge attempts to show that these are incompatible and not merely that the future cannot, in fact, be known.)

Other philosophers respond to this issue by arguing that what the foreknower "sees" is initially nothing like visual perception. Rather, the purported knower uniquely has cognitive access to the descriptions and thus the true propositions that accurately convey how the future will unfold. The most obvious way to explain this ability is via omniscience. God is a good candidate for having foreknowledge; God's beliefs about the future are (arguably) justified because among God's beliefs are 'I am God' and 'God has no false beliefs', even if there is never a time at which God comes to know these two statements (because God has always known them). However, omniscience might not be a necessary condition of foreknowledge, as it seems possible that God (if God exists) could grant someone the ability to foreknow the future. Assuming that the receiver of this ability knew that God provided it, the purported foreknower's true beliefs about the future seem sufficiently justified.

12. The claim that the future murderer *would* commit murder is not the same as the claim that he *might* commit murder. If the precogs have knowledge of the conditional future, then they know something more than that someone possibly commits a future murder. They know that he would actually commit murder if left free in the relevant situation. Some philosophers find it controversial to blame and hold accountable someone for what they (merely) would do apart from what they actually do. This is a difficult issue; it might raise another conceptual difficulty for Precrime's viability.

13. If this sort of reasoning is roughly accurate, then Lester Friedman's analysis of Anderton's situation must be amended. Friedman implicitly argues (*Citizen Spielberg*, p. 53) that the precogs' prevision of Anderton killing Crow is falsified by Anderton's

refraining from killing him in the way the precogs had originally foreseen. However, it is unlikely that the precogs' original prevision included Anderton's discovery of what they foresaw. Therefore, the situation that the precogs had foreseen was not exactly the one that obtained. This does not falsify the original prevision so much as it supercedes it, calling for a new prevision for what actually transpires. Dick's version of the story does a better job of capturing the twists brought on by the future murderer having access to his own prevision.

14. Luis de Molina, *On Divine Foreknowledge: Part IV of the Concordia,* trans. Alfred Freddoso (Cornell: Cornell University Press, 1988), Disputation 49, section 11.

15. The Molinist, then, would disagree with Friedman's implicit assessment of Spielberg illicitly having it "both ways" when it comes to the "conundrum" of "freewill and predestination" (*Citizen Spielberg,* p. 55). Assuming that knowledge of the conditional future is possible, then events can be "predetermined" at least in the (albeit misleading) sense that God has foreseen them but has allowed them to actually transpire. Nevertheless, our choices remain free; God's prior knowledge of how we would act does not render our choices unfree.

16. However, for a sophisticated attempt at arguing that not even God is properly justified with respect to true statements descriptive of how free agents would choose, see Scott A. Davison, "Foreknowledge, Middle Knowledge, and 'Nearby Worlds,'" *International Journal for Philosophy of Religion* 30:1 (August 1991): 29–44.

17. The first issue that must be dealt with is whether internalism or externalism about epistemic justification is preferable. If some account of externalism is defensible, then it is conceivable that the Precrime police rely on the precogs' previsions in a way similar to how we (in fact) rely on our eyes for our visual beliefs. Just as we do not need to know exactly how vision works for the beliefs generated by it to be justified, the Precrime police need not know exactly how the precogs come by their previsions. All they would need to know (or be justified about) is that previsions are successful in preventing homicides. For a good introductory discussion of the internalism/externalism debate—and epistemology generally—see Jack S. Crumley II, *Introduction to Epistemology* (San Francisco: McGraw-Hill, 1998).

18. The seminal contemporary source for this type of objection is Robert M. Adams, "Middle Knowledge and the Problem of Evil," *American Philosophical Quarterly* 14:2 (April 1977): 109–17.

19. The objection to Molinism here is damaging because Molina believed that God possessed knowledge of the contingent future logically prior to his act of creation. In a sense, there are no actual agents at this logical moment because God has yet to create anything. But if there are no actual agents at this logical moment, then they cannot make any actual choices. Thus, logically prior to creation, God cannot know how free agents would choose if created and left free in a specific set of circumstances. This greatly hampers God's providential control in creation and is tantamount to showing Molinism to be false. Put in terms of the movie, if Marks never actually murders his wife and her lover, then this was never a part of the actual future. If it was never a part of the actual future, then (so goes the objection) there is nothing for the precogs to foreknow about

Marks (except, perhaps, what he probably would freely do). Because this applies generally, it follows that Precrime is incoherent because it operates on unjustified beliefs (or visions) of the conditional future.

20. The most sustained defense of Molina's views can be found in Thomas Flint, *Divine Providence: The Molinist Account* (Ithaca, NY: Cornell University Press, 1998).

21. For more on this sort of defense of Molina, see William Lane Craig, "Middle Knowledge, Truth-Makers, and the 'Grounding Objection,'" *Faith and Philosophy* 18:23 (2001): 337–52, and Dean A. Kowalski, "Some Friendly Molinist Amendments," *Philosophy and Theology* 15:2 (2003): 385–401.

22. That the precogs have this sort of knowledge in the original novella is established by the fact that Dick's Anderton realized that the three previsions were out of phase with each other. The first indicated that Dick's Anderton would murder the retired army general if left free, but the second, knowing that Anderton was aware of the first prevision, indicated that Anderton would refrain. (This is further reason to believe that Friedman's assessment requires modification; see note 13.)

23. The outcomes of both scenes seem suspect. Once Anderton sees his own name on the wooden ball, the precogs (probably) should have received revised previsions regarding the murder of Leo Crow (unless they are incapable of this sort of knowledge). Similarly, once Anderton reminds Burgess that Fletcher's team is no doubt on its way, the precogs should again have received a revised prevision (perhaps seeing Burgess committing suicide, assuming suicide is indeed akin to self-murder). In any event, if the arguments of the last section hold up, it is not clear that the decisions of Anderton and Burgess to make different choices somehow falsify the relevant prevision or Precrime. Presumably, neither original prevision included the future murderer being privy to its contents. Therefore, once Anderton or Burgess discovers the contents of the original prevision, it becomes obsolete. This scenario is effectively portrayed in Dick's original version; see notes 13 and 22.

24. Friedman, *Citizen Spielberg*, 51.

25. Friedman, *Citizen Spielberg*, 54.

26. This implicit argument is reconstructed from Spielberg's comments in *Spielberg on Spielberg*.

27. There might be many intermediate steps listed before the final, unacceptable result is reached. However, the idea is that regardless of how many intermediate steps are included, each allegedly represents a small step from the last with no clear way to stop the slide until the final, unacceptable end results.

28. Furthermore, it seems that Agatha's predictive abilities are intensified once Anderton takes her from the temple; presumably, being (physically) near people somehow heightens a precog's knowledge of the actual and conditional future. (This claim is bolstered by the movie's conclusion, which divulges that the precogs have been moved to an isolated, undisclosed location to live the rest of their lives in peace.) If so, security around the temple could be increased so as to make it nearly impossible to remove the precogs from the "milk" in the temple. Moreover, the milk itself might play an important role here. We are told that it calms the precogs. Therefore, the alleged problems gener-

ated by Agatha's extensive knowledge capabilities can be abated if she is not allowed in situations that intensify them.

29. Professor of political science Joseph Foy has shared (via personal correspondence) grave reservations about the sufficiency of the sort of checks and balances proposed here. He is inclined to believe that the threat of political misuse remains too great. He thus, in effect, agrees with Spielberg's position. I am grateful to Professor Foy for reading an earlier draft of this essay and sharing with me his insights about the movie and its political implications.

30. It also (of course) leaves many of the philosophical issues germane to the short story untouched. Should Dick's Anderton be allowed to kill the army general and then subject himself to self-exile rather than being prosecuted to the full extent of the law?

Appendix
Discussing Five Spielberg Films

This appendix contains plot summaries for five of Spielberg's important and controversial films: *Schindler's List, Amistad, A.I., Minority Report,* and *Munich.*[1] Each plot summary is between one thousand and fifteen hundred words and is accompanied by a handful of discussion questions. The idea is to provide material that will be of benefit to classroom instructors, book club leaders, or anyone who wishes to ponder and better appreciate Spielberg's work. Consider reading the relevant essays in this volume by Ebertz, Baggett and Foreman, Dunn, White, Kowalski, and Foy (respectively), after watching the films, to stimulate further discussion.

Schindler's List (1993)

Screenwriter: Steven Zaillian (based on the book by Thomas Keneally)

PLOT SUMMARY

It is 1939 and Nazi Germany overruns Poland in two weeks. Polish Jews are required to register in Krakow. Nazi Party member Oskar Schindler arrives in the city. He throws lavish dinner parties at which high-ranking Nazi officials are the guests of honor. The officials take photographs with Schindler and soon befriend him.

Two years pass and the Krakow Jews are forced to enter the oldest part of the city known as the ghetto. Their homes and businesses are taken from them and their new accommodations are appalling. Schindler contacts the Jewish Council, the "Judenrat," and makes a proposition: If a number of Jews will invest in his new enamelware business, Schindler will return their monies in less than a year. But, more important, since the factory is outside the ghetto and Schindler will bankroll his workers with items profitable on the black market, the Jews will have opportunities to acquire other goods. This, according to Schindler, is better than money given their current situation. Begrudgingly, the Jews agree.

Itzhak Stern, a member of the Judenrat, becomes Schindler's production manager and accountant. An extremely bright man, he quickly realizes that hiring Jews to make Schindler's pots and pans will save many from being "deported" to another part of Europe. Stern has heard of others being deported, which really means being sent to the Auschwitz concentration camp and certain death. Stern hires a rabbi, a musician, a history professor, and even an elderly one-armed man because he (rightly) suspects that these will be the first to be evacuated from the ghetto. If you are not needed for the Nazi war effort, then you simply are not needed, especially if you are Jewish.

With Stern busy managing the factory, Schindler begins keeping his part of the bargain. He again sends his new Nazi friends extravagant gifts. As it turns out, these Nazi officials oversee war contracts to private businesses. All of Schindler's bids are approved; his business booms and he quickly becomes a rich man.

In the winter of 1942, Nazi officer Amon Goeth arrives in Krakow. He has been deemed the commandant for Plaszow, the new labor camp to be built outside of the city. A sign of things to come, Goeth's first official business as commandant is overseeing the construction of a barracks. The lead engineer, a highly educated Jewish woman, informs the guards and finally Goeth that the foundation must be refashioned or else the barracks will fall over. But Goeth does not like her tone—or the fact that she is educated—and orders one of his officers to immediately shoot her in the head. After her assassination, Goeth orders that her instructions are to be followed.

The following March, Goeth conducts the "liquidation" of the ghetto. Nazi troops forcibly remove Jews from the ghetto; those who are uncooperative are summarily shot. Some attempt to hide. Everyone else is marched to Plaszow. As darkness falls, the liquidation continues in the form of a "search and destroy" mission. Goeth sends in troops armed with stethoscopes, dogs, and, of course, rifles. No attempt is made to relocate the hiding Jews. Those that are discovered, either by a careful ear, by a canine nose, or simply by accident, are viciously shot.

Schindler's factory now lies dormant. To correct this, Schindler arranges a meeting with Goeth. As Schindler drives up to Goeth's villa overlooking the labor camp, Goeth is shooting Jews with a high-powered rifle. Those not working efficiently—and even some who are—meet a bloody end. Schindler bribes Goeth into allowing Schindler's workers to leave the camp, thus reopening his factory. However, Goeth does not allow Stern to leave. Stern will oversee Goeth's end of the business—part of the bribe—from inside the camp.

Business is again good for Schindler. His Nazi contacts and other acquaintances throw him a birthday party. Two Jewish girls present Schindler with a cake. They very nervously wish him a happy birthday from all of the workers. Schindler returns the sentiment by kissing the older girl—in front of the high-ranking Nazi contacts and officers. This gets Schindler thrown into prison. Soon after, however, he is freed by one of his contacts. The Nazi contact informs Schindler that he should not become too friendly with the Jews because "they don't have a future; that's not just good old-fashioned Jew-hating talk—it's policy now."

New workers arrive at Plaszow. To make room for them, Goeth orders that all current workers be examined by doctors to assess their general health. In a most embarrassing display, the Jews—men and women—are stripped naked and forced to run in circles in front of Nazi doctors. Those who are deemed unhealthy are either shot or "deported." Some of the Jewish women desperately prick their fingers and gently smear the blood on their cheeks in the hope of making themselves appear healthier than they really are. Meanwhile, however, the children are rounded up and placed on trucks. It seems that part of Goeth's ploy was to distract the adults so that the children could be removed from the camp without detection. Some children are lucky enough to escape—by hiding in floors, chimneys, or latrines—but most are not. The adults shriek in terror when they realize that the examination was part of a ruse to deport the children.

In April 1944, Goeth is ordered to exhume and burn the bodies of the ten thousand Jews killed during his tenure in Krakow and Plaszow. The sky over Krakow is filled with ash, which falls like gray snowflakes. The remaining Jews are to be shipped to Auschwitz. Stern informs Schindler that he is coordinating the final evacuation, with himself on the last train. By this time, Schindler's only goal is the safety of his workers; he now cares nothing for profit. He arranges another meeting with Goeth at which he "buys" his workers. If Schindler is willing to give Goeth enough money, Goeth is willing to hand over Jews to Schindler so that he can set up another factory in a different camp. Schindler and Stern type up a list of eleven hundred Jews; they are to arrive at Schindler's new factory near his hometown in Czechoslovakia. As a result of a clerical error, the women are sent to Auschwitz rather than Czechoslovakia; however, Schindler, after discovering the mistake, procures their safety by bribing a Nazi officer with diamonds—a precious commodity in postwar Europe.

With Nazi Germany's surrender in 1945, the war is over. Schindler must flee, for fear of being tried for war crimes along with other members of the Nazi Party. The "Schindler Jews" see him off, presenting him with a document signed by each and every survivor that describes Schindler's commendable efforts on their behalf, as well as a gold ring smelted from the fillings of Jewish teeth. Schindler breaks down at this gesture, murmuring that he could have saved more people, if only he had sold his car, his jewelry. Stern calmly assures him that he has done enough, reading to him the inscription on his ring: "Whoever saves one life saves the world entire."

DISCUSSION QUESTIONS

1. Were the acts of the Nazis against the Jews morally wrong in an objective or universal sense, or is this a subjective or relative judgment? Explain.
2. How would you characterize Oskar Schindler at the beginning of the film? Is his character different at the end of the film? If so, how? What might account for this transformation?
3. It is often believed that tragedies like, and perhaps especially, the Holocaust create pressing philosophical problems for theists (believers in God). Do your best to articulate this problem. How might the problem be resolved, if at all?
4. What might have been the motivation behind Spielberg's choice to shoot the film in black and white? What is the significance of the few scenes that are shot in color? Were these cinematic choices effective?
5. Spielberg is sometimes criticized for creating an engrossing Hollywood depiction of Holocaust survivors and the Holocaust generally. Are such criticisms warranted? Explain.

Amistad (1997)

Screenwriter: David Franzoni

PLOT SUMMARY

It is 1839. The Spanish ship *La Amistad* suffers insurrection near Cuba. But the mutineers are not sailors or soldiers—they are its cargo. They wish to return to Africa. They make their wishes clear to the two remaining sailors; however, the white sailors manage to dupe the Africans. They do not sail east, but instead go mostly north up the American East Coast. After passing a small but decadent candlelight cruise, the *Amistad* is soon intercepted and boarded by an American survey brig. The Africans are moved from their dark wooden cell to a dank metal one in New Haven, Connecticut, awaiting their day in court for murdering the crew of the *Amistad*.

The major players line up to be heard at the pending arraignment. The preteen queen of Spain, Isabella II, immediately sends her American ambassador with a treaty of 1795 in hand to recollect her property. In a reelection year, President Martin Van Buren sees the whole matter (at least initially) as an inconvenience, telling his chief of staff, "There are three to four million Negros in this country, why should I concern myself with these forty-four?" He sends Secretary of State John Forsyth to New Haven to appease Spain and thereby make the whole matter go away. Others, however, stake their claim to the Africans. Two leading abolitionists, Messrs. Tappan and Joadson, neither of whom are lawyers, (improperly) present the court a writ of habeas corpus in the hope of buying time to arrange proper defense for the Africans. Two American naval officers come forward, arguing that because they salvaged the *Amistad* they have a right to its cargo. An attorney representing the two white Spanish sailors presents Judge Andrew T. Judson a bill of sale (receipt) executed June 26 in Havana, Cuba; the Africans belong to them. The attorney baldly declares, "I do hereby call upon this court to immediately surrender these goods, and that ship out there, to my clients Jose Ruiz and Pedro Montes." All of this makes it difficult for Judson and District Attorney Holabird to proceed with the case.

It is clear that Tappan and Joadson have the weakest legal position; after all, they attempt to argue for the Africans' freedom on moral grounds. After the arraignment, Roger S. Baldwin, attorney at law, introduces himself to the two abolitionists. Baldwin is a real-estate and property lawyer, exactly what the abolitionists seemingly need. However, they (and especially Tappan) smugly smile at Baldwin and inform him that what they really need is a criminal attorney, a trial lawyer. They leave in their carriage headed for Washington, D.C.

Arriving in the nation's capital, Tappan and Joadson request an audience with one of the country's biggest political players, former president John Quincy Adams. Adams, now a congressman from Massachusetts, has a reputation of being sympathetic to the abolitionist movement—much like his father before him, former president John Adams. The younger Adams agrees to see Tappan and Joadson, but inexplicably chooses not to aid them. In fact, he claims that he is neither a friend nor a foe of the abolitionist movement. Joadson, an ex-slave from Georgia who is now a free and learned historian of American politics, interjects. He reminds the former president that his record consistently shows otherwise. Adams warns Joadson that erudition is useless unless it is accompanied by a modicum of grace. With that, he takes his leave of the two abolitionists.

The two men thus agree to meet with Baldwin again to discuss strategy. Baldwin believes that the case is not as difficult as it might appear. He begins by asking the two others whether the Africans were born slaves, as on a plantation. If they were, then they are possessions and "no more deserving of a criminal trial than a bookcase or plow." If they were not born slaves, then "they were illegally acquired" and their situation is a matter of "wrongful transfer of stolen property." Either way, Baldwin believes that the case is won. Tappan indignantly demurs, saying, "Sir, this war must be waged on the battlefield of righteousness. . . . It would be against everything I stand for to let this deteriorate into an exercise in the vagaries of legal minutiae. . . . It is our destiny as abolitionists and Christians to save these people. These are people, Mr. Baldwin." Despite Baldwin's apparent lack of ethical or religious convictions, Tappan and Joadson agree to his terms of a "two and one-half dollars a day" retainer.

However, the trial does not go as smoothly as Baldwin envisioned. He has some difficulty convincing the court that the defendants are not from Cuba and were not born on a Cuban plantation. That is, Baldwin must now prove that the defendants are indeed Africans. He attempts to show that none of them know any Spanish. He also points out that they do not appear to be familiar with Cuban customs or dress. The court asks for documentation (something that Ruiz and Montes's attorney apparently has), but Baldwin does not have any. Furthermore, the defendants cannot testify on their own behalf because of the language barrier. The opening arguments do not go well for Baldwin and the abolitionists.

Baldwin and Joadson work hard to connect with the Africans (that is, the defendants, who they hope are from Africa). They meet with the man who appears to be the Africans' leader; however, the language barrier remains. They thus hire an American linguist, but he is not familiar with the Africans' dialect. They then receive a warrant to inspect the *Amistad*. Accidentally, Baldwin discovers a hidden manifest. It seems to indicate that the *Amistad*'s cargo was purchased from another ship, the *Tecora*—a notorious transatlantic slave-transport ship. This is the break Baldwin needs. The manifest appears to show that the *Amistad*'s cargo originated from the Ivory Coast, most likely Sierra Leone. These African locales are under the protectorate of Great Britain, which has already outlawed slavery. It thus indeed seems that the defendants are Africans who were taken illegally.

The other major players become concerned. Isabella puts more pressure on President Van Buren. The southern states do the same—most notably in the person of Senator John Calhoun—threatening that this case might bring the country that much closer to civil war. Van Buren's advisors remind (inform?) him that he has the power to disband the jury and have the judge remove himself for any number of reasons. A new judge could be handpicked. The trial could reconvene without a jury. Baldwin would be forced to argue the case over again, but this time to a judge who might be less sympathetic. Baldwin is furious when he hears about the executive branch's involvement. Joadson again calls on former president John Adams. Adams is more receptive this time. He advises that Baldwin and Joadson discover the African's story, to truly know who they are. After all, quips Adams, if he has learned anything about the law, it is that "in a courtroom, whoever tells the best story wins." Invigorated by the former president's advice, the two find someone who speaks Mende, the African dialect spoken by the defendants. They discover that the African leader is named Cinque and that he saved his village from a man-eating lion; this is why the others look up to him. Baldwin reminds Cinque that they also admire him because of his role in the insurrection. He calls this the second lion that Cinque slew. Cinque recounts the horrific events of their capture and transatlantic voyage. The two come to know the Africans' story indeed.

Baldwin puts Cinque on the stand to substantiate the claim that the defendants are from Africa. Holabird attempts to discredit Cinque's testimony by pointing out the seeming inconsistencies in it. Baldwin calls a British naval officer to the stand to explain how and why Cinque's testimony is not inconsistent. Listening and watching the proceedings now from his defendant's chair, Cinque becomes emotionally charged. He stands and shouts, "Give us, us free! Give us, us free!" The new judge is swayed by Baldwin's arguments. Cinque's testimony is also persuasive. Van Buren and his advisors are shocked to hear that the judge rules in the Africans' favor.

Calhoun puts more pressure on the president. Van Buren decides to appeal the lower court's decision to the Supreme Court—currently stocked with seven judges from southern states. Baldwin is forced to inform Cinque that they must argue the case one last time. Cinque is first confused. Enraged, he shouts, "What kind of place is this? Where you almost mean what you say? Where laws almost work? How can you live like that?" Not knowing where else to turn, Baldwin writes to Adams, pleading for his assistance with the case before the Supreme Court. The former president finally agrees. He, too, begins to know Cinque and the Africans. By knowing their story, Adams remembers better his story—America's story—and this proves to be the key to finally securing the Africans' freedom.

DISCUSSION QUESTIONS

1. Evaluate Baldwin's basic argument in approaching the *Amistad* case and contrast it with Tappan's approach. Which seems like the stronger argument? Explain carefully.
2. What should be done with state-sanctioned laws that seem obviously unjust?
3. Is Adams correct when he suggests that in the courtroom what really matters is who tells the best story? If not, why not? If so, what does this say about the judicial system?
4. What role, if any, should foreign relations and policy play in dictating domestic policy?
5. Reconsider Cinque's cry upon learning the case must be presented to the Supreme Court: "What kind of place is this? Where you almost mean what you say? Where laws almost work? How can you live like that?" Would Cinque have good reason to be disillusioned with America today? Justify your answer.
6. Spielberg is sometimes criticized for taking too many liberties with the historical events surrounding the *Amistad*, with adding the (fictitious) Joadson character and downplaying the (actual) role of abolitionist Christians as two prime examples. Is this criticism fair? Is a filmmaker obligated to represent historical events as closely as possible when crafting a film based on them? Explain.

A.I.: Artificial Intelligence (2001)

Screenwriters: Steven Spielberg and Ian Watson (based on a short story by Brian Aldiss)

PLOT SUMMARY

Global warming takes its toll on the earth's future. Many of the world's heavily populated coastal cities—New York, Venice, Amsterdam—have been submerged by the sea. Millions of people are displaced. Governments now enforce new reproductive regulations; couples must have a license to bear children. But robotic technology is on the verge of offering aid to childless couples. Sophisticated androids, "mecha," have already been filling many roles for humankind, the "orga." Mecha serve as domestic help in the form of maids and butlers. Some serve more controversial roles, including sex surrogates. Cybertronics, a cutting-edge robotics company, believes that it can provide childless couples surrogate children—diminutive mecha that can genuinely love their parents like any orga child. According to Professor Allen Hobby, these mecha children will never grow old or become sick. They will forever love their parents.

Hobby seeks a suitable couple to test his prototype, David. Henry Swinton, a Cybertronics employee, and his wife Monica have recently lost their young son Martin to a tragic disease. Martin has been in cryogenic stasis until a cure can be found for his ailment. Although Monica insists on reading to him regularly, Martin must be considered deceased. Only a miracle will change this. Hobby believes that the Swintons are perfect for David. One day, Henry abruptly brings the young mecha home with him. Monica is appalled by the suggestion that this "doll" could ever replace Martin. Henry assures his wife that up until the imprinting process, David can simply be returned to Cybertronics with no strings attached. However, if the Swintons decide to "imprint" David, then he is theirs forever. The imprinting process is irreversible. He will forever love his parents. Should the Swintons decide to return David after the imprinting process, then Cybertronics will destroy David.

Monica is clearly uncomfortable with David in the house, especially during the day, when Henry is at work. Stealthily, but not intentionally so, David follows her around the house (including into the bathroom). David does not sleep or eat, making bedtime and dinnertime awkward. David's mannerisms are contrived and graceless. He speaks formally, always referring to the Swintons as "Henry" and "Monica." But after a while, Monica takes to David. While Henry is away, she begins the imprinting process. By pressing down on the back of David's neck and uttering a sequence of specific words, she will cause David to love her forever. After she completes the process, David gazes into her eyes and asks, "What were those words, Mommy?" Startled, Monica asks, "What did you call me?" "Mommy," David replies and immediately puts his arms around Monica's neck. They embrace and tears well in Monica's eyes.

For all outward appearances, Monica has become David's mommy. As any child would, David makes unfortunate decisions. He makes his parents late for an important date and spills his mother's very rare and expensive perfume. He also asks difficult questions, including, "Mommy, will you die?" Realizing that David will probably not expire, Monica tells him not to worry about it. She will live a very long time, perhaps as long as fifty more years. David looks up at her and whispers, "I hope you never die."

But Henry was not present at the imprinting process; his relationship with David remains strained. David does not love Henry, only Monica. David thus seems to compete with Henry for Monica's affections. Perhaps to diffuse the situation, Monica activates Teddy, Martin's old "supertoy" in the form of a teddy bear. Teddy possesses artificial intelligence and speech capabilities and is self-mobile. He seems to be a perfect companion for David. One of the first things David asks Teddy is, "Is fifty years a long time?" "I don't think so," answers Teddy in his incongruously deep (and judicious) voice.

The miracle the Swintons no longer hoped for comes true: Martin is coming home. The Swintons' orga son arrives in a wheelchair. His muscles have atrophied and he must be nursed back to health. Eventually, he leaves the wheelchair, but the braces that electronically stimulate his muscles remain. Martin first sees David as a curiosity, little more than his new supertoy. But it does not take long for him to see David as a threat. He vies with David for Monica's affections. Unfortunately, Martin's jealousies know no bounds. He first convinces his mother to read *Pinocchio* to David and him. David immediately recognizes the similarities between himself and the wooden marionette. He, too, wants to be a "real boy." Martin goads David into ingesting food during dinner. David does not heed Teddy's wise words, "David, you'll break." He instead swallows the spinach and must be cleaned. Much as during a hospital operation, technicians open David up and clean his circuits. As Monica looks on and worries, Martin is disdainful. Martin later convinces David to sneak into his (their?) mother's bedroom and, while she sleeps, snip a lock of her hair. David wants to know why they cannot simply ask Monica for her permission. Martin responds that it must be a secret, otherwise it will not mean as much. David noiselessly enters the bedroom late one night and puts the scissors to his mother's hair. The Swintons awake. Henry grabs the scissors, but not before they break Monica's skin.

It is Martin's birthday party. He invites his friends to the family pool for swimming and cake. Martin's friends marvel at David. He is like no mecha they have ever seen. One of the boys gets too close and frightens David. The young mecha asks his brother to protect him. But David's fear turns to panic and the two boys fall into the pool. David, who of course does not breathe, is not fazed by the water. He continues to grasp on to Martin for protection as they sink to the bottom of the pool. But Martin cannot breathe. The adults, including Henry, dive into the pool and finally free Martin from David's panicked grasp. Henry and Monica are now at breaking point. Monica finally agrees to return David to Cybertronics, knowing that her mecha son will then be destroyed. But she cannot go through with it. She leaves David in the woods just outside of the Cybertronics grounds. David is confused. He asks, "Is it a game?" Monica, now in tears, apologizes for not telling him about the world. She leaves him some money and tells him to avoid "Flesh Fairs."

David's subsequent travels are nothing if not fantastic, but his self-directed goal is clear: he must find the Blue Fairy, for she will make him a "real boy" so that his mother will take him back and love him forever. Teddy reminds him that *Pinocchio* is merely a story, to which David responds, "A story tells what happens." But how can they find the Blue Fairy? David and Teddy soon meet up with other renegade mecha; they are captured and forced to participate in a Flesh Fair—the very thing that Monica told David to avoid.

The Flesh Fair represents orga angst against mecha. Many orga see the mecha as a threat to the future of humankind. To quash their fears, captured mecha, most of whom have pain receptors like David, are subjected to terrible ends. Some are decapitated, others are burned with acid. The crowd cheers. David is petrified. He turns to the closest adult for protection—a mecha named Gigolo Joe. Joe is aptly named; he is a male "love-mecha." When it is David's turn to be destroyed, the Flesh Fair crowd is alarmed. He appears to be a real boy. A fracas ensues, and Joe, Teddy, and David somehow escape. Together the three work to find the Blue Fairy. Joe believes the answer lies in Rouge City. All they need to do is ask Dr. Know; if anyone knows the location of the Blue Fairy, he does. Before David's fantastic journey is through, he travels to the end of the world ("where the lions weep"), meets his maker, and has one last visit with his mother.

DISCUSSION QUESTIONS

1. What is it to love another person? Is it possible for a sophisticated android to love? Explain.
2. Is Monica's choice to imprint David morally undesirable or circumspect?
3. Are Flesh Fairs somehow morally inappropriate? Explain.
4. When Joe and David have an audience with Dr. Know, his answers are only helpful once the two mecha cross the categories "fact" and "fiction." What might this mean? What does it mean with respect to the movie?
5. Does Dr. Know actually know anything?
6. Spielberg is sometimes criticized for "ruining" Kubrick's movie by turning it into nothing more than a modern-day Pinocchio story. Is this criticism justified? Explain.

7. Some critics bemoan Spielberg's denouement of the film—the so-called multiple endings. What is the significance of the various endings, respectively and jointly?

Minority Report (2002)

Screenwriter: Scott Frank (based on the short story by Philip K. Dick)

PLOT SUMMARY

In 2046, the U.S. homicide rate reaches epic proportions. But in the same year, the U.S. government authorizes a federal grant to conduct experiments in "precrime." By 2049, the Precrime unit is operational. By 2054, the pilot Precrime unit in Washington, D.C., runs so effectively that homicide, at least within a two-hundred-mile radius, has become a thing of the past. The program is a success, and Precrime is about to go national.

Precrime is the latest advance in criminal science. The police can now "see" homicides before they actually happen. In fact, the police "see" the homicides through the eyes of others, namely the "precognitives." The three "precogs," as they are commonly known, are accidents of genetic research and advancement. To some, however, the accidents were unfortunate at best. The precogs are the children of "neurorine" addicts, inflicted with a condition called Renning's syndrome as a result of their parents' addiction. The syndrome has grave effects upon a child's cerebral cortex. The world's top geneticists, in particular Dr. Iris Hineman, work to aid the children. However, for some of the children the "cure" afflicts them with a further highly unique condition, the ability to see the future—and more importantly, the ability to predict with seemingly absolute certainty homicides that are about to take place.

John Anderton is the chief of the Washington, D.C., Precrime unit. Tragically, his six-year-old son, Sean, was abducted from a public swimming pool just before the inception of Precrime. Anderton has not been the same since. His marriage crumbled under the strain of losing Sean and he has become a neurorine addict himself. His only refuge is his job and the solace that he is now able to prevent similar tragedies before they even take place.

Anderton's supervisor, Lamar Burgess, informs him that the Justice Department, in the person of Danny Witwer, will soon visit the Precrime division. Before Precrime goes national, the Justice Department wants to ensure that it runs as smoothly and effectively as possible. The primary concern is whether the system is infallible; if it is not, then the Precrime division could arrest innocent people—those who have committed no crime and will not commit a crime, at least not the one the precogs claim they will commit. Because Precrime police science is grounded in the idea that murders should be stopped before they happen, "previsions" are the only "evidence" the Precrime police have to make arrests; therefore, the precogs can never be wrong. If they are, then Precrime law enforcement seems unjust.

Fletcher, Anderton's lieutenant, informs Witwer that when the precogs foresee a murder a complicated computer-driven process occurs, culminating with the shaping of two wooden balls, or "eggs." One egg is inscribed with the name of the victim and the other is inscribed with the name of the murderer. Fletcher continues, "The information we need is embedded in the grain of wood. And since each piece is unique, the shape and grain is impossible to duplicate." Skeptical, Witwer directs his response to the entire unit present: "I'm sure you've all grasped the legalistic drawback to Precrime methodology. Look, I'm not with the ACLU on this. . . . But let's not kid ourselves, we are arresting individuals who've broken no law." After some protestation from the unit, Witwer continues, "But it's not the future if you stop it. Isn't that a fundamental paradox?" Just then, Anderton enters the room and the discussion. After affirming that it does seem paradoxical, he announces to Witwer, "You're talking about predetermination, which happens all the time." Anderton takes a wooden egg out of Fletcher's hand and rolls it on a table toward Witwer. Just before it falls to the ground, Witwer catches it, prompting Anderton to ask why Witwer caught the egg. "It was going to fall," replies Witwer. "You're certain?" inquires Anderton, to which Witwer answers affirmatively. "But it didn't fall. You caught it," Anderton goes on; and after pausing, seemingly for effect, he concludes, "The fact that you prevented it from happening doesn't change the fact that it was going to happen." Although not appearing completely satisfied with this explanation, Witwer nods and then departs to ponder Anderton's words.

Soon after, an alarm sounds, signaling that the precogs have foreseen another murder. Immediately, the computer begins processing the information and subsequently begins shaping and inscribing a wooden egg. It soon rolls to Anderton's station. The victim's name is Leo Crow. The second wooden egg slowly rolls down the plastic tube. To Anderton's horror, it reads "John Anderton." Will Anderton soon commit homicide—kill a man that he does not even know? Surely there has been some mistake. But the precogs are never wrong! Has someone tampered with the system and framed him for a crime that he will never commit? Placing the egg in his pocket, he quickly but quietly leaves Precrime headquarters. The quiet is soon broken.

Alarms sound and Chief Anderton is now a wanted fugitive for the "future murder" of Leo Crow.

Anderton desperately makes his way to Dr. Hineman's residence. Now a recluse, perhaps the inventor of Precrime will be able to inform Anderton how someone could tamper with the system resulting in a false prevision. With great effort, he finds Hineman. She reminds Anderton of what he already knows—the precogs are never wrong. Hineman further informs him that she is not aware of any way to fake a prevision—the precogs see what they see. Anderton is beyond despair. Hineman picks up her tea, and looking over the cup at Anderton, also informs him, "But occasionally they do disagree. . . . Once in a while, one will see things differently than the other two." Anderton is stunned. He was unaware of these "minority reports"; he, like everyone else, believed that the infallible precogs all "saw" the same murders in pretty much the same way. Anderton asks whether Burgess knows about these minority reports. Hineman admits that he does. Anderton despondently asks, "Are you saying that I've haloed innocent people?" Hineman replies, "I'm saying that every so often those accused of a precrime might—just might—have an alternative future. . . . But we felt their existence was an insignificant variable." Anderton quickly interjects, "Insignificant to you, maybe, but what about those people I put away with alternate futures? My God, if the country knew there was a chance . . ." "The system would collapse," Hineman finishes. Anderton staggers off to find his minority report, but to get it, he must find his way back into the Precrime "temple"—the room housing the precogs. If he has a minority report, it is stored in the precog Agatha.

Of course, entering the Precrime building will be difficult. Almost at every turn, he will be faced with retinal scans, or "eye-dents." He seeks the help of an ex-con doctor who agrees to give him a new set of eyes, thereby avoiding the danger of retinal scan. But he must keep his old eyes in order to enter the temple. Even if he successfully kidnaps Agatha—for that is what he must do—he still has to avoid the prying eyes of his former colleagues and their artificially intelligent, metal recon spiders. This will be a perilous task indeed.

Anderton does not know Leo Crow; he has never even met him. But just as Hineman told Anderton, "a series of events has started that will lead you, inexorably, to his murder." This series began with Anderton's visit with Hineman. It continues with his successful escape from the temple with Agatha. He must now keep her safe until he can access her memories. But how? Soon, Anderton begins to recognize some of the previsions from the Crow future murder. He looks at his watch; the time of the future murder draws near. Anderton—inexorably—drags Agatha up to the apartment where the future murder is about to happen. Agatha is desperate. She reminds Anderton that he can leave. She pleads with him, "You still have a choice! The others never saw their future. You still have a choice. . . . You can choose!" Nevertheless, Anderton slowly walks into Crow's room.

DISCUSSION QUESTIONS

1. Why is it so important that Precrime police "science" be infallible?
2. If Precrime is infallible and the precogs foresee someone committing murder tomorrow, is that person justly punished for his (future) act? Explain.
3. Assume that the precogs are not infallible, but their previsions are correct 99.9 percent of the time. Furthermore, let us also say that Precrime successfully eliminates homicide in this country. Is the *elimination* of homicide not important and beneficial enough to overlook or outweigh the statistical fact that previsions will be incorrect *one* time out of a thousand?
4. Are any of the following objectionable infringements on our basic (political) rights: pervasive "eye-dents," the metallic recon spiders, Precrime itself? Explain.
5. Is Agatha correct in her claim that Anderton can refrain from killing Crow? If so, how?
6. Spielberg and Frank significantly altered Dick's original short story. Is this somehow objectionable? What ideals or concepts might Spielberg and Frank have hoped to convey by changing the story in the ways that they did?

Munich (2005)

Screenwriters: Tony Kushner and Eric Roth (based on a book by George Jonas)

PLOT SUMMARY

In 1972, the international community turns its attention to Munich, Germany, where the world's greatest athletes have gathered to compete against each other in the Olympic Games. However, the joyous celebration of peace and brotherhood symbolized by the games quickly turns into a horrific display of the worst of humanity. In the early morning hours of September

5, eight members of the Palestinian terrorist organization Black September take eleven Israeli athletes and coaches hostage. Demanding the release of more than two hundred Palestinians and non-Arabs being held in Israeli prisons, the Black September agents engage in hours of intense negotiations before arranging transportation and passage to Egypt. During a botched rescue attempt, five of the eight members of Black September are killed, the other three wounded and captured by German police. All eleven Israeli hostages are murdered.

The Israeli government gathers together top political and military officials to plan a response to the Munich massacre. Deciding that a response must be dramatic, capturing the attention of the world so as to deter future attacks against Jews, Prime Minister Golda Meir and members of the Israeli army call in Avner, a member of the Israeli intelligence and special operations agency Mossad. The prime minister justifies her position by claiming, "We say to these butchers, 'You didn't want to share this world with us, then we don't have to share this world with you.'" Avner is assigned to lead a team of Mossad agents in seeking out and assassinating eleven Palestinians who were believed to have played a role in planning Munich. Avner is forced to officially resign his position in Mossad to give the Israeli government safe distance and plausible deniability. He must also leave his pregnant wife and the rest of his life behind in order to track down and dispose of the eleven in what becomes known as Operation Wrath of God.

Four other agents—Steve, the driver; Carl, the cleanup artist; Robert, the bomb maker; and Hans, the documents specialist—join Avner in his mission. Because they are no longer officially working for the Israeli government, Avner and his team must find each of the names on the list independently. Avner seeks the help of Andreas, an old friend from Frankfurt, who introduces him to Yvonne. After he convinces Yvonne that he is working for wealthy Americans, she helps him to get in contact with Tony—an Italian informant who agrees, for a price, to help Avner find the men on his list.

The information Avner receives leads his Mossad team to Rome. There they find Abdel Wael Zwaiter, one of the men responsible for the planning of the Munich massacre. Avner and Robert track him back to his apartment building. They confront him and, after some nervous hesitation, execute him. Carl then arrives to clean up after them in order to remove any evidence of who might have been responsible for the killing.

After Rome, the team head to Paris where they meet with Louis, the man for whom Tony worked. Louis helps provide them information on their next target, Mahmoud Hamshari. Posing as a journalist seeking an interview, Robert is able to wire Hamshari's phone with an explosive. Afterward, Robert leaves and joins Steve and Hans in the car while Avner stands lookout. Carl then calls the house from a phone booth to get Hamshari to answer. Their first attempt at this almost ends in tragedy, as Hamshari's daughter unexpectedly reenters the penthouse. The second attempt is successful; Hamshari, now alone, answers the phone. When he does, Robert detonates the bomb. Hamshari later dies from wounds he sustains in the explosion.

The agents then travel to Cyprus, where they wire the hotel bed of Hussein Abad al-Chir with explosives. When detonated, the bomb nearly kills Avner and a honeymooning couple who have rooms on each side of al-Chir's. After the killing of al-Chir, Louis provides Avner the names and locations of three additional targets—Kemal Nasser, Kemal Adwan, and Yussuf Najjer. The three are located in Beirut, and in order to get permission to enter Arab territories, Avner's team must join with Israeli military personnel to carry out the assassinations. The strike is quick but messy. In addition to the three targets, the strike force takes out other Arab militants, as well as a few civilians.

The team then travel to Athens, where they stay in a safe house Louis has provided for them. They are surprised to find that Louis has also made arrangements for members of the Palestine Liberation Organization (PLO) to share the safe house. Late at night, Avner begins to talk politics with one of the PLO members, Ali. When Avner tries to convince Ali that the Palestinians will never be successful in "taking back" a homeland that was "never theirs," Ali nonchalantly replies, "We have a lot of children, they'll have children, so we can wait forever, and, and . . . if we need to, we can make the whole planet unsafe for Jews." Here Avner begins to realize the depth of the nationalist sentiments and hatred driving both sides of this ceaseless conflict. Later, during the assassination of Zaid Muchassi, a Palestinian informant to the KGB, Carl kills Ali.

After the assassination of Muchassi, Avner and his team receive the name and location of Ali Hassan Salameh, the man who organized the Munich massacre. Salameh is the prime target for the agents of Mossad. However, their attempt to kill him in London is thwarted by men they assume are working for the CIA. Soon after, a Dutch assassin named Jeanette, who originally tried to seduce Avner to draw him into someplace private, kills Carl. In an act of revenge, Avner, Hans, and Steve decide to hunt Jeanette down. Robert refuses to join them. He pleads with Avner not to go, saying, "We're Jews, Avner. Jews don't do wrong because our enemies do wrong. . . . We're supposed to be righteous." They go anyway, and murder Jeanette while she pleads, almost naked, for her life.

Soon after Jeanette's murder, Hans is stabbed to death and Robert is killed in a bomb-making accident. Meanwhile, Avner is experiencing suicidal thoughts and is unable to sleep because of increasing paranoia. He and Steve finally track Salameh to one of his homes in Spain. Their attempt to assassinate him, however, is unsuccessful because Salameh's bodyguards surprise them. In a desperate attempt to avoid being caught, Avner shoots one of the guards. He is disgusted to discover the guard he killed was a teenage boy. Avner and Steve flee, barely escaping, and Salameh remains alive.

Avner leaves Israel to join his family in their home in New York to be safe. However, he constantly feels as though he is being watched and hunted. His relationship with his wife, Daphna, suffers; even their lovemaking is violent and haunted by the brutal visions by which Avner is possessed. The psychological torment he feels is apparent in all aspects of his new life.

In a park on the waterfront in Brooklyn, Avner argues with Ephraim, a top-level Mossad agent who helped oversee Operation Wrath of God, about what Avner's team had been asked to do and why. Avner tells Ephraim quite simply, "There's no peace at the end of this. Whatever you believe, you know that's true."

DISCUSSION QUESTIONS

1. In the movie, Prime Minister Golda Meir claims, "Every civilization finds it necessary to negotiate compromises with its own values." In light of the film, is such an assertion correct? Are there (philosophical) reasons to believe that such a position is flawed?

2. Yvonne pontificates that right and wrong should not be thought of as ethical questions, but instead as "ways of talking about a terrible struggle, parts of an equation, a dialectic." What does *Munich* teach us about such a perspective? Is Yvonne correct in her assertion?

3. Avner suffers emotionally and psychologically from his mission, and all aspects of his life are touched by his actions. Is it possible for anyone to commit such actions and not be (negatively) affected by them? Can soldiers refuse military missions on moral grounds? Are some military missions impermissible?

4. In making *Munich,* Spielberg claims he was not attempting to produce a documentary. Instead, he used "imagination and creativity" to produce an emotional response to the human condition. Does the blending of history and imagination enable us to accurately draw conclusions about the ethics of such things as counterterrorism? Or does a filmmaker like Spielberg lead

viewers to adopt his own beliefs and perspectives about such complex moral questions by showing history from a particular perspective?

5. The final image in the film before the movie fades to black is of the World Trade Center. Is *Munich* a critique of U.S. foreign policy following the terrorist attacks of September 11, 2001? If so, what can the United States learn from the philosophical objections raised in the film? Defend your answers.

Note

1. Some of the material in this appendix is adapted from Dean Kowalski, *Classic Questions and Contemporary Film: An Introduction to Philosophy* (New York: McGraw-Hill, 2005). I am indebted to Professor Joseph Foy for his help with composing the *Munich* plot summary and discussion questions.

Contributors

GARY ARMS is a professor of language and literature at Clarke College in Dubuque, Iowa. He is the author of two books, *Mythology Smart Junior* (1997) and *Spelling Smart Junior* (1999). He has also published two plays, *The Arranged Marriage* (1999) and *Emily Dickinson's Birthday Party* (2005).

DAVID BAGGETT is an associate professor of philosophy at Liberty University in Virginia. His research interests include the philosophy of religion and ethics. He is the coeditor of *Harry Potter and Philosophy: If Aristotle Ran Hogwarts* (2004), *Hitchcock and Philosophy: Dial M for Metaphysics* (2007), and *C. S. Lewis as Philosopher: Truth, Goodness and Beauty* (2008). He is currently in the process of editing *Tennis and Philosophy* (forthcoming).

ROBERT R. CLEWIS is currently an assistant professor of philosophy at Gwynedd-Mercy College near Philadelphia, Pennsylvania. He has written on Heideggerian wonder in Terrence Malick's film *The Thin Red Line* (*Film and Philosophy,* 2003). His monograph, *The Kantian Sublime and the Revelation of Freedom,* is forthcoming.

KEITH DROMM is an associate professor of philosophy at the Louisiana Scholars' College in Natchitoches. A contributing author to *The Philosophy of* The X-Files (2007), his other recent publications include "'Based on True Events': Filmmakers' Obligations to History" (*International Journal of Applied Philosophy,* 2006); "Wittgenstein on Language Learning" (*History of Philosophy Quarterly,* 2006); and "The *Hostile* Office: Michael as a Sexual Harasser," in The Office *and Philosophy* (2008).

TIMOTHY DUNN is an assistant professor of philosophy at the University of Wisconsin–Waukesha. He is the author of "The Value of Solidarity" (*Southwestern Journal of Philosophy,* 2005) and coauthor of "Moral Musings of a Cigarette Smoking Man," in *The Philosophy of* The X-Files (2007). He earned his PhD from Rice University, and his research interests include ethics, egoism, and social/political philosophy.

ROGER P. EBERTZ is currently a professor and chair of the Department of Philosophy and Religion at the University of Dubuque, Iowa. His research interests include epistemology and ethical theory. He has published articles appearing in such journals as the *Canadian Journal of Philosophy,* as well as an essay entitled "Socratic Teaching and the Search for Coherence," in *Knowledge, Teaching and Wisdom* (1996).

MARK W. FOREMAN is an associate professor of philosophy and religion at Liberty University in Virginia. His research interests include medical ethics and Christian apologetics. He is the author of *Christianity and Bioethics: Confronting Clinical Issues* (1999).

JOSEPH J. FOY is currently an assistant professor of political science at the University of Wisconsin–Waukesha. He earned his PhD at the University of Notre Dame and served as a Manatt Fellow for Democracy Studies at the International Foundation for Election Systems. He is the editor of *Homer Simpson Goes to Washington: American Politics through Popular Culture* (2008), as well as a contributing author to *The Philosophy of* The X-Files (2007) and *The Executive Branch of State Government* (2006). His current research interests include the ethics and logic of power, democracy studies, ethnic peace and conflict, and politics and popular culture.

DEAN A. KOWALSKI is currently an associate professor of philosophy at the University of Wisconsin–Waukesha. He is the editor of *The Philosophy of* The X-Files (2007), author of *Classic Questions and Contemporary Film: An Introduction to Philosophy* (2005), and coauthor of *Moral Theory and Motion Pictures: An Introduction to Ethics* (forthcoming). He has published a handful of articles on the freedom and foreknowledge problem, including "Some Friendly Molinist Amendments" (*Philosophy and Theology,* 2003) and "On Behalf of a Suarezian Middle Knowledge" (*Philosophia Christi,* 2003); most recently, his "Hobbes and Locke on Social Contracts and

Scarlet Carsons" appears in Joseph Foy's anthology *Homer Simpson Goes to Washington* (2008).

MICHEL LE GALL has taught in the history departments of St. Olaf College and Carleton College in Northfield, Minnesota. His research interests and specializations include the Near East and North African studies. He is the coeditor of, and a contributor to, *The Maghrib in Question: History and Historiography* (1997), as well as numerous articles, including a contribution to *James Bond and Philosophy* (2006).

THOMAS RILEY is an associate professor of philosophy at Clarke College in Dubuque, Iowa. He earned his PhD from the University of Iowa and now specializes in metaphysics and epistemology. He is also concerned with pedagogy, and has coauthored "Validity, Analogy, and the Holy Grail" (*Teaching Philosophy*, 2003).

JAMES H. SPENCE is currently an assistant professor of philosophy in the Department of Philosophy and Religion at Adrian College in Michigan, and has previously taught at Louisiana State University and the University of Tennessee at Knoxville. His research interests include moral and political philosophy, and his publications include "What Nietzsche Can Teach You: Eternal Return in *Groundhog Day*," in *Movies and the Meaning of Life: Philosophers Take On Hollywood* (2005).

CHARLES TALIAFERRO is a professor of philosophy at St. Olaf College in Northfield, Minnesota. His research interests include the philosophy of religion and the philosophy of mind. He is the author or editor of seven books, most recently *Evidence and Faith* (2005). He is a regular contributor to philosophy and popular culture volumes, including *Superheroes and Philosophy* (2005) and *James Bond and Philosophy* (2006). He has taught at the University of Notre Dame and the University of Massachusetts, and was a visiting scholar at Oxford University, New York University, and Princeton University.

CHRISTOPHER R. TROGAN is currently an assistant professor of English and humanities at the U.S. Merchant Marine Academy in Kings Point, New York. He was a contributing author for *The Philosophy of The X-Files* (2007) and has published other articles on the relationship between ethics, epistemology, and aesthetics. He regularly teaches courses in philosophy and literature.

V. ALAN WHITE is a professor of philosophy at the University of Wisconsin–Manitowoc. He was a contributing author for *The Philosophy of The X-Files* (2007). His interests include free will, the philosophy of time, and pedagogy, and his essays have appeared in *Analysis, Philosophy, The Review of Metaphysics,* and *Teaching Philosophy,* among others. A former Carnegie/CASE Professor of the Year for the state of Wisconsin, he has an Internet page, *Philosophy Songs,* that is known internationally for its parody and middling tenor vocals.

JOHN W. WRIGHT is currently an assistant professor of communication and theater arts at the University of Wisconsin–Manitowoc. He holds a PhD in theater from Louisiana State University and his research interests include the aesthetics of ethical imagery. He has directed more than a dozen productions in the past ten years, including *Rosencrantz and Guildenstern Are Dead, The Laramie Project, Dangerous Liaisons,* and Alan Ball's *Five Women Wearing the Same Dress.*

Index